C000185841

POLISH FAMILIES AND MIGRATION SINCE EU ACCESSION

Anne White

This edition published in Great Britain in 2011 by

The Policy Press
University of Bristol
Fourth Floor
Beacon House
Queen's Road
Bristol BS8 1QU
UK

t: +44 (0)117 331 4054
f: +44 (0)117 331 4093
tpp-info@bristol.ac.uk
www.policypress.co.uk

North American office:
The Policy Press
c/o International Specialized Books Services
920 NE 58th Avenue, Suite 300
Portland, OR 97213-3786, USA
t: +1 503 287 3093
f: +1 503 280 8832
info@isbs.com

British Library Cataloguing in Publication Data
A catalogue record for this book is available from the British Library.

Library of Congress Cataloging-in-Publication Data
A catalog record for this book has been requested.

ISBN 978 1 84742 820 2 hardcover

Cover design by The Policy Press
Front cover: image kindly supplied by www.istock.com
Printed and bound in Great Britain by TJ International, Padstow
The Policy Press uses environmentally friendly print partners

FSC
Mixed Sources
Product group from well-managed
forests and other controlled sources
Cert no. SGS-COC-2482
www.fsc.org
© 1996 Forest Stewardship Council

Contents

List of figures and tables

Figures

Tables

Acknowledgements

Many people helped with the research for this book. Above all, I am grateful to the 102 interviewees in Poland and England and also to the 1,101 respondents who participated in the opinion poll organised on my behalf in Poland. Many other people also helped in essential ways with the research, for example by finding interviewees, sharing ideas and information, hosting me during my visits to Poland or taking over my teaching and other duties while I was on a semester's study leave. I am particularly grateful to: David Bull, Barbara Cieślińska, Debbie Clough, Tomasz Dudziński, Peter Duncan, Iwona Erturan, Barbara Everett, Małgorzata Fabiszak, Krystyna Formejster, Michał Garapich, Eliza Giner-Wajda, Krystyna Iglicka, Ewa Iwanowska, Jacek and Mateusz Janowiak, Paweł Kaczmarczyk, Agnieszka Kiełkiewicz-Janowiak, George Kolankiewicz, Danuta Kosturska, Agata Kościelska, Magda Kowalik-Malcolm, Olga and Leszek Kózka, Ewa Kucięba, Marta Lewandowska and Mr and Mrs Lewandowski, Janina and Magda Łosiewicz, Anna and Romuald Melerowicz, Mariola Milewska, Joanna Napierała, Joanna Nikiel, Nina Parish, Jacek Partyka, Violetta Parutis, Urszula Pienczykowska-Partyka, Małgorzata Pietrzycka, Magda Pokrzywa, Renate Rechtien, Renata Rogers, Anna Rydzewska, Sławomira from the Dom Nauczyciela in Suwałki, Krystyna Sobkowiak, Joanna Szymanowska, Paweł Walawender, Maggie Ward-Goodbody and the head of Kindergarten 1 in Sanok. My husband, Howard, and daughters Tamara and Lucy, were supportive at every stage of the research.

Most of the research was financed by the British Academy (Small Grant SG-48522, 'Family migration as a livelihood strategy in contemporary Poland'), and the project was completed during a semester of study leave from the Department of European Studies and Modern Languages, University of Bath.

ONE

Introduction

For the time being we've chosen England. (Anna, Bristol, 2009)

This book explores the reasons why so many Polish families, with children, have come to live in the UK since 2004. However, the scope of the book is much broader than this. Family migration from Poland can only be understood in the context of how people make their livings in particular places in Poland, and why people living in those places choose to leave. The book is therefore about migration from Poland in general.

It is also about the experiences of Poles in England, and the factors that shape their thoughts about how long to stay. Here the focus is narrower, concentrating on working-class families. Other researchers have published articles about more highly educated and/or young childless Polish migrants[1] or, more commonly, explored the experiences of a range of different people.[2] However, families are worth studying separately because they are in some ways a special group.[3] While some migrants may be compared to tourists, who come and go, hardly having to engage with UK society or public services, Polish parents need to engage. As this book demonstrates, they are also likely to remain in the UK. Hence their experiences and requirements are particularly important to policy makers as well as to UK society more generally. If the parents are not highly qualified and do not speak much English, they may need particular support.

Mass migration by Polish families to the UK, and to European Union (EU) countries in general, is a new phenomenon. Home Office data suggest that the number of children arriving in the UK doubled year by year from 2004-06, peaked in 2007 and then began to fall slightly.[4] By the second quarter of 2007 an estimated 170,000 Polish-born children (under 19 years old) were resident in the UK.[5] By 2008, Polish-speaking children formed the largest group of 'non-English speaking newly-arrived migrant schoolchildren' in England.[6] Looking at emigration more widely, a Polish study estimated that in 2007 0.34% of Polish school students left the country.[7]

The research interviews suggest that Polish families do not usually arrive in the UK intending to settle. This chapter opens with a typical comment: "For the time being we've chosen England". Like migrants everywhere, but perhaps even more so in the context of EU-endowed mobility, many Poles simply do not know how long they will remain abroad. This is why it is sensible to explore why people make certain decisions which have a bearing on whether they stay or return, instead of asking directly how long they will stay and then producing statistics about their answers.

The main sources for the book were 115 interviews with Polish women, 82 in Poland and 33 in England; interviews and conversations with key informants; an opinion poll conducted in Poland; and participant observation as a volunteer English teacher. Most of the project was funded by the British Academy. The book presents many verbatim quotations from the interviews, with the aim of presenting migration through migrants' eyes.[8] At the same time, it is structured around certain concepts (livelihood strategies, migration culture, networks, transnationalism, integration and return migration), most of which are introduced briefly here in Chapter One.[9] Since the book is designed for a wide range of readers, this chapter does not provide a detailed review of the scholarly literature on each topic. Instead, it concentrates on developing ideas which are particularly relevant to this book and which inform the analysis in subsequent chapters.

Causes of migration: a livelihood strategy approach

The dynamics of the global economy help shape migration across the world. However, people also migrate because of specific factors in the 'sending' country (in this case Poland) and the 'receiving' country (in this case the UK). Migration scholars often use the term 'pull factor' to refer to aspects of the receiving society, such as higher wages, which are attractive to migrants. By contrast, 'push factors', such as low wages, propel migrants from sending countries.

The terms 'push' and 'pull' are sometimes criticised for suggesting that migration is like a simple machine. One of the main aims of this book is to show the actual complexity of the migration process. However, 'push' and 'pull' are useful metaphors for analysing migrants' motives, particularly since migrants themselves often have a sense of being pushed and pulled in different directions. Indeed, it is helpful to extend the metaphor. Most often, pushes and pulls are used to explain the first decision to migrate, but in fact migrants already living abroad also experience pulls and pushes, which influence their thoughts about how long to stay.[10] Unemployment in the UK, for example, might be a push factor resulting in return to Poland, whereas homesickness might be a pull factor. This raises the question of whether return is motivated by much the same kind of reasoning as the original migration journey, an issue discussed in Chapter Ten.

Pull and push factors can be studied in their own right. They include, for example, the nature of the UK labour market, with its demand for flexible, low-paid labour; the government's decision to open access to the UK labour market in 2004 for citizens of A8 (East-Central European) member states; or the level of unemployment in Poland. However, it is not the purpose of this book to contribute to migration scholarship on this macro level.[11] Rather, the book explores *how individuals interpret pushes and pulls*. Not all unemployed Polish people migrate to the UK, for example, so it seems useful to look at why some people's experience of losing a job in Poland pushes them to the UK while others stay in Poland or perhaps choose an alternative migration strategy and go to Germany or Iceland instead.

Migration strategies are a subset of 'livelihood strategies'. As used in international development, the livelihood strategy approach is about enhancing opportunities for people to make better livings *in specific places*, taking into account their own understanding of what is locally feasible and appropriate. Livelihoods became a focus of attention for international donors because of the realisation that poor households can only be helped effectively if all their means of subsistence are taken into account. To understand how a family subsists, it is not enough to know how much money the household breadwinner earns in his main job. For example, a family with young children thinking about moving from Poland might have to take into account not only how much extra money the husband could gain by working in the UK, but also the fact that they would lose free childcare from the wife's mother and sister in Poland, so that she might have to give up paid employment. The livelihood strategy approach draws attention to the whole range of resources and potential resources, such as second jobs, social networks, time, health and skills, available to a given household. According to the Department for International Development, 'a livelihood comprises the capabilities, assets (including both material and social resources) and activities required for a means of living'.[12] An important function of the concept is to draw attention to social resources such as being able to ask favours from relatives: 'livelihood is never just a matter of acquiring [material resources].... It is equally a matter of ownership and the circulation of information, the management of skills and relationships, and the affirmation of personal significance [involving issues of self-esteem] and group identity.'[13]

The livelihood strategy approach is useful, therefore, because it (a) helps us understand all of a household's resources and the role of all household members in contributing to the family livelihood; (b) focuses attention on links between the individual, the household and the wider community; and (c) explores connections between material and non-material resources, especially social capital (understood as the ability to call on other people, outside the household, for favours and for help).[14] It is not a 'theory' explaining why people migrate, but merely a way of understanding how individuals and households make decisions in local contexts. Olwig and Sørensen have commented that, although 'a basic assumption in migration studies is that the search for a better livelihood is a main cause of migratory movements ... such studies rarely take in-depth research into specific livelihoods as their point of departure'.[15] There are exceptions, for example my own work on migration from small towns to cities within Russia,[16] or Mandel's mapping of the different livelihood strategies employed by women in Benin. Mandel discusses, for instance, why some women are better placed than others to devolve their domestic responsibilities on to other women, so that they themselves can travel back and forward across nearby international borders.[17] Jacobsen, applying a livelihood strategy approach to refugees, shows how 'refugees' pursuit of livelihoods can increase human security because economic activities help to recreate social and economic interdependence within and between communities, and can restore social networks based on the exchange of labour, assets and food'.[18]

Above all, to understand why people migrate, we need to know the *choice* of livelihoods available in a given location. The decision to migrate or return from emigration usually takes place after the potential migrant has considered and rejected local livelihood options or if they believe that there is simply no alternative option.[19] It is important to study how migrants perceive the merits of alternatives to migration and why these are considered to be unattainable or unsatisfactory. In keeping with the aim of this book to see migration through migrants' eyes, the livelihood strategy approach is used to see beyond Polish economic statistics and to study people's perceptions of their local economies: not only the quantity of work available, but also its quality and acceptability. If the work is poorly paid and/or in the shadow economy these may be reasons for preferring to migrate. Also significant is how much people expect to add to their basic wage by doing overtime or taking a second job. Households are tempted to adopt migration as their livelihood strategy when they feel they cannot put together a sufficient portfolio of different local income sources. For the purposes of this book, it is particularly important to note that in small towns and rural areas the range of opportunities can be quite limited, and this helps explain the popularity of migration from such places.

'Livelihood' is a better adjective than 'survival', the label commonly used to describe such household strategies.[20] Everyone has a livelihood strategy: strategies are not restricted to people who merely wish to survive, but can include people who want to be rich. For example, migration can lead to survival in the sense of escape from extreme poverty, but it also offers the chance to become wealthy, by local standards. Accumulation strategies[21] may combine with survival strategies from the outset, as when a migrant earns abroad to feed his or her family but also hopes to save money to buy a house. In other cases, accumulation gradually replaces survival as the objective as the migrant accumulates more and more material goods. Furthermore, 'survival' may be a bad label for the reason that labour migration, like other strategies, is for many migrants not primarily an escape route from poverty but, rather, a response to opportunity, which can be taken up by 'people of intermediate social status'.[22]

The situation is complicated by the fact that interviewees tend to present their livelihoods as being about survival in societies where it is not acceptable to be openly acquisitive. Polish interviewees, for example, often asserted that they migrated "for bread, not coconuts" (luxuries). If they had not migrated, they quoted the saying that "if you have bread, don't go looking for buns". It would be greedy to ask for more than plain bread.

In fact, the distinction between bread and buns (or even coconuts) is not so clear-cut. Once again, it is useful to study the sending society carefully in order to understand what constitutes that minimum standard of living, the pursuit of which will trigger a change in livelihood strategy. Poles, for example, often assert that they go abroad to secure a 'normal' standard of living,[23] but since Poland is a relatively wealthy country, a Pole's understanding of normality tends to encompass escaping a hand-to-mouth existence, rather than avoiding actual starvation:

I used to clean in private houses, and the women were really very nice, I was happy because they treated me like a daughter. And they tried to give me stuff to eat because they said I was terribly thin. I said that we had everything in Poland ... and we only went to Greece to earn money for extras, not for food. (Celina, Grajewo)

Normality can be defined by comparing the speaker's own (implicitly abnormal) standard of living against various standards and patterns of consumption located in memories of the communist past, impressions of lifestyles abroad and, probably most importantly, simple observation of what goods are in the shops today and the more comfortable lifestyles of some neighbours and friends.

As this discussion of normality suggests, decisions about livelihood strategies are made in a cultural context. Pine and Bridger argue that 'strategies are not necessarily "economically rational" according to models of supply, demand and efficient self-interest. However, in terms of cultural meaning, local knowledge and understanding, and within the context of social relationships and networks, they are often the best and most sensible responses people can make.'[24] For example, if a husband has a local job but the wife is unemployed, it would make economic sense for the wife to migrate and for the husband to take over her housework and parenting responsibilities. Nonetheless, because of prevailing norms about gender roles, this is often viewed as an unacceptable strategy, so the husband migrates instead.

Norms, in a sociological sense, are unwritten rules that help determine how most people behave within a given culture, including how they migrate. On the other hand, causation is circular: norms come into being partly because they are normal, the common form of behaviour. Hence it is possible for new types of behaviour, which are becoming more normal, to rise to the status of norms. If women across the globe are 'increasingly migrating as individuals rather than as dependants of other family members',[25] this may make such migration more socially acceptable, and therefore even more likely to occur.

Migration cultures are conventions about why and how people should migrate, which people should migrate and where they should go, as well as views about whether or not migration is a normal and sensible way of making a living, and about the costs and benefits of migration for the whole local community. In order to understand migration cultures, it is helpful to explore the full range of opinions in sending communities, not just the views of migrants themselves. As Byron suggests, 'accounts which include both migrants and their non-migrant counterparts tend to be more informative about the process than those which consider only the migrants'.[26] This is why the research conducted for this book included 82 interviews in Poland.

I am not arguing that all behaviour is culturally or economically determined. An important aim of the book is to explore the extent to which individual migrants are free to make their own decisions, or, in social science terminology, how much agency they enjoy. Different groups of migrants find themselves in different situations. For example, a childless university graduate from Warsaw will usually have more freedom of manoeuvre than a working-class family of six from a small town in Poland. Although it is conventional to distinguish between refugees and labour migrants, whose migration is seen respectively as 'forced' and 'voluntary', many labour migrants feel that they do not have much choice. However, as Faist suggests, 'mobility of persons is best viewed as ranging on a continuum from totally voluntary exit ... to totally forced exit, where the migrants are faced with death if they remain in their present place of residence'.[27] One of the reasons for studying small towns and working-class families in particular was the desire to understand the situation of migrant groups with *limited* agency and to dispel myths sometimes encountered in the UK about the unfettered mobility of Polish migrants.

Rather than asking 'how much choice' migrants have, one could ask 'how much do they risk?'. A significant aspect of the migration culture is the extent to which migrants view migration as being relatively risk-free.[28] This is discussed in Chapters Three, Five and Six, which consider, for example, the evidence that experimenting with migration to another EU country is viewed as less risky than experimental relocation to a Polish city.

Networks between sending and receiving societies

'Migrant networks are sets of interpersonal ties that connect migrants, former migrants and nonmigrants in origin and destination areas through ties of kinship, friendship and shared community origin.'[29] A place with strong networks to a receiving country is likely to be exactly the sort of location with a well-developed migration culture, shaped by a myriad of influences passing back and forward across international borders. Networks explain *how* many people migrate – with the help of other people – and also to some extent *why*. Where migrant networks are well established, the risks of migration are reduced and more and more people are encouraged to migrate. A process of 'chain migration' ensues, as one person joins the next. As Massey et al observe with reference to Mexico, 'When migrant networks are well-developed, they put a destination job within easy reach of most community members, making emigration a reliable and relatively risk-free resource'.[30]

Massey et al's formulation begs the question of why 'most' but not 'all' local people are able to access migration networks. If networks are formal organisations and institutions, such as recruitment agencies and job centres, the answer to this question might be that formal qualifications for the jobs on offer are the selection criteria, although applicants also need other kinds of 'human capital', notably confidence to entrust their migration to strangers. Often, by contrast, networks consist of the would-be migrant's friends and relatives, and their friends and relatives in turn. In such cases those who are able to migrate are the people with the right 'social capital'. They are able to exploit good relations with, or call in favours from, people who can help them go abroad.[31]

This book contributes to understanding migration networks by 'analysing the practice of network membership':[32] providing a close-up examination of how people in sending communities use or do not use networks. Chapter Five, for example, looks at whether – according to the unwritten rules of the local migration culture – potential migrants normally create access by asking existing migrants to help them, or whether they tend to wait to be invited. Can the network be seen as a climbing frame, onto which the migrant can scramble, or is it more like a net, where the potential migrant hopes to be 'pulled in' by someone else? Chapter Seven investigates the 'ends' of networks: where – to change the metaphor – does the chain break? Who are the people in the sending communities who do not migrate, and what impact does the transnational activity of other members of the community have on *their* lives?

Migrants abroad: transnationalism and integration

The term 'transnational[ism]' has been defined in different ways. At its simplest level, it refers to the connections which migrants keep with their home countries, the 'persistent and fluctuating ties that bind across borders'.[33] These can be networks, but the term 'transnationalism' is also used to describe activities, such as participating in organisations of fellow nationals in the receiving country, communicating with people in the sending country or frequently returning for visits. When transnationalism became a fashionable concept in the 1990s,[34] it served to some extent merely to draw attention to the existence of things which migrants had always done,[35] and its advocates have been accused of exaggerating the novelty of transnational practices.[36] Nonetheless, the extent of transnationalism has certainly increased, thanks to a variety of factors including cheap international transport and telecommunications, the internet and, for luckier categories of migrant, such as EU citizens, the relaxation of border controls.[37] This opens up opportunities which have qualitatively changed the lives of migrants, as well as the attractiveness of migration. So far this chapter has referred to sending and receiving countries as if they were quite separate places, but using the term 'transnationalism' draws attention to the fact that national borders are becoming less important. Instead of seeing the situation as one country sending and the other receiving, distinctions between sending and receiving are blurred. It is better to think of Polish society *spreading* between Poland and the UK.[38] Hence migrants today are much more likely to feel 'at home' when they are abroad.

Scholars disagree about whether transnationalism is a theory or simply a phenomenon (if it exists at all). This book accepts transnationalism as a real and in some respects new phenomenon, and uses the concept chiefly to understand the evolution of migrants' identities. Above all, transnationalism is important because it helps migrants maintain their former identities while they are abroad: it emphasises the 'portability of national identity'[39] in the modern world. National or perhaps, more precisely, ethnic identity,[40] can be brought from one country to another. This statement might seem trite, were it not for the fact that the concept of transnationalism is built on the understanding that identity is not something given at birth. Instead, it is constantly being maintained and re-constructed. When one interviewee's husband said "However long I live in England, even if I become a citizen, I will still feel Polish," he made the statement that his identity was unchangeable. However, the interesting question is, why would he still feel Polish? The answer is not so obvious, since migrants often lose many aspects of their former identities. For example, they may no longer be able to think of themselves as knowledgeable about popular culture. By using the concept of transnationalism we are drawn towards understanding how migrants actually construct identities for themselves, keeping alive a sense of where they are from. In this case, for example, installing Polish satellite television would be a way of keeping in touch with popular culture in Poland, and maintaining Polish identity in England.

'Transnationalism' directs attention in the right direction, but remains a vague guide. It may imply that ethnic identity is homogeneous: 'there is a danger in applying the concept of transnationalism in a way which stresses the across-the-board sameness of being Polish'.[41] Moreover, it is often criticised for seeming to refer to almost everything migrants do.[42] This book explores how Polish migrants make decisions about how long to stay in the UK, so the focus is narrowly on transnational practices which have a direct bearing on how settled a family feels in the UK. These are home making, maintaining ties with relatives and participation in Polish communities in England. The analysis takes into account the fact that much transnationalism is spontaneous (Poles are not forever consciously repairing their ethnic identities), and that some transnational activities can be too expensive for some migrants. Chapter Nine discusses the different reasons why different interviewees led 'Polish' lives, the extent to which they wanted and were able to do this and the outcomes: did they feel more, or less, at home in the UK?

Understanding transnationalism can also cast light on migrant integration into the receiving society. According to Snel et al, 'Despite limited knowledge on [sic] the relation between transnationalism and integration, the current prevailing political view is that the two are at odds'.[43] If this is the attitude of many politicians and members of the public, it can only be because integration is equated with assimilation, and because of normative assumptions: the belief that migrants 'should' cast off their old identities and adopt the ways of the receiving society. Transnationalism is seen as a disturbing new phenomenon that frustrates this objective, is hostile and exclusivist towards the receiving society and promotes 'ghettoisation' or 'segregation', where migrants remain immersed in their own cultures. However, 'parallel lives', to use the famous phrase from the 2001 Cantle Report,[44] are only one of many possible consequences of transnationalism. As Faist, Levitt, Morawska and other scholars have illustrated, in practice there are many ways in which migrants can combine involvement in the receiving society with the pursuit of diverse transnational activities.[45] Most of these are completely unthreatening to the receiving society and can indeed promote links between the migrants and their local communities, as illustrated, for example, by the Polish organisations discussed in Chapter Nine.

Contemporary scholars tend to understand integration as a half-way house to assimilation, without necessarily assuming that the migrant will complete the journey. Berry's fourfold acculturation[46] model is a useful starting point for understanding integration in this sense, by comparing different migration outcomes. According to Berry, there are four possible migrant orientations, which he refers to as 'strategies', but which are most often viewed as outcomes, rather than processes.[47] 'Marginalisation' is when migrants lose their original cultural identity but also fail to take on the culture of the receiving country. They are left with no clear sense of identity. 'Assimilation' is when migrants forfeit their original culture and replace it with the culture of the receiving society. 'Separation' is the opposite of assimilation, the equivalent of 'segregation', on the level of whole communities. The fourth outcome, 'integration', is the opposite of marginalisation. When they are 'integrated', migrants have acquired two identities. They have multiple contacts with the receiving society, while remaining comfortable with their old identities.[48] This is a way of understanding possible acculturation outcomes, rather than an attempt to sort all migrants into separate boxes. Indeed, individual migrants may sometimes combine elements of different orientations in different aspects of their lives. Nonetheless, integration is, overall, the type of acculturation which is least stressful for the migrant and which is generally preferred.[49]

Focusing mostly on integration as a process, rather than an outcome, Chapters Eight and Nine of this book consider separately the two interweaving strands of integration: integration in the sense of increasing contacts with UK society and in the sense of making a Polish home in England, with the help of transnational activities. This does not imply that adult migrants will think of themselves as having dual national identities; that will probably only be possible for their children. What is required is a mix of the two cultures in a proportion which is comfortable for the migrant at a given time. The concept of 'sufficient' integration is helpful here. A Polish student who comes to pick strawberries for a single summer will need to acculturise to a lesser extent than a Polish child who begins attending an English school. Markova and Black suggest that 'some groups [of East Europeans in the UK] have apparently unproblematic relationships within their neighbourhoods, even without "strongly" identifying with them or forming "strong" relationships. Public policy ... should not simply assume that all immigrants share the goal of integration over the longer term.'[50] The focus of this book is on understanding how Polish migrants view their integration and what they consider to be enough integration for them to feel comfortable about remaining in the UK.

The fourfold paradigm, if used carelessly, may seem to imply that it is up to the migrants to integrate into a (monolithic) receiving culture. The actual diversity and responsibilities of the receiving community should also be recognised. Integration in the sense of the individual migrant learning to operate in two cultures and having both co-ethnic and other networks can be combined, conceptually, with social integration viewed as a 'two-way process'[51] on a societal level, in which members of the (diverse) receiving community welcome newcomers and adapt to accommodate them. This process occurs in the UK when, for example, non-Polish shopkeepers, often Asian, begin to sell Polish foods, or state institutions supply interpreters.

Ager and Strang, in the *Indicators of integration* they produced for the Home Office, address these different dimensions of integration and their interconnections. They describe 'language and cultural knowledge' as a 'facilitator'. On another dimension, integration is about 'social connections', while the 'means and markers' of integration are employment, housing, education and health. Ager and Strang argue that 'whilst the four domains outlined ... under "markers and means" can be thought of as the "public face" of integration, they do not fully explain what integration is about for people as they experience it in their lives'.[52] Hence the significance of social connections. They suggest that:

> ... an individual or group [is] ... integrated within a society when they: achieve public outcomes within employment, housing, education, health etc which are equivalent to those achieved within the wider host communities; are socially connected with members of a (national, ethnic, cultural, religious or other) community with which they identify, with members of other communities and with relevant services and functions of the state; and have sufficient linguistic competence and cultural knowledge, and a sufficient sense of security and stability, to confidently engage in that society in a manner consistent with shared notions of nationhood and citizenship.[53]

'Sufficient' is used twice in this definition, and it is not specified with which community the migrant should identify. It is acceptable for him or her to 'identify' entirely with fellow nationals, but – by contrast – simply to be 'socially connected' with other communities (in the plural). The focus on providing opportunities for migrants 'within employment, housing, education, health etc' reminds us that migrant integration shares the same 'markers and means' as the integration of other social groups and suggests that not every aspect of migrant integration should be seen through an ethnic lens.[54] In addition to their Polishness, the interviewees' identities as working-class women had many implications for their integration. Their lack of useful formal qualifications and their time-consuming domestic responsibilities clearly limited the resources available for them to make satisfactory livelihoods in the UK.

This chapter has already discussed the merits of applying a livelihood strategy approach to the causes of migration, but it should be apparent that it is also useful for understanding the fortunes of migrants once they are in the receiving society. It helps explain how new identities are shaped and how integration occurs.[55] Newly arrived migrants search and experiment, reshaping their livelihood strategies in accordance with their changing perceptions of themselves, in their new environment. For example, to integrate into the foreign labour market they may need to come to terms with deskilling and working in jobs perceived as lower status than the jobs they had at home. From being the majority in their home country, they have to take on the role of an ethnic minority. They make choices about how much to become involved in networks bonding them to the receiving community, or alternatively binding them within the co-ethnic community. It is hard to separate the economic from the psychological and cultural: churchgoing, for example, could be seen as an expression of faith, but it is also a cultural activity and an opportunity for networking which might even bring material benefits.[56]

If making a living and adapting one's identity are parallel and overlapping processes, integration could be defined as the successful forging of a livelihood within the receiving community, where the migrant both earns a sufficient amount of money and also feels comfortable with the amount of identity change he or she has undergone. Again, the idea of sufficiency is significant. A migrant has to be able to understand his or her employer, but complete knowledge of English grammar, for example, is not necessary to construct a livelihood with confidence.

The literature on transnationalism serves as a corrective to the idea that the longer you stay, the 'more integrated' you necessarily become. Integration can be a linear process, but in the 21st century there is also potential for keeping elements of one's ethnic identity indefinitely, through the transnational practices already discussed. Is transnationalism, therefore, a kind of 'happy ending'? Is integration, in the sense of the migrants themselves picking and choosing the ingredients for new identities, a stress-free option? It is important not to be too optimistic about a migrant's freedom of manoeuvre. Highly educated and/or wealthy migrants may have considerable choice about whether or not to engage in transnational activities and to some extent can select from among a range of identities.[57] By contrast, rather than happily exploring different options, working-class parents often feel that they are battling against a series of obstacles thrown in their way. For example, with regard to acculturation, their efforts to learn the language of the receiving country may be thwarted by the unavailability of suitable language classes and their own lack of time. With regard to transnationalism, rather than sitting comfortably within their transnational networks, they are often more conscious of being tugged in different directions, caring responsibilities towards their children in the UK competing with caring responsibilities for relatives left behind in Poland.

Family reunification, gender roles and networks

As already suggested, dense webs of family and friendship networks connect Poland to countries across Western Europe. Individual families are located within these webs, and are emotionally tugged in different directions by ties to family members in various countries. These emotional factors play a role in explaining the decisions migrants make about when and where to go and when to return. Trust and being open to persuasion, for example, are often essential for family reunification abroad. The processes of persuasion and discussion that occur within households are a major theme of this book.[58]

Castles and Miller, in their account of the 'migratory process', suggest that family reunification is a predictable stage in that process:

> Although each migratory movement has its specific historical patterns, it is possible to generalize on the social dynamics of the migratory process.... Most economic migrations start with young, economically active people. They are often 'target-earners', who want to save enough in a higher-wage economy to improve conditions at home, by buying land, building a house, setting up a business, or paying for education or dowries.... As time goes on, many erstwhile temporary migrants send for spouses, or find partners in the new country. With the birth of children, settlement takes on a more permanent character.[59]

At first sight, this analysis seems entirely applicable to much Polish migration to the UK. Even the Polish language terminology mirrors that used by Castles and Miller, emphasising the role of the migrant in initiating the process. They state that 'temporary migrants *send* for spouses'; Poles say that migrants 'collect' family members. The novelty of migration patterns in the 21st century should not be overstated, despite enhanced opportunities for mobility. However, this book explores just how conventional or otherwise Polish family reunification really is. Are gender roles so traditional, and is family reunification so clearly a prelude to permanent settlement abroad?

With regard to gender roles, Castles and Miller suggest that 'as time goes on ... migrants send for spouses', but presumably it makes a difference if the time lapse is now usually months, rather than years. If the wife is easily able to make an 'inspection visit' before joining her husband, this may give her a right to veto which she would otherwise not have enjoyed. Given that independent migration by women is a global trend, it might also be the case that there are more examples today of wives being the pioneer migrants and subsequently inviting their husbands to join them abroad, rather than vice versa. It would seem surprising if, in 21st-century Europe, female migrants were simply shadows of their husbands,[60] and this book explores family migration in the context of expectations about gender roles. The power of children to influence family decision making should also not be ignored. As already mentioned, the pioneer migrant often has some persuading to do, so being open to persuasion is a key attribute for family members who are asked to follow the migrant abroad.

Being open to persuasion may derive from relationships within the individual family: happy families are more trusting. It can also be linked to patriarchal relations within the household, where the husband can impose his will. If the husband is regarded as 'head of the family', this is generally connected to assumptions that he is the main breadwinner. In this case, the wife, with her inferior earning power, can be expected to forfeit her job in the sending country and follow him abroad.

Clearly such attitudes towards gender roles are not particular to individual families but are rooted in the surrounding society. (A discussion of Polish gender roles follows in Chapter Two.) Life stage is also important. Women with pre-school-age children may not work for money and, even if they are employed, they may be less attached to their jobs than mothers of older children, who have been at the same workplace for a long time and see it as an important aspect of their self-identity. In this case, the mother's reluctance to leave her job and the children's reluctance to leave their schoolfriends can be mutually re-enforcing.[61] There are also other social factors which influence being open to persuasion, for example, regarding the status of certain occupations in particular sections of the sending society. Cleaning is a case in point. Many women migrants work as cleaners because the job requires only minimal foreign language knowledge. Where women in the sending country do not have any problems with exchanging their existing job to become cleaners, they are more amenable to family reunification abroad. For instance, some interviewees in Poland were entirely relaxed about the prospect of becoming cleaners abroad, as in the case of Marcelina, an unemployed shop assistant who was about to join her husband in Norway. Other women in more skilled occupations echoed the sentiments of Alina, a nurse and single parent, whose sister was encouraging her to go to the USA: "So, am I supposed to go and be a cleaner? I'd prefer to stay at home."

As Alina's example suggests, the reunification of nuclear families can be seen in the context of the wider transnational networks, where all sorts of family reunification takes place. The 'spouse invites spouse' model is only one of many.[62] In fact, parents join adult children, siblings join siblings and friends join friends. Rather than a husband inviting his wife, for example, a nuclear family might migrate together because a woman with children abroad had invited her sister and the sister's family to join her. Aleksandra, for example, explained that her sister-in-law decided to settle in England because her husband's siblings were already there with their own children: "One family encourages the next".[63]

There is a distinction between conventional family reunification on the one hand, where a migrant husband invites his family to join him abroad, and chain migration on the other, where women invite sisters, mothers, female cousins and friends to join them, usually to do care work or cleaning. Where the husband is not the pioneer migrant but the person left in Poland, a rethinking of gender roles within the household is almost inevitable, since men have to 'take on traditionally female responsibilities'.[64] The opposite side of the coin is that bonds between mother and daughter, sisters, female cousins and female friends may be strengthened by their experience of working together abroad.[65]

Gender relations also have their own dynamic within nuclear families living abroad. The very process of making the decision to migrate will have an impact on relations within families. 'In rejecting old strategies and searching for new ones, an opportunity is opened for household members to renegotiate … their role in decision-making.'[66] As families start to make new lives abroad, these relations are subject to even greater pressure. Integration is complex enough for individuals migrating alone, but the situation is more complicated still when a whole family is involved. It is unlikely that both spouses will be integrated equally and it is impossible for children, especially school-age children, to share exactly the experiences of their parents. This may lead to changing power relationships within the family, such as when children act as interpreters for their parents. Where the husband has migrated first, he is often more proficient in the new environment and his 'trailing' wife can become marginalised, especially if she is not in paid employment.[67] The opposite situation can also occur, however. It is hardly surprising if there is 'a recurring debate concerning the extent to which migration should be viewed as empowering or exploitative for women',[68] given the probability that a shift in power relations – in whichever direction – is so likely an outcome of migration. However, it is not just power relations between family members which are important, but also the quality of relations in general: how disposed family members are to cooperate with one another in forging a common livelihood strategy, how strongly they want to be together and so forth. An extra twist is added by the fact that the family may be migrating into a society where they encounter new norms about gender roles, perhaps challenging some patriarchal assumptions. Because of these contacts Polish men and women may 'start the process of reworking their values and norms in relation to gender issues'.[69]

'Temporariness' and migration timing

'Temporariness' has been widely identified as an aspect of East–West migration within Europe since 1989.[70] Although temporary migrants share the common characteristic that for official purposes they maintain residence in their home country, many authors recognise the actual diversity of temporary migration.[71] It can be short term or part time (for example, seasonal) or both. In fact, circularity, broadly understood to include frequent visits home by semi-settled migrants, is typical of almost all East–West migration within Europe today. Few migrants, it would seem, have uprooted themselves completely, in stark contrast to many émigrés of the Cold War period.

As Cwerner points out, time is an essential dimension of the migration experience: 'the time perspectives and symbols of immigrants affect in many ways their predicament in the "host" society'.[72] Yet, Cwerner argues, surprisingly little is written about temporal aspects of migration. Referring to his research among Brazilians in London, Cwerner suggests the need to supplement classic accounts of the stages of migration (for example by Castles and Miller, discussed earlier), to emphasise in addition the apparently perpetual temporariness, uncertainty and drift that characterise some contemporary migrants' lives.

Temporariness is inextricably linked to the idea of return. Referring to Elchardus et al and their discussion of the 'paradox between the migrants' will to return … and the forever delayed return',[73] Cwerner discusses how migrants have to cope with the fact that often they do not know when or whether they will go home. Of course, many migrants from East–Central Europe are seasonal workers who do not necessarily face this experience, although even they may be unsure about whether to extend their stay, or how many times they will need to undertake seasonal work abroad before they can finally settle down back at home. On the other hand, Polish migrants to the UK often seem to have come with genuinely open-ended plans.[74] Eade et al, writing in 2006, suggested that many Poles in London even pursued a strategy of deliberate open-endedness, a strategy which they labelled 'intentional unpredictability'.[75]

Is there anything new about open-endedness, as a feature of the current wave of migration from East-Central Europe? Gmelch, writing back in 1980, argued that 'most migrants simply do not have definite plans....They go on a trial basis, letting their decision of whether or not to return and when to return be guided by the opportunities they find in the new society.'[76] The novelty today lies not in the exploratory nature of migrant strategies, but perhaps rather in the feasibility of extending the exploratory stage for a much longer period and at less personal cost. It is possible for migrants to travel back and forward between the receiving and sending countries while they are making up their minds what to do, as well as to engage in other transnational practices, as discussed earlier in this chapter. Open-endedness might therefore be seen as a luxury that is the particular privilege of migrants without legal restrictions on their movement and with access to cheap international transport.

On the other hand, given that stress is often the result of uncertainty, it might be the case that too much open-endedness is actually not a luxury, but a burden, particularly for those with family responsibilities who cannot easily adopt a nomadic identity. Moreover, as already indicated, migrants can often be uncertain because they are in the uncomfortable position of being pulled in opposite directions – whether to stay or to go. Roberts, for example, points out that 'immigrants are potentially exposed to multiple, and often conflicting expectations of the duration of their migration. For instance, expectations that derive from communities of origin may clash with those present in communities of destination.'[77] There can also be competing opinions within a single migrant household, as suggested earlier in this chapter, about the best strategy to undertake, and this promotes protracted periods of uncertainty.

Methodology

Primary sources

Given that individual localities in Poland often have specific migration patterns and traditions, as well as diverse economic indicators, it seemed important to study some Polish locations in depth. The two main fieldwork sites were Grajewo, in the north-east region of Podlasie (*województwo Podlaskie*), population 22,309 (2008) and Sanok, population 39,231 (2008) in the south-east region of Podkarpacie (*województwo Podkarpackie*).[78] Podkarpacie is the Polish region with the highest rate of post-2004 migration; Podlasie is in third place.[79]

In 2007 I conducted a pilot survey consisting of 18 interviews. Nine were in 'Poland A', small towns and villages in Wielkopolska, a western region around the prosperous city of Poznań. In general this is a rich area with low rates of post-2004 international migration, about two thirds of the Polish average.[80] The remaining nine interviews, in 'Poland B' (the eastern and more underdeveloped half of the country) took place in Ełk and Suwałki (2007 populations 56,698 and 69,281 respectively)[81] in the north east. I then decided to concentrate the main part of the research in places where there was high migration, on the grounds that (a) where there was less migration people might not have strong opinions about how migration should be done, and (b) in places with high levels of overall migration there might also be a higher incidence of family migration to the UK. I excluded regions near the German border, thinking that much of the migration there would be to Germany and therefore temporary. I made research visits in March–April 2008 (Grajewo, 33 interviews); September 2008 (Sanok, 21 interviews); and March 2009 (Grajewo, 10 repeat interviews). My first hypothesis turned out to be correct: comparing the nine Wielkopolska interviewees and many of my interviewees in the UK, who came from low migration localities, with the interviewees in Grajewo and Sanok, it emerged that motivations and mechanisms for migration could be quite different in regions sending low or high numbers of migrants. High-sending regions had developed quite specific and elaborate cultures of migration, whereas elsewhere individual migrants appeared to be more autonomous. They were less inhibited about using recruitment agencies and less dependent on social networks.

The second hypothesis, that high-sending localities would also send high numbers of families to the UK, was not really confirmed, except in the case of Sanok, where 59.5% of respondents in the opinion poll thought that 'quite a lot' (*sporo*) of families with children had migrated to Western Europe.[82] Because of its particular link to London, dating from the 1990s, the town is rather special, so family migration is well established.

The 30 interviewees in England came from all corners of Poland, and from locations of different sizes, ranging from Warsaw to tiny villages (see Appendix 1). The main fieldwork sites were the cities of Bath (2001 'urban area' population: 90,144) and Bristol (551,066), as well as the nearby small towns of Trowbridge (34,401) and Frome (24,171).[83] Although I originally intended to conduct 10 repeat interviews in the UK as well as Poland, I only conducted three, since, after the formal interviews, I saw many interviewees quite often, and was able to keep up with their news in casual conversation. In addition to the formal interviews, I observed the Bath Polish community in action by teaching English at a Polish parent and toddler group and Saturday School in Bath. I also visited two toddlers groups in Bristol.

I aimed to have a large number of in-depth interviews with people who were roughly similar to one another. This was in order to generalise with greater confidence. I decided to confine my sample to women, in view of their special responsibilities for making decisions about migration with children. Such migration seems most often to take the form of mothers and children reunifying with husbands and fathers, who go abroad first and who are the family pioneers. I also tried to limit my sample to women without higher education because in Poland graduates (of any subject) often have good language skills as well as other resources, and I guessed that families of professional people who migrated might face a smaller number of challenges and that in general they might shape their livelihood strategies differently. For example, Toro-Morn's interviews with married working and middle-class Puerto Rican women in Chicago showed that working-class women followed after their husbands and sometimes only joined them in the USA after difficult household negotiations, including other members of the extended family. By contrast, 'middle-class women came with their husbands and had an agenda of their own'.[84]

I would have liked, in addition, to interview men and people with higher education, and to have conducted a case study of livelihoods in a Polish city. However, since I was doing all the interviews myself, such an expansion (implying several hundred interviews) would have made the project unfeasible. In fact, a handful of UK respondents were from cities, occasionally husbands were present at the interviews (see below) and the interviewees included a few women who had an incomplete higher education as well as five who turned out, during the interview, to be graduates (see Appendix 1). These conversations often provided food for thought, for example, about how even in apparently flourishing cities such as Wrocław, Warsaw and Kraków, there are many families who struggle to make ends meet.

The 72 interviewees in Poland included people who had returned from migration, those who had not yet migrated and/or those who had no future migration plans. Twenty had already migrated themselves and 23 had husbands who had migrated, making 33 households where one or both spouses had migrated in the past or were currently working abroad. In addition, four women had been abandoned by their migrant husbands, and some other divorced husbands were migrants. Nine adult children were currently migrants or had worked abroad. Including siblings, parents, aunts, uncles and cousins, 68 out of the 72 households had migrant family members.

The most interesting interviews in Poland were often with women who had returned from migration or who were considering migration in the near future, and I have drawn particularly on these. However, all interviewees were able to supply dozens of migration stories simply from their personal contacts. As well as their family members, everyone had friends who had migrated. My respondents were typically hairdressers, nurses, kindergarten teacher helpers, factory workers and shop assistants, and they had plenty of opportunities to chat to a range of people in their small towns. Of course, there may have been factual inaccuracies in some of these stories about friends and family members but, equally, there is no reason to suppose that interviewees' stories about themselves were totally 'accurate'. Moreover, stories about third parties could touch on quite intimate matters, such as growing estrangement between two spouses separated as a result of migration, matters which interviewees may not have wanted to talk about with reference to themselves and about which I never asked directly.

The interviews with mothers were loosely structured around a list of topics that I had memorised. I often opened the interview by mentioning my own migration history (working in Poland in the early 1980s) and the fact that I, too, was a mother. Comparing the number, age and sex of our children helped establish rapport. Usually the interviews were quite conversational in character. Since most interviews took place in interviewees' own homes I was able to form a superficial impression of their living conditions and also often to meet members of their families. Sometimes the presence of other family members was inhibiting, since, for example, it was hard to discuss openly the risks associated with a mother's plans to migrate if these might be disturbing for small children who were present. Occasionally a husband or mother dominated part of the conversation. Usually, however, it was helpful to meet other family members, particularly husbands who had their own views on things and could also fill in details of the family's migration history that the wife had forgotten.

The 115 interviews with mothers were backed up by interviews and conversations with key informants such as teachers and headteachers, a community development worker, the head of a UK job agency and job centre heads and employees in Poland (see Appendix 1). In addition, I commissioned an opinion poll to find out about views on parental and family migration in one of the regions where I did my fieldwork, Podkarpacie. The sample was 1,101 residents of the region, not including the city of Rzeszów. The poll was a telephone survey conducted by BD Center Consulting; I wrote the questions (see Appendix B). There are no cities other than Rzeszów, or even towns of over 67,000, in Podkarpacie; this was an attempt to access public opinion in small towns and villages in a high-sending region. The sample included both men and women. I also computed the findings for mothers of children under the age of 20, without higher education, and found that they differed little from the overall sample.[85]

The local media and other local publications could, in theory, help shape perceptions about migration trends within communities. However, my research (both the pilot project in different localities in 2007 and the Grajewo/Sanok research in 2008-09) revealed an almost complete silence on the topic of migration in those communities. To confirm my impression, I talked to librarians and consulted their databases of articles from the local press. When I called in at the offices of one local newspaper to ask why they did not publish more articles about emigration, the editor's response was "We should do". A librarian, speculating on why nothing had been written about migration from Grajewo, suggested that migration was such a feature of everyday life that it was taken for granted. On the other hand, I wondered if migration was too uncomfortable a subject to discuss. When an article about migrants abandoning their children did appear in a Podlasie newspaper, it blamed parents in the west of Poland for being so hardhearted as to leave their children in children's homes, and asserted that this did not happen locally.[86] Exceptionally, one newspaper, not local to Sanok but nonetheless covering the south-east corner of Poland, published some articles in 2007 about so-called 'euro-orphans', children left in Poland by one or both parents, who had migrated to Western Europe (see Chapter Seven).[87]

By contrast, the national media quite often carry reports about migration and sometimes interviewees' discussion of local friends and family seemed to be coloured by national media analyses. For example:

> The daughters are OK, perhaps they're more attached to their mother, but it's hard to bring up a boy on your own, it's hard....Those children must definitely feel the fact that their father is away. Euro-orphans, that's what they are. There was a television programme about them recently. (Maria, Grajewo)

Other interviewees were critical of the national media for presenting a picture that did not accord with their own first-hand impressions. Magda (Sanok) complained, for example: "On television you hear lots of people are coming back to Poland. Massive amounts.... But I don't think there are. You can't see it."

Translation issues

Where I use 'migrate' and 'migration' in quotations from interviews, the Polish words were usually the more colloquial *wyjeżdżać/wyjechać*, or the plural noun *wyjazdy*. I usually translate 'there' and 'here' (*tam* and *tu[taj]*) as 'in England/Bath/ Bristol' and 'in Poland/Grajewo/Sanok', or vice versa. These words are much more commonly used in Polish than in English. 'There' is the country from which you are absent. *U nas* ('in our place/country') is translated 'in Poland', which sounds more natural in English. The verb *ściągać*, used to express the idea of one migrant bringing over another, has been translated in various ways, mainly for stylistic reasons. 'Pull in' (in the sense of pulling in a chain) is sometimes appropriate; in other cases I have used 'bring over' or 'invite'. I tend to translate *święta* (religious holidays) as 'Christmas and Easter'. Where distances between towns are indicated, these are not as the crow flies, but by road, from information provided by Google maps.

Anonymity

All personal names have been changed, and I attempted to give interviewees names appropriate to their age group. Given the large number of pseudonyms required, and the limited number of common Polish names, I have used most names twice, but never for women from the same location. For example, one Ewa is labelled 'Ewa, UK' and the other 'Ewa, Grajewo'. Some husbands, children and friends of interviewees have also been given pseudonyms. In cases where the person was talking about sensitive matters such as her relationship with her husband, or criticising her neighbours, I have concealed the identity of the interviewee, not using even a pseudonym. The samples from Grajewo and Sanok were sufficiently large for anonymity not to be compromised by mentioning the name of the town, but in other cases I have normally concealed the precise location unless it is particularly relevant. The use of many small quotations from different interviewees also helps protect anonymity, by making it harder for the reader to follow the stories of individual women, something which would have been facilitated had I adopted a case study approach instead. There are also few references to contributions to internet discussion forums. Although in many cases contributors use pseudonyms, even these have not been indicated.

Structure of the book

Chapters Two to Seven consider the lives of people in contemporary Poland and broadly address the theme of why some Poles migrate. Chapters Eight to Ten consider the lives of Polish families in England and examine why some people consider return and others, becoming more integrated, are increasingly committed to remaining in the UK. Chapter Eleven, the conclusions, summarise, in turn, the main empirical findings and the book's contribution to migration theory.

Chapter Two provides some brief information about Polish society and the history of migration from Poland. Chapter Three examines the perceived shortcomings of local livelihoods in Poland, the economic 'push' factors promoting migration. Chapters Four and Five explore facets of the local migration culture in places like Grajewo and Sanok, attitudes that promote migration in certain circumstances and for certain objectives. Chapter Six focuses on one aspect of the migration culture: conventions about gender roles and migration. It discusses why fathers and/or mothers migrate and the increasing popularity of migration by both parents with their children. It investigates the role of economic versus emotional reasons for family reunification among the UK interviewees, and this leads on to Chapter Seven, which is about the negative emotional impacts of migration on Polish communities and families. I argue that whole family migration is often a response to widespread concern about impacts of single-parent migration such as damaged marriages and lonely children.

The latter part of the book examines the integration of Polish migrants as the context in which they are more or less likely to feel like staying in the UK for an extended period. Chapter Eight is about integration in the sense of building bridges into the surrounding UK community and being welcomed into it. Chapter Nine looks at integration in the sense of being able to make a Polish home in the UK, and constructing one's own Polish identity within the context of UK Polish communities. Chapter Ten investigates plans and thoughts regarding return. It explores why some pulls prove to be stronger than others and, in particular, why families are likely to make the decision to stay in the UK.

Notes

[1] See, for example, Bobek (2009); Fomina (2009); Parutis (2006); Trevena (2005).

[2] For example, Anderson et al (2006, 2007); most contributors to Burrell (2009a); Eade et al (2006); Garapich (2006, 2008, 2009); Goodwin and Goodwin (2009); Iglicka (2008); Osipowicz (2010); Ryan et al (2007, 2008, 2009). See www.bath.ac.uk/esml/polish-migration/publications.html for a bibliography of recent publications on Polish migration.

[3] A number of papers presenting ongoing research into different aspects of Polish family migration were presented at the 'Children, Families and the Migration Experience: Opportunities and Challenges' Conference, Middlesex University, 21 May 2010 (after this book was submitted for publication). See www.kronoweb.net/polishconference/Conference%20programme%20-%2021%20May.doc

[4] Home Office (2009) figures for people registering on the Worker Registration Scheme capture some of the inflow of mothers with children and suggest that at least 46,000 children under 17 years old came from Poland to the UK between May 2004 and March 2009. Home Office figures are for all registering Accession 8 (A8) migrants, that is, people from the East-Central European countries that joined the EU in 2004. Sixty-six per cent of the overall total were Poles; my total represents 66% of the number of dependants given by the Home Office, although there is no way of telling whether some nationalities were more likely than others to come with children. Some children have, of course, gone home. Nonetheless, the figures are probably much higher than the WRS figures suggest. By no means all mothers work – some are self-employed and not everyone who should register does so.

[5] UK Labour Force Survey data. Source: email communication (27 February 2008), regarding unpublished Institute for Public Policy Research data, from Dhananjayan Sriskandarajah, Director of Research Strategy, Institute for Public Policy Research (London).

[6] Pollard et al (2008, p 27).

[7] Walczak (2008, p 2). I give some local Polish figures in Chapter Six. For UK figures see, for example, Sales et al (2008) on several London boroughs, or Garapich (2008a) on Hammersmith and Fulham.

[8] See Corden and Sainsbury (2006) for the rationale and ethical dimensions of using verbatim quotation.

[9] The concept of return migration is discussed in Chapter Ten. Other concepts such as 'social capital', 'social remittances', 'norms' and 'community' are discussed as they are introduced, but not in detail.

[10] This is recognised by authors writing about return migration, for example, Gmelch (1980). For a review of pushes and pulls influencing return, see King (2000, pp 14–18).

[11] See, for example, Massey et al (1998) or Castles and Miller (2009) for a discussion of migration theories.

[12] DfID (1999, p 1). Ellis (2000, p 231) defines livelihoods as 'the activities, the assets, and the access that together determine the living gained by the individual or household'. Similarly, Kanji (2002, p 140), defines them as the 'wide range of activities that allow individuals to gain and retain access to resources and opportunities, deal with risk and

manage social networks and institutions'. Jacobsen (2002, p 99) suggests that 'the pursuit of livelihoods ... refers to the availability, extent and mix of resources, the strategies used to access and mobilize these resources, and the goals and changing priorities' of the individual or household.

[13] Wallman, S. and associates (1982) *Living in South London: Perspectives on Battersea 1871-1981*, London: Gower/London School of Economics, cited by Long (2000, p 197).

[14] 'Social capital' has been defined in numerous ways. In relation to livelihood strategies, it is used in the meaning developed by Bourdieu as a resource available to individuals.

[15] Olwig and Sørensen (2002, p 1). Olwig and Sørensen (like, for example, Duany) are chiefly interested in the fact that migrants pursue dual location livelihoods, which 'allow circular migrants to combine various resources from work, family, and the state' in two countries (Duany, 2002, p 360, writing about Puerto Rico and the USA). See White (2009b, pp 568-70) for a fuller discussion of migration as a livelihood strategy.

[16] Internal migration in Russia has many similarities with international migration from Poland to the UK. A major cause is the limited range of livelihoods available in small towns and villages, particularly livelihoods that would allow local people to save up for housing or higher education. Migrants from the provinces often perceived big cities, and Moscow in particular, as 'another continent', so there is an acculturation process, and migrants are often poorly integrated in terms of housing and jobs. See White (2007, 2009b).

[17] Mandel (2004).

[18] Jacobsen (2002, p 96).

[19] For an example of the latter situation, see, for example, Hossain et al (2003) on the migration strategies of extremely poor households in Bangladesh.

[20] Some writers (for example, Duany) use the terms 'survival', 'subsistence' and 'livelihood' interchangeably. Wallace (2002a) uses 'household strategies'.

[21] This is the term used by Pickup and White (2003, p 421); it can also be labelled a 'development strategy' (Kaczmarczyk, 2008b, pp 159-84).

[22] Castles and Miller (2009, p 23).

[23] See Galasińska and Kozłowska (2009); Galasińska (2010); White (2009b) (on similar discourse in Russia).

[24] Pine and Bridger (1998, p 11).

[25] Jolly with Reeves (2005, p 3).

[26] Byron (1994, p 63).

[27] Faist (2000, p 24).

[28] New economics of labour migration theorists claim that households choose migration as a strategy for one member as a way of reducing the risk associated with everyone remaining in the home locality (Castles and Miller, 2009, p 24). However, the interviewees in this research never suggested that migration was a way of avoiding keeping all their eggs in one basket. They did discuss how much, if anything, they risked by international migration.

[29] Massey et al (1998, p 448). For a discussion of migration network theory, see, for example, Boyd (1989); Castles and Miller (2009, pp 28-30); Faist (2000).

[30] Massey, D.S., Alarón, R., Durand, J. and González, H. (1987) *Return to Aztlan: The social process of international migration from Western Mexico*, Berkeley and Los Angeles, CA: University of California Press, cited by Palloni et al (2001, pp 1266-7).

[31] For a discussion, see, for example, Faist (2000, pp 14-15).

[32] Cassarino (2004, p 266).

[33] Harney and Baldassar (2007, p 191).

[34] Transnationalism was 'launched', although not invented, in 1990 at a conference of social anthropologists in New York; the proceedings were published as Glick Schiller et al (1992).

[35] Portes (2001, p 184).

[36] For critique, see Kivisto (2001); Portes (2001); Vertovec (2001).

[37] Vertovec (2001, p 574) also mentions political changes that have increased migrants' 'capacity for political organisation ... sending countries' more positive views of their emigrants, and the impact of migrant remittances on local economies and labour markets'.

[38] These are often referred to as 'transnational social fields'; Faist (2000) prefers 'social spaces', where 'space has a social meaning that extends beyond simple territoriality' (p 45).

[39] Sassen, S. (1998) 'The de facto transnationalizing of immigration policy', in C. Joppke (ed) *Challenge to the nation-state: Immigration in Western Europe and the United States*, Oxford: Oxford University Press, cited in Vertovec (2001, p 575).

[40] The distinction between 'ethnic' and 'national' is a vague one, but since 'national identity' could be construed as merely referring to citizenship, it seems preferable to use the term 'ethnic' to indicate that cultural attributes of Polishness are the main focus of discussion. As this book suggests, tension can exist where a migrant feels alienated from the state but culturally connected to the nation. For discussion and exploration of Polishness as a 'national' identity among migrants, see Burrell (2006).

[41] Temple (2010, p 297).

[42] The enormous diversity of practices that could be described as transnational has led scholars to categorise different kinds of transnational activities as being 'broad' or 'narrow', and so forth. Levitt suggests that 'cross-border practices vary by scope, intensity, goals, institutional context, and the socioeconomic characteristics of those who pursue them' (Levitt, 2003, p 179).

[43] Snel et al (2006, p 287).

[44] Cantle (2001, p 9): 'Separate educational arrangements, community and voluntary bodies, employment, places of worship, language, social and cultural networks, means that many communities operate on the basis of a series of parallel lives. These lives often do not seem to touch at any point, let alone overlap and promote any meaningful interchanges.'

[45] Faist (2000); Levitt (2003); Morawska (2003).

[46] Acculturation 'has been defined as culture change that results from continuous, first-hand contact between two distinct cultural groups' (Redfield, R. et al (1936) 'Memorandum on the study of acculturation', *American Anthropologist*, vol 38, cited by Neto et al, p 20). Properly speaking, acculturation in general terms refers to a collective process, while 'psychological acculturation' refers to changes in the individual group member (Neto et al, 2005, p 20).

[47] Ward (2008, p 107).

[48] The model has been elaborated by Berry in a series of works. For a recent exposition, see Berry and Sabatier (2010). For critique, see, for example, Rudmin (2003) and Ward (2008).

[49] Neto et al (2005, p 20).

[50] Markova and Black (2007, p xiv).

[51] See Spencer et al (2007, pp 5-6) for analysis of the two levels of integration, personal and collective, and also Ager and Strang (2004, p 6). On the related concept of social cohesion, see, for example, Hudson et al (2007). This book does not explore government policies to promote sustainable communities, or the controversy they have generated. Rather, the Home Office indicators are adopted because they are a useful tool for answering the research question, 'What determines decision making about how long to stay in the UK?'.

[52] Ager and Strang (2004, p 3).

[53] Ager and Strang (2004, p 5). The Home Office indicators were produced to facilitate the integration of people who had been granted refugee status in the UK. See Phillips (2009, p 213).

[54] For a discussion, see Garapich (2009).

[55] See Long (2000, pp 196-7) on the 'identity-constructing processes inherent in the pursuit of livelihoods'.

[56] Temple (2010, p 295).

[57] See, for example, Snel et al (2006); White and Ryan (2008).

[58] See, for example, Siara (2009) for Polish migrant internet forum discussions about gender roles and, on household discussions and disagreements: Al-Ali (2002); Bailey and Boyle (2004, p 231); Grasmuck and Pessar (1991, Chapter 6); Ryan et al (2009, p 72); Slany and Malek (2005, p 136); Toro-Morn (1995).

[59] Castles and Miller (2009, p 33). On women's migration see, for example, Ackers (1998); Passerini et al (2007); Slany (2008); Zontini (2004).

[60] See, for example, Ackers (2004) and Zontini (2004).

[61] Mincer (1978, p 764).

[62] See, for example, Ryan et al (2009, pp 69-70) for a discussion of some of the different patterns of 'family migration' from Poland to the UK.

[63] Interviewed in Sanok, 2008.

[64] Lukowski (1998, p 149), discussing households in Perlejewo in the mid-1990s.

[65] See, for example Guzik's stories (2005) about Polish women working in Italy (based on the experiences of her sister and friends).

[66] Grasmuck and Pessar (1991, p 161).

[67] Bailey and Boyle (2004, p 230).

[68] McIlwaine et al (2006, pp 4-5). See also the discussion in United Nations (2005, pp 14-18 and 62-64).

[69] Siara (2009, p 181).

[70] See, for example, Morokvasic (2004) and Wallace (2002b).

[71] For example, the ethnosurvey conducted by the Warsaw Centre of Migration Research in the 1990s identified six types of temporary migration; see Iglicka (2001, p 37). Iglicka points out (p 41) that short-term temporary migration was the most rapidly increasing category.

[72] Cwerner (2001, p 7).

[73] Elchardus, M. et al (1987) 'Temps, culture et coexistence', Studi Emigrazione, vol 24, no 86, p 146, cited by Cwerner (2001, p 12).

[74] As suggested, for example, by Eade et al (2006, p 11) and Home Office accession monitoring reports.

[75] Eade et al (2006, p 11).

[76] Gmelch (1980, p 138).

[77] Roberts (1995, p 44).

[78] GUS (2009a, p 90).

[79] Kaczmarczyk (2008b, p 37).

[80] Kaczmarczyk (2008b, p 37).

[81] GUS (2009a, pp 90-1).

[82] Twenty-two out of 37. Overall, 45.7% respondents in the south-east corner of Podkarpacie (where Sanok is located) felt that many families had migrated, compared with the below average figure of 37.6% in the west of the region. See Appendix 2 for details of the sub-regions.

[83] Figures are from the 2001 Census and are for the 'urban area' extending slightly beyond city boundaries (ONS, 2004).

[84] Toro-Morn (1995, p 718).

[85] Podkarpacie cannot be considered typical of all Poland. Apart from being the region with the most international migration since EU accession, it has a rural population of 53%, compared with 32.6% for Poland as a whole, and this helps account for the fact that is also untypical of Poland in other respects: with an even higher proportion of practising Catholics, larger households and more traditional gender roles. It is also a poor region and, even in towns, incomes are lower than the Polish average and local people display higher than average pessimism about prospects for the future (Strzeszewski, 2008).

[86] Anon (2007a).

[87] *Super Nowości*, at www.pressmedia.com.pl/sn. It seems that the material was also used by *Super Nowości's* partners, interia.pl and polskalokalna.pl. One article, featuring comments from Sanok, appeared on the Sanok website isanok.pl ('Sieroty emigracji', attributed to 'admin').

TWO

Post-communist Poland: social change and migration

This chapter provides some background information about Poland as a whole, giving the context for the more detailed examination of livelihoods in specific Polish locations that follows in Chapters Three to Seven. The term 'post-communist' is used, the adjective preferred by political scientists, in preference to 'post-socialist', a label used by some sociologists and anthropologists. The Polish political system from 1944-89 was far from 'socialist', as social democrats understand the term. Communist party rule, however, was a reality.

Social and economic change since 1989

After the collapse of the communist regime in 1989, the Polish government immediately introduced 'shock therapy' to reform the economy. Although in the short term this created a deep recession, Poland also returned to growth more quickly than the rest of East-Central Europe, and by 1996 gross domestic product (GDP) had outstripped 1989 levels.[1] During the recession of the early 1990s, factories closed and others laid off workers: registered unemployment rose steeply from 0.3% in January 1990 to 16.9% in July 1994. It then began to fall, before rising again from 1998, peaking at 20.6% in January–February 2004, on the eve of EU accession. As the economy recovered (and perhaps also as a result of migration) unemployment then began to fall, arriving at a low of 8.8% in October 2008. With the global economic crisis, unemployment climbed to 11% by April 2009.[2] So many Poles have experience of unemployment (37% in late 2007)[3] that it is not surprising if they are anxious about losing their jobs and pessimistic about the Polish labour market.

National opinion polls show growing satisfaction with living standards over the 1990s, followed by increasing discontent around the turn of the century. When asked to compare their social standing in 2004 with their position in 1994, 38% of respondents in a national poll felt they had dropped down the social ladder, 46% believed their status was unchanged and only 17% believed that their position had improved.[4] Again, it is easy to see why many Poles believed, around the time of EU accession, that migration would be a better livelihood strategy than staying at home. Economic growth in the 21st century and greater political stability since 2007 has promoted increasing optimism. By 2009 Poles were expressing considerably greater satisfaction with their living standards than at any time in the post-communist period. In May 2009, 42% of Poles felt that they and their families lived 'well', while 44% said 'neither well nor badly' and only 14% answered 'badly'.[5]

As these figures suggest, the transition to a market economy has created 'winners', but also 'losers'. There is, in addition, a sizeable group who are ambivalent about their status. In terms of the distribution of income across society, Poland is slightly more equal than the UK and comparable to Ireland.[6] It appears that regional economic disparities are somewhat decreasing in Poland, and they are less pronounced than, for example, in Germany.[7] Nonetheless, economic differences remain significant and they find political reflection. The terms 'Poland A' and 'Poland B' crudely capture the difference between the wealthier, western part of the country, and regions to the east of the River Vistula. The June 2009 elections to the European Parliament showed Poland still neatly divided between east and west. The most popular party in the eastern constituencies was Law and Justice (PiS, Prawo i Sprawiedliwość), which presents itself as a champion of 'transition losers'.[8]

However, 'A' and 'B' are simplistic labels that fail to capture the actual socioeconomic diversity of Poland. Within each half of Poland, there are significant differences and within a single region even neighbouring small towns and rural districts can be very dissimilar. For example, unemployment in Grajewo was 17.7% in January 2009, nearly twice the figure in neighbouring Mońki.[9] Small towns across Poland also share similarities that distinguish them from larger places. Everywhere, for example, small towns dependent on just one or two major factories are vulnerable to unemployment. A national survey in March 2009 discovered an exact correlation between size of settlement and level of optimism about the possibility of finding a job on the local labour market. Those believing it would be 'difficult' or even 'impossible' to find a job locally included: 79% of villagers, 67% of small-town residents, 58% in medium towns, 47% in smaller cities and 24% in cities of over 500,000 population.[10]

Gender inequality is another aspect of post-communist Poland. Under the communist regime, on paper women enjoyed equal rights and there were high numbers of women in paid employment – by 1970, 80% of all women aged 15 to 54.[11] However, as elsewhere in the Soviet bloc, women were disproportionately represented in low-paid sectors of the economy and had little access to managerial jobs or political power. Social attitudes were often conservative, despite the rhetoric of equality. Most women combined paid employment with a heavy burden of domestic work. This was not entirely a male breadwinner model of gender relations, however, since the state and workplace also assumed responsibility for supporting families. Following the collapse of communism, women were badly affected by the retraction of state childcare services and other support for working mothers, which has made it harder for women to take paid employment in an already constricted labour market. Sexist attitudes and sexual exploitation of women are more open than under the communist regime, as is discrimination in the workplace.[12]

However, 20 years have passed since the collapse of communism, and it is important to distinguish problems of the early 1990s from the current situation. Since migration is gendered, it is helpful to try to establish how women stand on the Polish labour market and how Poles view women's and men's roles within the family. A June 2009 national opinion poll showed that even in 2009 women were just as pessimistic as in 1993 about their prospects on the labour market – 59% believed that women had fewer chances than men to find a job.[13] Women's pay is about 60% of men's, a similar proportion to that in the UK and USA. In another recent survey of Polish women, 47% felt that women were discriminated against in the workforce, while 31% disagreed.[14]

Nonetheless, there is evidence of changing opinions about women's roles. Overall, it seems that women are increasingly enthusiastic about paid employment. When a national opinion poll asked whether having a job was beneficial, overall, for a woman's 'family life', in 1993 only 28% agreed that it was; by 2009 42% agreed, with 24% feeling that the pros and cons were equally balanced.[15] In 1993, only 48% of women felt that women with paid jobs were more respected than housewives; in 2009, the figure had risen to 67%.[16] As elsewhere in Europe, it seems that belief in the 'male breadwinner' is to some extent being superseded by enthusiasm for a dual carer/dual earner model.[17] A survey in 1994 found that only 35% of respondents supported a 'partner-like' marriage where both spouses worked and they shared childcare and housework. In 2004, the figure had risen to 56% (51.5% of men and 60% of women).[18] Moreover, surveys tend to suggest that there is much more enthusiasm for 'partner-like' marriages among younger and better-educated Poles. For example, in the 2004 survey 63.5% of 18- to 24-year-olds supported the 'partner-like model'.[19] However, enthusiasm for equal roles within the household is greater than actual practice. In 2007, only 15.5% of couples claimed they did equal quantities of housework, as well as an equal amount of paid work, and in 19.3% of households the wife had no paid employment.[20] Women continue to do most of the cooking, laundry and childcare, including supervising children's homework (a recurring theme in this book).[21] They are also likely to have caring responsibilities in the extended family.

Close relations with the extended family remain very important for many Poles. A 2007 survey, for example, found that 73% of adult Poles saw their parents, 58% saw grown-up children living separately and 41% saw siblings at least once a week. These were more or less identical to responses given in a survey in 1997, suggesting that mass migration has not weakened ties between those left in Poland.[22]

With regard to relations between children and parents, there is some evidence that these too are more egalitarian than in the past. 'The role of modern fathers has also changed – there is an increasing tendency for children to treat their fathers as partners rather than authorities who impose values and life styles.'[23]

Young people today, who have grown up in the post-communist era, differ in some respects from the rest of the population, and also from their own parents when the latter were young. Surveys show, for example, that the young are optimistic.[24] A 2008 survey concluded that one third of students were 'very happy' with life.[25] The different levels of optimism which surveys show to characterise differently-sized locations in Poland partly reflect their different demographic profiles: city dwellers seem to be happier, but this could be partly because Polish cities contain exceptionally high proportions of students, by European standards.[26]

The proportion of young people going to university has increased hugely in the post-communist period. By the early 21st century nearly 50% of the 19- to 24-year-old age cohort were students, although only 11.5% of the total population had university degrees. The number of workplaces for graduates has not increased correspondingly and this has contributed to what Fihel and Kaczmarczyk describe as the 'brain overflow' since 2004, with many Polish young people migrating to Western Europe immediately after graduation because they could not find, or did not even try to look for jobs in Poland.[27]

Foreign language knowledge is closely related to age and this has an influence on the direction of migration flows. Surveys conducted between 1997 and 2006 showed an increase from 37% to 45% of Poles who could make themselves understood in a foreign language, and this was largely because of increasing knowledge of foreign languages among young people in particular. In 2006, 77% of 18- to 24-year-olds, but only 59% of people aged 25-34 and 41% of people aged 35-44, felt they could communicate in a foreign language.[28] The language concerned was usually English, as suggested by the following data about which languages were spoken by 18- to 19-year-old school students.

Figure 2.1: What foreign language do you speak well enough to have a conversation with a foreigner?

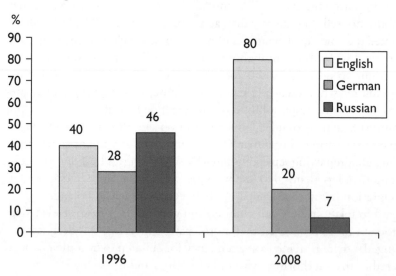

Source: Badora et al (2009, p 127)

Migration from Poland

Poland has a history of shifting borders and of migration, both forced and voluntary. From around 1860, ethnic Poles (mostly impoverished peasants) and Jews (escaping poverty and persecution) began emigrating en masse from eastern parts of Poland. More than 3.5 million had left by 1914.[29] The USA was the most common destination, but Poles also migrated to European countries as well as to Canada, Australia and other destinations. In addition, hundreds of thousands of Poles worked in German fields and mines.[30] Between the two world wars nearly two million more Poles migrated 'for bread'.[31] The Second World War and its aftermath entailed the mass displacement of Poles, Germans, Ukrainians, Belorussians and Lithuanians, as the borders of Poland shifted to the West. For the first time, too, the UK acquired a Polish diaspora, with the settlement of former soldiers and airmen.[32]

During 1944-89, the Polish communist regime attempted to control and limit emigration. It permitted and encouraged the exodus of most of Poland's remaining Jews as well as the migration of ethnic Germans to East and West Germany (1,372,000 in the years 1950-90).[33] Other migration was highly restricted. However, the communists could not prevent labour migration. Many departing 'Germans' were ethnically Polish. In addition, and despite the difficulty of acquiring a passport for foreign travel, migration resumed to North America, with over 100,000 Poles arriving in the USA between 1950 and 1980.[34] Moreover, from the early 1970s Polish 'tourists' began travelling to Western Europe on holiday visas and by the 1980s hundreds of thousands of undocumented traders and temporary workers were shaping livelihoods in Western Europe; as time went on, these stays often became more extended.[35] Migration soared in the 1980s as Poles – particularly young and highly educated people – left the country in response to economic chaos and political repression following the suppression of the Solidarity movement. More than two million Poles migrated during the 1980s, about 45% of them to West Germany.[36]

After Solidarity's victory in the 1989 elections and the collapse of the communist regime, more highly educated Poles tended to cease migrating, and some returned to Poland.[37] However, labour migration grew, in response to the economic hardship of the early 1990s. Germany was still the favourite destination, especially from south-western parts of Poland, where some local communities became almost entirely dependent on migrant remittances.[38] Other countries also became popular, with networks often building up around Polish communities first established in the 1980s. In Greece and Italy, Polish women typically worked as undocumented cleaners and care workers. Working in Brussels became a normal livelihood in north-eastern Poland. With the setting up of regular coach services, by the mid-1990s 'it [wa]s as if Belgium were next-door'.[39] At the same time, migration continued to North America. Indeed, the introduction of 'diversity visa lotteries' to the USA in 1990 resulted in a concerted effort by Poles to buy up lottery tickets, with the result that about a third of the winners were Polish.[40] According to interviewees, this was a time when many families from eastern Poland departed for the USA. However, overall labour migration in the period 1989-2004 was often risky and undocumented. High migration localities in Poland developed a specific migration culture, in Morawska's phrase, a kind of 'toolkit'[41] for finding ways around the obstacles to migration. Migrants necessarily depended heavily on knowing the right people and relying where possible on family members.

Labour migration between 1989 and 2004 was typically not migration for settlement. Money earned abroad was spent in Poland – often on everyday consumption – and the family home remained in Poland. The practice of 'earning there but spending here' is labelled 'incomplete migration' by Polish scholars, following Marek Okólski.[42] It can be viewed as the result of push factors in Poland. It is unlikely that many of these labour migrants would have chosen to migrate, had they found acceptable jobs in Poland, where they had left their children and often also their spouses. Moreover, the third possibility – resettling abroad – was equally out of bounds for most. Morokvasic in effect adopts a livelihood strategy approach when she writes of 'a context in which possibilities of immigration and settlement and those of regular employment [in Poland] are extremely limited'.[43] Her phrase 'settled in mobility' captures the perpetually transient existence of these lone migrants. Given the undocumented nature of so much migration[44] it was hard to bring children to live abroad, although families did begin to settle, particularly in places where there was employment for both sexes, such as Brussels and London. Polish migrants before 2004 also included young people hoping to have an adventure and gain life experience as well as make some money and escape unemployment at home. Iglicka argues that in the 1990s international migration was 'becoming a way of life for some specific segments of society: older, less educated persons who were unable to adapt to Poland's new market economy and young people, mainly vocational school graduates, sometimes unemployed or in the process of seeking a job in Poland'.[45]

In 2004, when Poland joined the EU, it was younger people who seem particularly to have responded to the pull factors of open access to UK and Irish labour markets,[46] as well as cheap international transport. Poles rapidly became the largest group of foreign-born UK residents. By the end of 2004, according to Polish figures, there were perhaps 150,000 Poles staying in the UK for a period of over two months; by the end of 2007, this figure had climbed to 690,000.[47] In a textbook description of transnationalism, a Polish journalist observed:

> Emigration has ceased to be a great trauma. It no longer forces people to break their ties with their home country. The passengers on cheap airlines who arrive back in Poland for a few days with hand luggage only are no different from their contemporaries who on Friday evening hurry home on the Warsaw-Lublin train. The journey lasts the same time.[48]

Although, as already mentioned, unemployment in Poland peaked at the beginning of 2004 at 21% and therefore constituted a powerful 'push' factor, opportunities to travel and improve English language skills were also important motivations for this new wave of migrants. EU commissioner Danuta Hübner asserted that 'Young people will treat migration to the West as an adventure and the opportunity to gain experience'.[49] A handbook for Poles planning to work in the UK asserted that 'More and more Poles are deciding to work abroad not only to put aside a little money, but also to get experience of work and life abroad'.[50] Kaczmarczyk suggests that 'most recent Polish migrants are under 35, relatively well-educated, single and with language skills, and migrate to Ireland and the UK, while the longer-term migrants [those who began migrating before 2004] are less well-educated, have poor language skills and go to Germany, Italy and Spain'.[51] The adventure seekers included many students and recent graduates, including students from prosperous Polish cities. The labour migrants included 'the very large number of low skilled residents of stagnant small towns and villages for whom Poland can offer no career prospects'.[52] It would seem, therefore, that age, education/skills and size of home town are particularly relevant variables in determining whether migrants go to the UK or to continental Europe.

It is important to note, however, that even in the UK the typical migrant is not highly educated and not from a city. Well-educated Polish migrants from cities are better represented in the UK than in other countries, but three quarters of migrants to the UK are *not* university graduates, 41% come from towns of under 100,000 population and 31% come from rural areas.[53] Moreover, although many are childless and single when they arrive, it is common for young migrants to marry people they meet in England, usually Poles. Marriages are often soon followed by the birth of children.[54] Finally, as already explained at the beginning of Chapter One, the number of Polish children arriving in the UK directly from Poland increased substantially after 2004.

Overall, migration has touched a large proportion of the Polish population since 1989. A 2007 survey conducted in Poland found that 9.5% of Poles had worked abroad at some time in the past 10 years and 0.9% were currently still working abroad. However, different proportions of the local population migrate from different regions in Poland. The highest migration regions since 2004, Podkarpacie, Świętokrzyskie and Podlasie, have 2.23, 1.68 and 1.55 times the national average. The lowest region, Mazowieckie, surrounding Warsaw, has only 55% of that average.[55] This book is largely about the high-migration regions of Podkarpacie (Grajewo) and Podlasie (Sanok) and the high incidence of migration from these locations is suggested by the data presented in Table 2.1.

My own survey in small-town and rural Podkarpacie showed that one third of respondents had had a close family member in Britain during the course of the previous year. Studies of individual towns and villages reveal the localised nature of migration trends, both with regard to the incidence and the direction of migration, within a single region.[56] For example, within Podlasie there are towns and villages closely connected to Belgium, whereas others have retained their long-standing associations with the USA. A rough idea of the most popular destinations in the two fieldwork regions from 1997-2007 can be gauged from Table 2.2. These are just the most popular destinations for temporary work abroad. My interviewees mentioned almost every country in Western Europe, from Finland to Malta.

Table 2.1: Percentage of Poles working abroad

	Poland	Podkarpacie	Podlasie
Respondent works abroad or had worked abroad some time in last 10 years	10.4	15.7	14.4
Member of household works abroad now	7.3	14.7	9.4

Sources: Gwiazda and Roguska (2008, pp 100, 102); Strzeszewski (2008, pp 102-3)

Table 2.2: Which country have you worked in (at any time over the period 1997-2007)? (%, in rank order)

Poland		Podkarpacie		Podlasie	
Germany	46.4	Germany	29.8	Germany	41.8
UK	14.7	Italy	21.0	Belgium	16.3
Italy	8.4	UK	16.3	USA	14.8
Netherlands	7.5	USA	14.4	UK	13.1
USA	6.2	France	8.3	Italy	7.4

Source: Gwiazda and Roguska (2008, p 101); Strzeszewski (2008, p 102)

Official statistics about permanent resettlement abroad paint a similar picture. Nationwide, Germany was the most popular country, followed by the UK, but in Podlasie and Podkarpacie the favourite destination was the USA, although the UK was catching up (see Table 2.3).

Table 2.3: Numbers of Poles permanently resettling abroad, 2007

	Poland	Podkarpacie	Podlasie
Germany	13,771	133	61
UK	9,165	547	194
USA	3,078	583	293

Source: GUS (2008a, pp 466-7)

Overall figures for Podkarpacie and Podlasie suggest differences between the two regions in regard to geographical attachments. In Podlasie there is more attachment to the local area, the region, Poles, Poland and Europe than in Poland as a whole, while in Podkarpacie the figures are slightly below average in all cases except for attachment to a person's own town or village.

Migration can be a sensitive subject, prompting soul searching in Poland about the state and fate of the nation. Traditionally, 'migration for political reasons has higher moral status than economic migration.... In Polish emigration ideology, political exile is a sacred act in the fight for freedom while economic migration is a necessary evil.'[57] Although many Poles probably feel ambivalent about the current wave of migration, there are those who consider it shameful or even morally dangerous – testifying to increasing levels of acquisitiveness in society and leading to the erosion of family values. Pope John Paul II himself expressed similar views[58] and they are common in Catholic and conservative circles. The newspaper *Nasz Dziennik* (*Our Daily*), for example, reported that:

> Archbishop Wesoły Szczepan read a homily, in which he touched on the theme of labour migration. He reminded his listeners of the fact that many middle-aged Polish women were working in Italy as domestic servants, "humiliated and despised". That young people go to the British Isles and, although they have university degrees, they work as waiters and kitchen porters. Often, they leave their families in Poland. "Are a few extra euros more important than the family?" the Archbishop demanded.[59]

The opposite approach, in this politicised subject area, is to blame the incumbent government for the wave of migration. For example, the liberal newspaper *Gazeta Wyborcza* initiated an internet forum discussion about migration in 2006 by laying the blame not on selfish migrants but on the situation in contemporary Poland, under the conservative government of Jarosław Kaczyński. '*Gazeta Wyborcza* journalists are trying to discover what has to change in Poland to make emigrants return, what should change so that young people would see a future for themselves in Poland, and not the UK.'[60]

Despite the fact that they came from particularly conservative and Catholic parts of Poland, interviewees in Grajewo and Sanok tended to discuss migration matter-of-factly. They rarely moralised about migration or seemed to regard it as shameful and unpatriotic. Insofar as they attributed 'blame', it was attached to local economic conditions. They did not appear to be embarrassed talking about migration, which was so much a feature of their everyday lives and the lives of everyone they knew. It was simply 'normal', as the following quotations suggest.

> Anne: Do you think it's bad that so many people work abroad?

> Anita: Is it bad that so many people work abroad? [pause] We're used to the situation as it is today, here in this part of Poland. And for me it's not surprising that people go to work abroad. It's normal here. *It's normal here.* (Grajewo, 2008)

I suspect there isn't a single household without someone who works abroad. In every house, to earn extra money. They even take unpaid leave from work. Perhaps they have work here which is even quite good work, but all the same, they take unpaid leave and they go abroad. There's always some profit in it. *That's how we live.* (Magda, Sanok/village)

While a person is healthy and strong, and *can* migrate, *there's no sense sitting at home.* (Beata, Grajewo)

The uncertain economic situation combined with very intensive migration over the past 20 years would seem to have created conditions where migration has become a normal livelihood strategy from many parts of Poland, and places like Grajewo and Sanok have acquired a 'migration culture' in the sense that migration is an expected part of everyday life. The following chapters examine more closely how local conditions and expectations prompt individuals and whole families to migrate abroad.

Notes

[1] See, for example, Blazyca (2009, p 219).

[2] GUS (2009c).

[3] Gwiazda and Roguska (2008, p 93). The figure refers to late 2007.

[4] Derczyński (2004, p 6).

[5] Feliksiak (2009, pp 4-5). More highly educated people and those under 45 were the most likely to answer 'well'.

[6] The Gini coefficient in 2002 was 0.345 (cf USA 0.408, Sweden 0.250) (UN, 2008). The higher the number, the more unequal the distribution of income. A score of '1' would indicate that one person earned all the wealth in the country. A score of '0' would indicate equal distribution.

[7] Eurostat (2009, pp 43, 46).

[8] Raciborski and Kublik (2009).

[9] Urząd Pracy Podlasia (2009).

[10] Wciórka (2009, p 7).

[11] Lovenduski and Woodall (1987, p 158).

[12] See, for example, Hardy et al (2008, pp 102-3) on women as transition losers.

[13] Anon (2009a, p 7). In 2009, 29% felt that chances were equal, as compared with 25% in 1993.

[14] Zadrożna (2006b, p 4): 3,487 women participated in the survey.

[15] Anon (2009a, p 6). Zadrożna (2006b, p 3) found that 43% disagreed that it was 'bad' for the family if the wife worked. In other words, this was an almost identical finding.

[16] Anon (2009a, p 7).

[17] See Aboim (2010, pp 172-3).

[18] Fuszara (2005, pp 13-14).

[19] Fuszara (2005, p 15).

[20] Gwiazda and Roguska (2008, p 108).

[21] Szczepańska (2006, p 5). For similar findings see Wachowiak (2002).

[22] Szczepańska (2008, p 4).

[23] Bojar (2005, p 286).

[24] See, for example, Feliksiak (2009).

[25] Zagórski (2008).

[26] Eurostat (2009, p 32).

[27] Reference is to the five-year Master's degree that has been standard in Poland until very recently. See Gwiazda and Roguska (2008, p 109); Fihel and Kaczmarczyk (2009, pp 42-4).

[28] Strzeszewski (2006, p 2).

[29] Iglicka (2001, p 13); Sassen (1999, p 80).

[30] Castles and Miller (2009, pp 88-9).

[31] Iglicka (2001, p 13).

[32] Sword (1996); Burrell (2009b). Four hundred thousand East European workers, mainly Polish, also settled in the UK between 1947 and 1951 under the European volunteer workers schemes. See Kay, D. and Miles, R. (1992) *Refugees or migrant workers? European volunteer workers in Britain 1946-51*, London: Routledge, cited by Stenning et al (2006, p 7).

[33] Iglicka (2001, p 33).

[34] Slany, K. (1991) 'Emigracja z Polski w latach 1980 do głównych krajów emigracji zamorskiej i kontynentalnej: aspekty demograficzno-społeczne', *Przegląd Polonijny*, vol 4, pp 15-36, cited by Iglicka (2001, p 22).

[35] Iglicka (2001, pp 43-4).

[36] Okólski, M. (1994) 'Poland', in S. Ardittis (ed) *The politics of East-West migration*, New York, NY: St Martin's Press, cited by Iglicka (2001, pp 25-6).

[37] Iglicka (2002).

[38] See Kicinger and Weinar (2007, p 53) for a discussion of research on Opole Silesia, in the context of an extensive literature review of recent Polish migration scholarship, published in Poland. Working papers and bulletins available on the Centre of Migration Research website (www.migracje.uw.edu.pl) are an invaluable resource for analysis of recent Polish migration trends. Like Kicinger and Weiner (2007), some publications are in English.

[39] Lukowski (1998, p 147); Wasek (2007).

[40] Morawska (2001, p 66).

[41] Morawska (2001, p 63).

[42] See, for example, Okólski (2007, p 3).

[43] Morokvasic (2004, p 10).

[44] The 2007 Warsaw Centre of Migration Research ethnosurvey found that even in 2007 only 60% of people working abroad were doing so legally. In Belgium and the USA the percentages were around 30% and in Italy 6% (Kaczmarczyk, 2008b, pp 253-4).

[45] Iglicka (2001, pp 41-2).

[46] The UK, Ireland and Sweden were the only 'old' member states not to restrict access for a transitional period.

[47] Fihel and Kaczmarczyk (2009, p 26), using 2008 statistics from the Polish Central Statistical Office (GUS).

[48] Piechota (2009).

[49] Lipiński (2006, p 2).

[50] Rudnik (2005, p 14).

[51] Kaczmarczyk (2008a).

[52] Fihel et al (2006, p 46).

[53] Fihel and Kaczmarczyk (2009, pp 34, 37).

[54] There were 25,632 births in England and Wales in 2008 to mothers born in the 12 new EU states (ONS, 2009b).

[55] Kaczmarczyk (2008b, p 37).

[56] Particularly important in this respect were the ethnosurveys conducted in a number of small towns and villages by Warsaw University Centre of Migration Research in 1994-99 (see Frejka et al, 1998; Iglicka, 2001; Jaźwińska and Okólski, 2001) and in 2007 (Kaczmarczyk, 2008b). For the town of Mońki, see Cieślińska (1997) and Osipowicz (2002). For a comparison of two villages in Opole Silesia (a traditional sending region) and Świętokrzyskie (a new sending region) see Elrick (2008).

[57] Garapich (2008c, p 130).

[58] Garapich (2009, p 48).

[59] AKJ, KAI (2007).

[60] Redakcja (2006).

THREE

Small-town livelihoods

This chapter discusses how people make a living in contemporary Poland. A range of livelihood strategies available to people without higher education, especially inhabitants of small towns and villages, are explored. The chapter explains why livelihoods are often seen as being so inadequate that labour migration is chosen in preference. In keeping with the livelihood strategy approach, as well as main jobs in the legal economy, other assets are also considered that can contribute to household livelihoods, such as second jobs and state benefits.

As discussed in Chapter One, a merit of the livelihood strategy approach is that it focuses on the whole portfolio of resources to which a household has access. The common Polish word *kombinować*, meaning 'to find a clever way of getting something done', often using personal connections, tends to exemplify the idea of *combining* various assets. A good combination of local assets may make emigration seem unnecessary. For example, Luiza, a nurse in Grajewo whose cousin was trying to persuade her to come to Iceland, was resisting persuasion. In order to support her mother and three children in Grajewo without migrating, Luiza did overtime whenever possible. After describing how much money she spent on breakfast for her family of five, she demanded: "And how about dinner and supper? Well, it's a pity, but you need money. That's why you find different ways to make ends meet [*dlatego człowiek kombinuje jak może*]". Urszula and her husband had four children. Urszula's brother, who worked in Italy, helped the family with occasional gifts of cash. In addition to these foreign-earned remittances, the household had extra income from local sources:

> It's hard … but somehow we manage. Grandmother helps a bit.… My husband works at the bus factory.… It's not well paid. He does overtime when it's available. To make a bit of extra money. Those are the different ways we survive [*Tak kombinuemy*].

By contrast, there are households where a combination of liabilities, such as poverty and many children, precludes migration as a livelihood strategy.

> I have some neighbours with six children. And the little girls used to come and play with my younger daughter. My friend in America sometimes sent me clothes which her daughter had outgrown and when mine had grown out of them too I gave them to my neighbour. Unfortunately they had no chance of migrating. The husband had worked at the chipboard factory but lost his job and they were very hard up. In the end he found some occasional jobs, the odd job here

and there. The children grew up a bit and last year, when the youngest
girl was already eight, the wife could allow herself to go to Germany
for the summer to pick strawberries. (Beata, Grajewo)

While subsequent chapters look more closely at configurations of assets within
individual households, this chapter concentrates more on local economies as a
whole, although without an extensive focus on economic 'facts', for example
statistics about the availability of local jobs. Instead, the perceptions of local
people, parents who might be tempted to migrate with their children, are
explored.[1] Former migrants and non-migrants alike tended to hold identical
negative perceptions about their local economies, suggesting that there is a large
potential for migration from places like Sanok and Grajewo. This chapter begins
by considering interviewees' negative feelings about their regional and small-town
identities. Grajewo is then considered as an example of a small town with a long
migration tradition, where unemployment remains an important migration motive,
low wages are a constant complaint, and almost complete pessimism about the
future was encountered.[2] Subsequently, the discussion turns to Sanok, which has
had high levels of migration to the UK since the 1990s. Here, the push factor
is low wages. In Sanok, there was slightly more optimism about an increasing
availability of jobs, but interviewees were still pessimistic about finding jobs which
paid decent wages. The options for additional earnings in both towns are also
considered, with the conclusion that these are limited.

The chapter then turns to some further aspects of Polish livelihoods which all
interviewees complained about and which – judging from the opinions of the
small UK sample, backed up by other evidence – typify cities as much as small
towns. These are unequal and unfair access to paid employment, with particular
problems for women; insecurity of employment, both in the sense that much
employment is short term and also that it is frequently undocumented, without
payment of taxes and national insurance contributions; and the risky quality of the
alternative strategy of setting up small businesses. Given that these problems existed
in cities as well as smaller places, it is hardly surprising that the interviewees were
sceptical about whether it was worth seeking alternative livelihoods elsewhere in
Poland. The chapter examines small-town interviewees' opinions as to whether
it was worthwhile to commute or move permanently to cities in Poland. Finally,
complaints about child benefit are considered, a subject which I was never
asked about directly in the interviews but which emerged as a major theme in
conversations both in Poland and the UK.

There are many other livelihood strategies, from investing in the stock market
to selling mushrooms picked in the forest. A 2007 survey identifies 24 such
strategies.[3] Some (for example, accumulating debts, or receiving gifts of money)
are mentioned in later chapters, but unfortunately many must be ignored due to
space constraints and the limitations of the interviews, which were not intended
to gather detailed information about household finances.

Table 3.1: Strategies to improve household finances (% respondents adopting such strategies)

	Poland	Podkarpacie	Podlasie
Economising	75.5	78.3	75.1
Overtime at main job	30.5	19.8	34.5
Second job, seasonal work	24.6	21.5	26.0
Rendering small services (household repairs, cleaning, childcare, help with harvest, etc)	11.7	13.1	13.8
Taking out loans	31.9	29.1	27.4
Help from friends and family	20.1	21.5	19.4
Obtaining extra qualifications	15.2	12.4	14.0
Working abroad	7.8	12.8	9.5

Source: Gwiazda and Roguska (2008, pp 77-80); Strzeszewski (2008, pp 77-80)

Regional differences and pessimism induced by living in 'Poland B' and/or in 'small towns'

There are many people in Poland who are satisfied with their livelihoods. As pointed out in Chapter Two, by May 2009 nearly half of Poles felt that they and their families lived 'well'. In some cities, satisfaction levels are well above the Polish average. Among residents of the major cities, those in Kraków are the happiest with where they live, while Poznań apparently contains the highest proportion of people 'very happy with life in general' and 'very happy about prospects for future'.[4] Inhabitants of the other big cities in Poland A, Wrocław and the 'Tri-City' (Gdańsk, Gdynia and Sopot) are also more optimistic about future prospects than Poles on average.[5] The mayor of Wrocław asserted in May 2008 that the city 'offered good job opportunities and was developing rapidly', so that parental migration 'was not much of a problem'.[6]

UK interviewees from Wrocław and the Tri-City expressed the opposite point of view, which indicates that people can feel poor in even the apparently most flourishing cities, and that satisfaction with life, as suggested in Chapter Two, is closely related to socioeconomic status, which cuts across regional differences. Stenning's study of Nowa Huta, Kraków's industrial suburb, similarly draws attention to 'experiences of loss and dislocation among the old working class'.[7] Moreover, as Chapter Two suggested, individual regions display considerable internal diversity. The two interviewees who lived within 30 kilometres of Poznań were very satisfied with their livelihoods, but the seven who lived in towns and villages slightly outside this radius complained bitterly about their local areas. They never mentioned that they lived in 'Poland A'.

If poor people in 'Poland A' did not identify with that label, by contrast, interviewees from 'Poland B' were quick to mention their regional identities, without any prompting. This self-identification seemed to contribute to their overall pessimism, verging on fatalism, about the futures of their small towns. For example, Alina (Grajewo) asserted: "It's Poland B. Agricultural, poor. It was always worse here. That's the kind of region it is."

To a lesser extent interviewees also blamed their problems on the fact that their towns were small. For example, Czesława observed: "It's better in Kraków because there's more jobs, those big centres, and they pay more or less reasonably I suppose. So you can get by, in cities. But in Sanok it's poor." UK interviewees from 'small' Polish towns made exactly the same point. Marzena said "X is a small little town, of course the big factories are in the city, Gdańsk and around Gdańsk," while Ilona explained: "I live in a small town called Y.... It was hard to find a job there [in 2005] and that's why my husband came to England." Marzena and Ilona were describing towns of 60,000 and 47,000 as 'small towns'. If they seem small to local residents, it was in the sense that there was a small range of livelihood options. Although opinion poll data cited in Chapter Two illustrated that inhabitants of small towns across Poland tend to be pessimistic about the local labour market, it is not the case that absolutely all small towns are depressed, as illustrated, for example, by Zuzańska-Żyśko's study of small towns in Silesia.[8] It seems rather that to some extent towns are perceived as small because they have too little to offer.[9]

Grajewo and Sanok: small-town employment problems and migration traditions

Grajewo is the administrative centre of Grajewo *powiat* (district) and has the associated range of institutions including the local council and a hospital; it also has one vocational school, preparing students to work in the hotel industry. Grajewo, however, is not in a tourist area, being just outside the Mazurian Lake District. The town consists of housing estates constructed during the industrialisation of the 1970s–1980s and streets of small houses, often built by migrants to the USA.[10] Warsaw, about 200km south west, is the site of the nearest airport. For all the claims about how easy it is to come and go between Poland and the UK, this shows that flights are not so accessible to all Polish people. Białystok, the regional capital and nearest city, lies 80km south east of Grajewo. It is too far for most Grajewans to consider it a feasible daily commute. The Belarusian and Lithuanian borders are also about 80km distant, the Russian border slightly closer. Few of my interviewees had crossed these borders, although a handful had gone shopping or sightseeing in Lithuania.

Grajewo has a long migration history and was the site of an early 20th-century recruitment agency smuggling America-bound migrants across the Russian-German border to the Baltic coast,[11] as well as a place where German employers hired temporary labour. Temporary migrants to East Prussia may have constituted as many of 10% of Grajewo's population during the 1930s depression.[12] Interviewees who had grown up in the communist period in former East Prussian villages north of Grajewo recalled how their schoolfriends and indeed almost the entire population of some villages had emigrated to Germany. Migration to the

USA also continued under the communist regime and a teacher[13] who came to work in Grajewo in 1980 had the impression that "half of Grajewo lived in the USA". Krystyna, a hairdresser who moved to Grajewo in 2000, remembered that "When I moved here I was amazed because in almost every family someone had emigrated to the United States."

A number of interviewees commented that Grajewo was a pleasant place, particularly in the summer when you could go cycling in the surrounding countryside and have barbecues on the allotments. In some respects, it had changed for the better in recent years:

> The housing cooperatives contract cleaning firms and they really try hard. They just clean and clean all the time. They keep the place tidy. And in the summer they look after the greenery, get things done. So it has changed. Overall, Grajewo is quite an ordinary town, but it's a clean one. (Anna, 2008)

A 2007 survey of Grajewan public opinion revealed widespread dissatisfaction with the limited range of leisure facilities,[14] particularly the lack of a long-promised swimming pool. Interviewees often complained about how little there was to do in Grajewo, making comments such as: "All we have is a cinema and three churches" (Edyta) and "In Grajewo all the shops are the same" (Anita). Unsurprisingly, interviewees concluded that the shortage of leisure opportunities and chances to socialise were one reason why so many young people migrated:

> When you talk to them, they all want to go ... abroad. Young people just sit on the benches outside the entranceways to their blocks of flats, well, they could go to the cinema, but not everyone can afford to go out once a week, for example to the cinema.... They have nowhere to meet. (Kazimiera)

Nevertheless, a scarcity of jobs emerged as the most important migration motive. Most respondents seemed convinced that Grajewo had never really recovered from the recession created by the transition to a market economy in the early 1990s:

> The job situation is a complete disaster at the moment. A disaster.... Lots of workplaces have shut down, disappeared. Or else to cut costs, they all wanted to cut costs, to pay less: supposing a factory employed 100 workers, it would cut the staff to 50.... They didn't use to worry about such things [in communist days], they would employ heaps of workers, but afterwards they started to lay people off.... People like me lived through those years, somehow I pulled through, but all sorts of things went on, you didn't know what to expect. Everything hung by a thread, at any moment they could have torn up my contract. Somehow that time passed for me, but lots of people [who lost their

jobs] are sitting at home unemployed.... No one will take them on
at their age. (Małgorzata, 2008)

Unemployment in Grajewo at the time of the interviews was well above the
national average. In January 2004 unemployment was 26.2% (compared with
a 20.6% Polish average). Shortly before the two fieldtrips unemployment rates
were still 20.1% and 17.7% in Grajewo *powiat* (December 2007 and January
2009 respectively) compared with Polish averages which had fallen to 11.2%
and 10.5% in these months.[15] Interviewees felt that Grajewo's main disadvantage
was the shortage of businesses, apart from the Pfleiderer chipboard factory and
the Mlekpol dairy, the town's two main factories, which had survived from the
communist period.[16] As Kazimiera lamented, "In general, we just don't have many
businesses in Grajewo. Not many workplaces. In general, in our whole region,
not just Grajewo.... The region's not developing, economically. What could we
do, anyway? Attract more tourists? That's the only thing."

A constant refrain was that 'there were no prospects' in Grajewo, and this made
interviewees doubtful about whether their own children would want to stay in
the town. They tended to feel that if there was some small improvement, it was
because of emigration, not because new businesses were starting up:

> I don't know if there's any future here for young people, there's not
> much for them. Young people, my daughter for example, don't expect
> to stay in Grajewo.... They hope to find a future some other place
> with more prospects, because Grajewo is really just a town for retired
> people. It's quiet, because there's hardly any industry. (Barbara, 2008)

Those jobs available tended to be poorly paid: most wages were below the Polish
national average, which was 2,944 zl per month in 2008.[17] To quote Kazimiera
again: "The pay is bad. For example, a man can go to work on a building site or
a woman to a shop, and they'll earn 800 zl [a month]. And pay 500 zl for their
flat. So there's no *good* work."

While Sanok suffers from many of the same problems as Grajewo, it has certain
advantages. It has easier access to international travel because it is just 75km south
of Rzeszów, which has an international airport. Rzeszów is not a large city (2007
population 166,454);[18] the nearest big city is, in fact, Lviv, in Ukraine (160km
east). Kraków is 200km north west. Sanok is in the south-east corner of Poland,
even closer to international borders than Grajewo. The Ukrainian border is
about 50km distant, the Slovak border roughly 60km. A number of interviewees
mentioned visiting Slovakia; fewer had been to the Ukraine.

Like Grajewo, Sanok is the *powiat* administrative centre, but, with a population
of 39,231, it has more to offer, and there is a wider range of further education
and leisure activities to keep young people in the town. Sanok is the largest town
in the Bieszczady mountains and is also a tourist base in its own right, with a
16th-century castle, old market square and literary associations. (Tourists can sit

beside a statue of the good soldier Švejk on a bench near the square.)[19] The town centre nestles round a steep wooded hill, the park, which has been beautified with EU money; an attractively restored synagogue houses the Polish headquarters of the Carpathian Foundation, promoting intergovernmental cooperation across the Carpathian Euroregion.[20] Like Grajewo, Sanok possesses a number of large housing estates built for factory workers in the late communist period. There are also streets of migrant-built individual houses, but these are often grander than migrant houses in Grajewo. Interviewees agreed that in recent years Sanok had changed for the better, at least in appearance.

Sanok does not have such a strong USA connection as Grajewo, although interviewees mentioned migration to the USA in the communist period and Podkarpacie as a whole has a long history of migration to North America. Perhaps it is because Sanok did not have such strong transatlantic migration networks that it was easier to set up new European networks in the 1990s. These predominantly linked Sanok to London. In April 2008, 677 people listed themselves as living in 'Sanok + London/Londyn' on the social networking site *Nasza Klasa*.[21] Jadwiga explained: "Lots and lots of people from Sanok go to London. Perhaps because they have more friends there.... In the 1990s some of my [women] friends, and other people I know, they began going to England." Magda, from a large village near Sanok, commented "I suspect that there isn't a single household without someone who works abroad.... Most of them are in London."

Like Grajewo, Sanok has two major factories: the Autosan bus factory and Stomil, which produces rubber items such as washing machine parts. As in Grajewo, industry in the town has experienced restructuring and downsizing:

> Autosan was a huge employer, 30 years ago there were 8,500 workers, now there are 1,000, or even just 900. It's amazing. 8,500! When I used to go by the factory [on my way to work] there were traffic jams because so many people were [crossing the road] and walking through the factory gates, so the cars had to wait 20 minutes. And today? You see a couple of people going in. (Czesława)

As in Grajewo, employment at one of these major employers was seen as an anchor for household livelihood strategies. Other family members could have insecure jobs, but if the breadwinner worked at the bus factory or 'in the rubber' (to use the local expression), this inspired a certain confidence about the future.

In September 2008, when the fieldwork was carried out, registered unemployment was 11.4% in Sanok *powiat*,[22] slightly above the Polish average of 8.9%[23] but nowhere near the levels in Grajewo. In January 2004 unemployment was 25%, similar to the rate in Grajewo, so there had been a significant improvement. Unlike in Grajewo, there was some confidence among interviewees that more local workplaces had been created. However, there were also plenty of suggestions that, if there was more employment, it was because there had been so much emigration. Interviewees sometimes displayed a definite reluctance to believe any comforting assurances from official sources that the economy was actually improving. Moreover, even if there were a greater number of job vacancies, average wages were still very low, just as in Grajewo.

Interviewees in both towns, therefore, had a strong incentive to try to supplement their basic livelihood strategies, or to change them altogether. One obvious solution would be to work overtime or find an additional job. However, in general, a difference between cities and small towns is that small towns offer fewer opportunities than cities to earn additional money (*dorabiać*) through overtime or an extra job.[24] This applies to both Sanok and Grajewo. In Grajewo, Teresa, for example, suggested that although there were small jobs that could be done for acquaintances such as window cleaning, other cleaning, or looking after small children and older people, you would need to be quite desperate to do any of these jobs because they only paid pennies. The fact that in Grajewo, for example, Jolanta was paying her *full-time* childminder only 400 zl a month in 2009 suggests how low such earnings can be. Several nurses in Grajewo were interviewed and most complained about the fact that colleagues in cities were able to find extra nursing jobs, whereas this was almost impossible in Grajewo. Nurses are sometimes asked to give patients injections at home, since many medicines in Poland are injected rather than taken orally. However, interviewees said that this was not a source of additional earnings because people were so poor that they did not have the heart to take money from them. Some skilled manual workers find additional income sources. Barbara's husband, a plumber on a Grajewo housing estate, was able to make extra money by doing private repairs, which were 'always' needed, and Halina mentioned that her husband, a Sanok bus driver, collected people from Rzeszów Airport.

Poland-wide employment problems

The rest of this chapter considers some further aspects of Polish livelihood strategies which seemed to be perceived as problems both by small-town and city residents, and which, in the case of the UK interviewees, helped to motivate their decision to migrate. The discussion begins with problems linked to local employment opportunities.

Unequal access to the labour market

Six interviewees in Poland were unemployed when interviewed, but many interviewees in both countries had experienced periods of unemployment in Poland, particularly when, as mothers of small children, they were trying to re-enter the job market. In the UK, many mothers take up part-time work, but this is less common in Poland than in the UK: in 2007, only 3.8% of adult Poles in Poland worked part time, compared with 47.7% who worked full time.[25]

Government statistics suggest that women constitute around 70% of economically inactive 35- to 44-year-olds,[26] although many housewives do not register as being unemployed, so official figures reveal only part of the picture. The national opinion poll cited in Chapter Two indicates that in June 2009 59% of women believed that women had fewer chances than men to find a job,[27] but in Sanok and Grajewo, there seemed to be even wider acceptance that women had particular difficulties. The obstacle was not so much overt discrimination as the rigid gendering of the labour market, connected with well-defined local views on gender roles. For example, Celina, a cleaner who was trying hard to migrate, complained that "Here in Grajewo, women don't have chance. Not women. If it's a bloke, he'll find something quicker, won't he? But women can only work in shops or clean somewhere." Some women asserted that anyone could get a job in a shop, if they were prepared to accept 800 zl, but interviewees' experiences suggested that it was not so easy. Teresa's daughter, for example, had gone to London. She did have a job in a shop after leaving secondary school in Grajewo but she lost the job when the shop shut down, and although she looked hard she could not find anything else in Grajewo. She then became very disillusioned about the prospect of finding anything at all; hence her decision to migrate to England.

Some interviewees felt that women of all ages were disadvantaged, and Teresa's daughter's experience would back up that impression. However, many interviewees thought that young women had more of a chance of finding shop jobs. According to Bożena (Sanok), for example: "Men can do repairs, building work, there's Stomil, Autosan – not often, but more than before. Women can only work in shops and even they want *young* women. Women my age [45] don't have a chance." Many women even in their thirties, in both towns, had searched for work for years. The situation is worse still for women over 40. In a Polish survey, 42% of women said that in their current workplace, or when looking for work, they had found that women over 40 could not get jobs.[28] Beata, for instance, said that she had been told at the Grajewo Job Centre that "she was too old for employers" when she was only 41. She took a succession of jobs abroad, returned to Grajewo at the age of 46, but again found nothing. In 2009, aged 49, and on the brink of departure to Cyprus, she complained again about her most recent attempts to get a job in Grajewo: "There was absolutely no question about it: no work at all. I did the rounds, searching for something. But there was nothing…. It's just my age. I don't feel so old!"

For unemployed women over 40, migration often seems to be the only livelihood strategy remaining:

> Mothers go abroad too. Usually if the mother had never worked and always looked after the children and the father went out to work, and the mother for example doesn't have a degree … and when the children are a bit older then she goes abroad. Because if she hasn't got a degree and hasn't been employed for some years, it's hard for her to return to work, here in Poland…. Usually she goes to pick fruit, just for the harvest season, for two months. (Rosanna, Wielkopolska, 2007)

Czesława told the story of a friend who earned three to five times as a carer in Italy what she would have made in Poland, and concluded: "There are lots of cases like that, they go off for three months … because who will give them a job in Sanok if they're over 50?" Maria made a similar comment about her cousin, from a town near Grajewo:

> She goes to Germany and works on strawberry and asparagus farms. For three to four months a year, but it's enough to live on for a whole year in Poland.… Her children are already big.… She lost her job in Poland, they shut the factory … but she's still a long way off retirement. So, what's she supposed to do? Just twiddle her thumbs?

Notwithstanding the particular problems of women, some interviewees also told stories illustrating that unemployed middle-aged men could have great difficulty finding jobs. Maria's husband, for instance, had been told by the Grajewo Job Centre that they could not find him a job because he was too old, at around 45. Felicja described the problems her husband had experienced during a recent spell of unemployment (ending when he found a job as a lorry driver based 99km from Sanok):

> My husband had a lot of problems finding a job, but that's his age. It's different if you're a young person looking for a first job, but if you're over 40, or indeed 50.… 'I'm really sorry, sir, but you're a little too old', they say, or just 'At your age…'. They prefer young people.

Chapter Two referred to Poland's current 'over-supply' of graduates. This is particularly a problem in small towns and villages: 'local labour markets in rural areas and tiny towns, not being able to offer good prospects for young and well-educated people, became a "trap" for a relatively large group of people who effectively became economically redundant'.[29] Most interviewees did not have any children who were old enough to have already graduated, but their impressions were that it could be difficult for young graduates on the small-town job market. However, interviewees in both the UK and Poland also told stories of young graduates who had searched hard even for city jobs, without finding anything commensurate with their qualifications. Overall, there was a perception that graduate unemployment was a national problem, and this added to interviewees' feeling that they understood why so many people migrated.

The situation for school leavers was often said to be even worse than for graduates. Jolanta, for example, interviewed in the UK, had gone to a catering college in a central Polish city and spent several years unable to find more than temporary work, not using her diploma. In the small towns, interviewees asserted that young people would go abroad straight after secondary school:

> Young people who have just left school don't have jobs.... [If they don't have any higher qualifications] it's definitely harder for them to get a job. Most often they go abroad, to England, to Ireland, lots of people, lots of people, precisely those young people who just left secondary school.... Just from our street five people have gone abroad immediately after leaving school. (Rosanna, Wielkopolska, 2007)

> Huge numbers of them go abroad after leaving school. They leave secondary school and they don't have any prospect of getting any sort of job, so they go off abroad. (Jadwiga, Sanok)

A final aspect of unequal access to employment was the perceived prevalence of favouritism and nepotism. Interviewees made numerous comments about how you had to know the right people to get a job, both in small towns and in cities. Agnieszka (Polish city/UK) commented, for example, that "in Poland you need good contacts to get a job, that's the main thing, not qualifications", while Danuta made similar comments about Grajewo. However, she attributed them to what she perceived to be its small-town disadvantaged status: "You need to have the right acquaintances. Perhaps it's easier in big towns where there are more offices and firms, but what is there here? Two factories, a few shops and the town council where it's simply incestuous."

Job insecurity

A further common complaint about employment in Poland was the perception that many jobs were insecure, being temporary and/or in the shadow economy. Region-wide, 36.6% of inhabitants of Podkarpacie and 26.1% of inhabitants of Podlasie were worried about losing their jobs in 2007,[30] but these average figures say little about the situation in specific localities:

> There are no permanent jobs. There's just temporary work for a fixed period, and that's why [people migrate]. Perhaps if they had steady work, well paid, just enough to cover the basics ... then it would be a different situation. (Joanna, Grajewo)

Even the major factories in Sanok and Grajewo could not be counted on to provide secure employment. In Grajewo, the chipboard factory – like other factories in the town – had a history of laying off workers temporarily when orders were in short supply. During my visit to Grajewo in March 2009 I was repeatedly told that, whatever the state of the world economy, 'crisis' on the Grajewo labour market was nothing new.[31] In Sanok, too, some interviewees complained about their husbands' jobs at the big factories being insecure. Halina told the story of a meat processing factory in Sanok which had made large numbers of employees redundant, and "people who had worked there went off to do the same sort of work in Ireland. I know that lots of people from that particular firm went.... Lots of people, it was such a big factory, and suddenly...". Similarly, in Grajewo, Anita's husband had worked in a meat factory in Ełk which had suddenly made many workers redundant; this was when he started migrating to Germany.

Short-term contracts were commonplace. Kindergarten staff in Sanok, for example, were employed on a succession of 10-month contracts. Danuta said that her family put up with this situation, rather than migrating, simply because her husband had a permanent contract as a forester. "One member of the family has a steady job. That's good." However, this is not a problem confined to small towns. Jolanta was from a city in central Poland where she described the job situation as "very poor". Explaining why her husband went to England, she said: "My husband did work before we came but not on a permanent contract. For a season, or for a few months. The most was 18 months at a time. But for very poor pay. Not what we wanted." Jolanta herself had worked on and off at the same factory: they would give her a temporary contract, lay her off, and then take her back, again on a temporary contract.

Short-term jobs were often undocumented. In Sanok, Elwira suggested that 80% of local jobs would be without a contract or social insurance, and although this percentage is hard to believe, it illustrates a perception that it is hard for people to find jobs outside the shadow economy. In Wielkopolska, Rosanna asserted "Lots of people work illegally, they don't have a contract, because the employers simply won't give them one, it's more convenient for them if the employees don't have a contract." Interviewees who could only find work in the informal economy were especially dissatisfied with their livelihoods. For Dorota in Grajewo, this was a major reason why she wanted to go to England:

> I work for some neighbours, at markets, I travel round with them. It's on the black market, too, they don't register me because they can't afford to, it's their own business. I used to work unregistered in a shop, they didn't want to register me, because of those contributions they have to pay. And if they do register someone then they say goodbye after six months.... It's not very pleasant [in that respect] in Poland and I'm not at all surprised that people go to work abroad.

Overall, there was often a perception that the private sector was a place of exploitation, and this also shone through in the UK interviews (see Chapter Eight).

Self-employment as an alternative livelihood strategy

Given that interviewees perceived so many obstacles to accessing a reasonably paid, steady job in their local area, it is not surprising if individuals are tempted to set up their own businesses. It was true that some interviewees could not imagine themselves in such a role. Maria (Grajewo), for example, felt that "the best thing is a steady job, where you know you will get paid at the end of the month. And to do well in business you have to have a flair. Not everyone is born with that talent." However, becoming self-employed was a common livelihood strategy. One of the Grajewo interviewees, Małgorzata, worked in an insurance office and she asserted that "lots" of new small firms were springing up in Grajewo. However, she said that they never employed more than 20 people, echoing the observations of other interviewees, that even if new firms were opening, they did not have a noticeable impact on the overall labour market. This often happened because they were family firms, employing only relatives. Small building firms, second-hand clothes shops and hairdressing salons are a feature of both towns. According to Elwira, a hairdresser, there were 50-60 hairdressers' salons in Sanok alone.

One stimulus to such enterprise was the availability of loans from the local job centre, subsidised by the EU, to start a small business. These were non-refundable if the business was a success and still operating a year later. Among the interviewees, Marta took advantage of this scheme, as an alternative to going abroad, a strategy which she felt might threaten her marriage. A year on, she was pleased with her shop selling second-hand clothes from England. According to the Grajewo media (e-grajewo.pl):

> There has been a growth in the number of unemployed people receiving subsidies from the job centre to set up their own businesses: most often these are builders, beauty and hairdressing salons and garages doing car repairs. Increasingly the applicants are young people returning from abroad.... In 2008, 77 people from Grajewo *powiat* received the subsidy.[32]

An official at the Sanok Job Centre commented in September 2008 that there had been such high take-up for the scheme that they had already run out of the allocated funds. Over 50% went to builders, although often the applicant was not a qualified builder, but had simply gained experience by working on building sites in Western Europe. Last year the job centre had checked up on these businesses and they found they were doing extremely well and could not keep up with the demand for house repairs. On the other hand, people who set up little shops and kiosks had mixed fortunes. The market was saturated, so they tended not to last very long.[33] Interviewees had the same impression about Grajewo:

> What kind of business can they open in Grajewo? A shop, a hairdresser's, when there's one on every corner? Some kind of shop? There have been so many shops which lasted just six months or a year and then shut down, because people don't have money to buy things. There's no point in a young person investing here with a view to staying in Grajewo. (Luiza, 2009)

Some interviewees could name a few examples of local people who had invested money earned abroad in businesses in Grajewo and Sanok, but no one could think of many. This accords with the evidence of other surveys that, like migrants in other societies, Polish migrants more often spend their money on consumption than on investing in business ventures at home. Among the interviewees, there were just two examples. In Grajewo, Irena ran a shop selling bathroom fittings; her husband was still working from time to time in London. The couple had not ruled out migrating to the UK, where their daughters were students, but were put off by their perception of a language barrier. In Sanok, Iwona's husband imported putty from the UK. Here, the whole family had returned from London, were doing quite well and were intending to stay in Poland.

The UK interviewees included a number of families who had migrated to England because of business failures in Poland, and there were also interviewees in Poland who had tried to set up a business but not succeeded. The reason was usually attributed to lack of custom: people in small towns did not have money to spend. For example, Eliza, in Grajewo, had been unable to find a job after becoming a mother, so eventually:

> When our daughter was four I opened a little cake shop, but you know that, with that kind of product [not an everyday purchase], there are ups and downs, there were times when we did make some money, but one thing led to another and it made no sense any more and my husband and I decided to shut it down [at which point he began to migrate].

Being aware of such examples can make other people wary about opening anything. Jolanta, for example, had a certificate qualifying her to work as a beautician, but was hesitant in setting up her own business. She remarked "It's a very good profession but just at the moment it's rather risky to set up a business in Grajewo." Several UK interviewees had simply become exhausted with running a business in Poland and this helped shape their decision to migrate. Renata, for example, explaining the family's decision to come to England, said that, "the main thing was that we'd had enough of running our own business where there were non-stop problems with everything. I couldn't do anything with it, that really made me fed up, I'd had enough."

Internal migration as an alternative livelihood strategy

It might be supposed that migration within Poland would be a popular strategy, an alternative to local employment or self-employment, to be tried out before undertaking the more extreme option of international migration. As already indicated, in small towns there is a perception that Polish cities offer a wider range of jobs and more opportunity for extra earnings. Some interviewees had direct experience of this. Magda's husband, for example, was able to replace his former strategy of working in England by working in Kraków and taking on enormous quantities of overtime:

At the moment my husband is working in Kraków … because it's easier to get work and you can earn more money.… Although the way it is they have to work 14 hours a day, not eight hours like people work in Sanok.… He works from 8am until 8pm for the minimum rate, which is 8 zl, and later in the evening he gets 10 zl. That's the overtime he does. 14 hours is a bit much!… He comes back to Sanok every week … and when he's in Kraków he stays with friends.… It's long hours, and though the money isn't too bad, it isn't as good as in England.

Interviewees in both Grajewo and Sanok also knew people who worked on building sites in Warsaw and returned home at the weekends.

It happens that people do go to work outside Sanok, particularly in Warsaw: you can get a job quicker there. On building sites, on motorways, it's easier there [than in Kraków].… They work a month in Warsaw and then come home to Sanok to see their families, that's the system.… It's worth it for them. (Jadwiga)

However, interviewees were not convinced that it was worthwhile commuting *daily* from a small town to a larger one. Wages might be slightly higher, but buses, trains and petrol were also expensive relative to earnings. Sanok is unfortunately placed in that there is no thriving medium-sized or larger town within easy daily commuting distance. Grajewo is just 16km from the more prosperous small town of Ełk, but many Grajewan interviewees would not consider commuting even this distance. Interviewees in prosperous Wielkopolska told of different experiences. Teresa claimed that in her tiny town, 60km from Poznań, there was a labour shortage because so many people commuted to the city. On the other hand, Marcelina said that her brother had stopped commuting just 20km to Poznań from another small town because it was simply not worthwhile financially. He had gone to Liverpool in England instead. Marcelina herself could not imagine what job she could get in Poznań that would make it worth commuting from her village, where she was unemployed. Instead, she was planning to go to Norway.

In villages where there is almost no paid employment, there seems little choice but to commute or to move place of residence altogether. Three of the Sanok interviewees were commuting by bus into Sanok to work at kindergartens in the town. They complained about the unreliability of the bus services and the price of tickets. Danuta, for example, was paying 130 zl a month for her ticket, from a wage of 860 zl. Czesława described how her husband had worked as a builder and decorator in England just to earn the money for a car so that it would be possible for them to commute into Sanok from their village:

He didn't have a job in Sanok and even if he had somehow got one, they pay such a pittance.… [He did it] so we could buy a decent car and get into town, because we live quite a way, 10km from Sanok. So we have to commute and a car made it easier.

Now living in the UK, Sylwia and her husband had lived in a village in northern Poland, 8km from the nearest small town and two hours by train from a city. At one time they both worked in the small town (he as a postman, she as a hairdresser), but they could only afford to have one car and to use public transport was complicated. Sylwia's husband also tried working in the city but it did not seem worth spending four hours a day on the train just to make ends meet. (As an example, she said they could not afford medicine for their child.) This contributed to their decision to move to England. In a more extreme case, Barbara and Marek, who had four children, lived in a village with no employment. They commuted to work at a factory 7km away, but in 2004 their wages were reduced to 600 zl a month, the bus ticket cost 200 zl, and so Marek went to England.

Some city employers pay for buses to collect labour from surrounding villages: for example, I interviewed a furniture manufacturer in Poznań who felt forced to do this because of the shortage of local craftsmen. However, although such practices may alleviate some of the inconvenience and cost of commuting, they do not necessarily make it an acceptable strategy. In the UK, Katarzyna complained that her brother-in-law was poorly paid and never at home: the only reason he agreed to being bussed to work in a city over 100km away was because "he had no choice".

If interviewees were generally unenthusiastic about commuting from villages and small towns as a livelihood strategy, but could sometimes see it as being viable, there was, by contrast, almost universal agreement that it made little sense to move permanently to a city in Poland rather than going abroad. To relocate permanently to a city was a promising strategy for young people who had studied there and then found 'good' work after they graduated, but for working-class, small-town families it was simply not worthwhile, and many UK interviewees seemed to take the attitude that it had not been worth considering. In general, Poles are not very mobile within Poland. According to a 2010 CBOS (Centre for Public Opinion Research) survey, 65% live in their birthplace and only about one fifth have moved more than once during their adult life. Most of these internal migrations are within the same administrative region (*województwo*) and most are for family reasons, with only 28% moving because of work.[34] Iglicka comments that 'the relatively low [geographical] mobility of the Polish workforce is caused both by cultural factors and also by the inflexible housing market. Changing one residence for another is very expensive, which discourages people from moving in search of work, or better work. This is especially true for people who earn only average wages, or less.'[35] CBOS found that housing was the most commonly mentioned barrier to internal migration, an opinion shared by the Confederation of Polish Employers.[36] The interviewees entirely concurred that housing costs, plus the general cost of living, would be unaffordable. Even to rent temporarily and scout around for a job in a Polish city was felt to be unrealistic (whereas this was exactly what people often did in foreign countries). Typical comments included the following:

> In Poland there is no future in taking a child from a small town and moving to a city. You just can't afford to keep yourself there. (Justyna, Wielkopolska, planning to resettle with her child in England)

> Pay in Kraków is nothing to write home about, compared to the cost of living. (Patrycja, UK)

> Very few people go from Sanok to Warsaw. After all, you have to live there, too. It seems that earnings are higher, but living costs, renting a flat is awfully expensive. You don't often hear of people moving. (Bożena, Sanok)

Some interviewees thought it might also be hard to find employment, and that you needed to know the right people:

> No because salaries in Warsaw are only a few hundred zl higher than in Sanok – it isn't worthwhile. And it can be hard to find work, which is kept for friends. You might as well do some easy manual job in the UK and get paid more than you would do working in a Polish office. (Marta)

Some interviewees suggested that you might as well move abroad rather than to a city in Poland because you would be among strangers wherever you moved; in other words, the fact that the Polish city was Polish seemed to count for nothing. For example:

> My husband and I were thinking about moving somewhere else, but we came to the conclusion that either we would stay in Sanok or, if we moved, it would be to somewhere abroad. Because if you move somewhere else in Poland, all the same everything will be foreign [*obce*]. Strange people, strange places. (Rozalia)

Thanks to easy international transport foreign countries do not seem so far away. As Beata said: "In Warsaw they would certainly have earned more than they did in Grajewo, but in Iceland they earn even more than that. And besides, they can often fly home, can't they? Come back for visits?"

A handful of interviewees with a strong self-identification as villagers or small-town residents mentioned attachment to a quiet or rural way of life as a reason not to move to a more populous location. Paulina, aged 25, gave her village identity as a reason for not living in a town, even a small place like Sanok:

> We haven't even thought of [moving to live in a city]. Somehow, we were born in the village, we grew up there. We did live for a while in Sanok but then we came back. It was better for us in the village. Our families, our parents. And somehow if you grow up in a village you have a different way of looking at things.

> I can't see myself in a city. Actually I come from the country, I was born in a village. (Anna, Grajewo)

Among the UK interviewees, a handful had moved very short distances within Poland, for example when they got married, and one had moved when she went to college to obtain a vocational qualification. The only family that had moved a considerable distance within Poland was untypical in many respects and obviously seen by their acquaintances as pursuing an extraordinary livelihood strategy. They moved out of Warsaw to a village in the mountains, where they hoped to set up a guest house.

> Iwona: We moved to near Jelenia Gora.

> Anne: That's a long way.

> Iwona: That's what they all say in Warsaw! They don't say England is far away, but they think Jelenia Gora is far!

The failure of this new business prompted their move to England.

People seem to be feel that migration inside Poland would be less experimental and more final than migration to the UK. This is especially true if the choice is between a whole family uprooting itself within Poland and just one family member migrating abroad, at least for a trial period. Overall, however, the most important factor inhibiting internal migration is the assumption that there is a problem with Polish livelihoods in general, that is, it is not worth moving because it would be hard to make ends meet anywhere.

Child benefit

An additional source of income that was mentioned by many interviewees, from all parts of Poland, was child benefit. They felt that it ought to be a substantial top-up to family incomes. It should constitute a significant element in the household's livelihood and should be paid to all families: it was owed by the state to families as a right, as it had been under the communist regime. Child benefit is now means tested and awarded only if the family income is less than half of the average monthly wage.[37] In 2008-09 fewer than half of Polish families received it.[38] Many interviewees, although poor, were not quite poor enough to qualify. Their grievances were threefold: (a) the size of the benefit was too small;[39] (b) it was humiliating and annoying to have to provide so much paperwork, annually, for so tiny a return; and (c) it was unfair that they personally had had their entitlement rescinded because they had missed the threshold by a few zlotys. In these circumstances, it was hardly surprising that interviewees often remarked on the generosity – as they perceived it – of child benefit in the UK.

> 48 zl a month isn't enough even for nappies, and what about milk etc? Ridiculous money, like they're making fun of you. It's a waste of time to stand in the queue and apply. (Olga, Sanok)[40]

> We have 64 zl child benefit. Isn't that ridiculous? Yes? It's bizarre. And you have to go and fill out so many forms so they'll give it to you. And then in the end it turns out you're not entitled to it because you earn 'too much', 20 zl too much, or 15, or five. So it's hard for families to live in Poland....That's another reason why people migrate. (Czesława, Sanok)

> Policy towards families isn't ideal, in Poland. We used to get child benefit and this year they took it away because they calculated our income and there was some extra item and we turned out to have 3.11 zl more than the threshold! And they took away our child benefit. Just imagine. We lost almost 300 zl and for us that's quite a bit of money. (Urszula, mother of four, Sanok)

It was noteworthy that although they did not in general blame the Polish state for migration, interviewees were adamant that in this respect the state was squarely to blame, and, as the quotation from Czesława illustrates, they drew a direct link between inadequate benefits and migration. Furthermore, their conviction that the state had a role to play in supporting families suggests a firm belief in a triangle of responsibilities for family welfare, rather than a simple male breadwinner/ female carer family model.

Conclusion

This chapter has illustrated the usefulness of adopting a livelihood strategy approach, exploring how interviewees felt about and compared available livelihoods in Grajewo and Sanok as a background to understanding local people's decisions to migrate. The towns were chosen as examples of localities in Poland where average wages are perceived to be very low and many jobs are insecure. Households therefore feel they need to diversify their strategies to find additional sources of income, and compare various options. In part, such comparisons are based on the objective realities of the environment, but they also rest on prejudice, for example, the assumption that 'it's not worth moving to a city', or that official assertions that the economy is improving must be untrue. Despite the incentive to develop new household strategies, in such small towns it is hard to obtain a better paid or second job. Women returning to work after childbearing have particular difficulties finding any job at all, especially if they are over the age of 40. Being a housewife is often not an option of choice, particularly given the small size of child benefit: interviewees complained about this at length and perceived the state to be derelict in its obligations towards families. Establishing a small business is an alternative strategy and start-up capital is available from the EU. However, many small businesses do not survive for long, largely because purchasing power is low and there is insufficient custom. There is therefore a paucity of local livelihoods in small towns. Other problems, which are not specific to small towns, include the insecurity of much employment, especially in the private sector. This is why the state sector, or a well-established local factory, was seen as a much preferable place of employment, although one which was often unattainable.

In such circumstances, migration is an obvious alternative. However, migration to a Polish city is rarely adopted as a livelihood strategy, except by students. Families perceive it to be too complicated to find housing in the city and it does not seem to be financially worthwhile, given the higher cost of living. The remaining potential strategy is international migration and Chapters Four and Five discuss how and why this is so commonly adopted.

Notes

[1] Because I conducted 43 interviews in Grajewo and only 21 in Sanok, there is a preponderance of quotations from Grajewo respondents, but I have tried to maintain a balance as far as possible.

[2] The Warsaw University Centre of Migration Research ethnosurvey found that in 2007 unemployment still remained an important migration motive in Mońki, Grajewo's neighbouring town, as it had been everywhere in Poland around the time of EU accession. Meanwhile, unemployment had receded as a migration motive in the other three locations studied (Kaczmarczyk, 2008b, p 181). As noted in Chapter Two, Grajewo has higher unemployment even than Mońki.

[3] Qestions 26 and 27 of a cross-regional CBOS survey of 38,866 Poles. See Gwiazda and Roguska (2008, pp 77-80) and Strzeszewski (2008, pp 77-80). For a discussion of a piece of qualitative research investigating individual coping strategies for dealing with transition as 'trauma' in Podkarpacie (not quite the same as livelihood strategies), see Długosz (2008), although this does not examine migration.

[4] Zagórski (2008, p 13).

[5] Zagórski (2008, p 13).

[6] Kozerawska (2008).

[7] Stenning (2004, p 116).

[8] Polish small towns are a neglected topic. In addition to Zuzańska-Żyśko (2006), there is one other recent monograph: Cieślińska's 1997 study of Mońki, near Grajewo.

[9] See White (2004, 'Introduction'), for a discussion of 'small towns' as a category in post-communist Russia.

[10] For a chronology of Grajewo, see Modzelewski (2009).

[11] Giza and Tefelski (1998, p 129).

[12] Korneluk (1988, p 84).

[13] Not a formal interviewee.

[14] Glińska (2007, pp 17-18); Pawluczuk (2007, pp 17-18).

[15] Wojewódzki Urząd Pracy w Białymstoku (2005, p 27); Urząd Pracy Podlasia (2009); GUS (2009c).

[16] www.pfleiderer.pl, www.mlekpol.com.pl. See Modzelewska (2004) for an overview of the Grajewan economy.

[17] Information on Grajewo from the PUP (job centre) director, Grajewo, 1 April 2008; Polish figure from GUS (2009a).

[18] GUS (2008a, p 96).

[19] For a history of Sanok (unfortunately with nothing about migration), see Bańkosz (2008). I have been unable to discover anything about Sanok's migration history from the internet and the public library had no information.

[20] International Carpathian Foundation Network: www.carpathianfoundation.org.

[21] http://nasza-klasa.pl, accessed 22 April 2008. The figures for Sanok were much higher than for anywhere else in Podkarpacie, and much higher for London than for other towns in England. Grajewo had 77 users in London (both spellings).

[22] www.ezeto.pl/pupsanok/?c=mdTresc-cmPokaz-148; www.pup.sanok.pl/?c=mdTresc-cmPokaz-15; and www.ezeto.pl/pupsanok/?c=mdTresc-cmPokaz-73 (website of Sanok Job Centre).

[23] GUS (2009c).

[24] For a discussion of the same phenomenon in post-communist Russia, see White (2004).

[25] Strzeszewski (2008, p 115).

[26] GUS (2007a, p 156). In Sanok, for example, the total number of women who were registered unemployed when I did my fieldwork was 839, out of a registered total of 1,474 (57%). 'Informacja sygnalna o sytuacji na rynku pracy w powiecie sanockim wg stanu na 30.09.2008' (http://ezeto.pl/pupsanok/fck_pliki/file/StatystykaPUP/1817_broszura_wrzesien_2008.pdf).

[27] Anon (2009a, p 7). In 2009, 29% felt that chances were equal, as compared with 25% in 1993.

[28] Zadrożna (2006a, p 24).

[29] Fihel and Kaczmarczyk (2009, p 42).

[30] Gwiazda and Roguska (2008, p 97); Strzeszewski (2008, p 99).

[31] See, for example, Anon (2009b) on the travails of the Grajewo dairy.

[32] Anon. (2009) '18,6 tys. zł na własną firmę', e-grajewo.pl/wiadomosc,186_tys._z_na_wasn_firm.,8761.html.

[33] Interviewed 18 September 2008.

[34] Kowalczuk (2010, pp 1, 3-5).

[35] Iglicka (2008, p 65).

[36] Kowalczuk (2010, p 10).

[37] Cerami (2005, p 139).

[38] 3,260,000. See Anon (2009c).

[39] From November 2009 child benefit was increased by 40%, to 68 zl for a child under 5, 91 zl for children aged 5-17 and 98 zl up to age 24 (Anon, 2009c).

[40] Twenty-four-year old Olga was not an interviewee, but answered questions via *Nasza Klasa*, 4 September 2008.

FOUR

Local migration cultures: compulsion and sacrifice

> They had no work in Sanok, neither him, nor her. And the situation simply forced them to migrate. (Aleksandra, explaining why her sister-in-law's family went to England) (Sanok, 2008)

Chapters Two and Three looked at the economic push factors that help explain migration from contemporary Poland. However, decisions to migrate are also influenced by non-economic factors in the sending locality, such as the climate of opinion regarding migration. This climate of opinion can be conceptualised as a 'migration culture'. As defined in Chapter One, migration cultures are conventions about why and how people should migrate, which people should migrate and where they should go, as well as views about whether or not migration is a normal and sensible way of making a living, and about the costs and benefits of migration for the whole local community. By knowing the migration culture one can better understand decisions that may seem irrational from a strictly financial point of view. For example, one interviewee's husband was unemployed in Grajewo but reluctant to work in Germany, despite the efforts of the local job centre to help in this regard. He was still hoping for an American visa even though he had already been refused one six times. He stated bluntly, "In the west of Poland they go to Germany, here in the east we go to the USA."

The examples of migration cultures in this chapter and Chapter Five are drawn primarily from Grajewo and Sanok, but this does not imply that the towns are identical, still less that they are typical of all of Poland. Elrick argues that 'it is preferable to speak of "cultures" of migration, which evolve in different geographical contexts, and not just a single, national "culture" of migration'.[1] Clearly, different Polish localities have different cultures, as illustrated by the case studies in Elrick's article, where one village had a long tradition of international migration and the other did not. Nonetheless, there is no reason to suppose that Sanok and Grajewo are untypical of other Polish places where migration has become a way of life, and their migration cultures do have common features linked to the high incidence of migration.

Although the examples given here are primarily from Grajewo and Sanok, some of the issues discussed are more widely relevant. Hence reference is also made to interviews with people from other parts of Poland, including the UK interviewees. Everywhere, for example, there is a tension between a perception that migration is an unpleasant necessity and migration viewed as an experimental response to opportunity. Rafał came to Bristol (UK) from Silesia after he was invited by a friend. Nonetheless, his explanation of why he came to England – "we *had* to *try out* something new" – encapsulates this view of migration as being both a necessity and experimental.

Horváth suggests that a 'migration culture' can be understood as ways of doing things connected to migration, but also as an environment where it is expected that people will migrate.[2] The two meanings are linked. A location with a strong migration culture – strong in the sense of having a history of migration which has produced some fairly binding conventions about how and where to migrate, and networks of people who can help one another do it – is also likely to be a location where certain groups are expected to migrate or, at least, where individuals, when faced with unemployment or some other urgent reason to change their livelihood strategy, may assume that migration is the only option. This chapter explores the rational and irrational bases for perceptions that people are 'forced by the situation'. This phrase, used by Aleksandra in the quotation at the start of this chapter, recurred again and again.

To understand a culture it is helpful to analyse how people talk about the things they do: in this case, how interviewees talked about situations where they, or people they knew, decided to migrate, or might decide to migrate in the future. What does it actually mean when people say they are 'forced' or (as explored in Chapter Five) 'tempted' to migrate? With regard to compulsion, there are situations when a household has no income and migration is a strategy to avoid starvation, but objectives other than starvation can also be considered necessities. This chapter examines the ideas that a 'decent' or 'normal' lifestyle, home ownership and higher education for their children are necessities that force Polish parents to migrate. In such circumstances, the perception that migration is forced is often accompanied by a discourse of parental self-sacrifice. Migration may also be seen as forced because it is a strategy adopted when all else fails and stories are discussed of how migrants arrived at migration after trying out various other livelihoods first.

Discourse of 'forced' migration to achieve a 'normal' lifestyle

> I went *because the situation forced me*, not in search of any luxuries.... I was divorced, I had no work, and three children, and I had to secure some kind of living for my children, so that's why I went abroad to work. (Alicja, Grajewo)

> I never imagined that my husband would emigrate, but *the situation forced us to*. (Teresa, Wielkopolska; she and her daughter were both ill and the household was continually short of money needed for medical treatment)

In the above quotations the interviewees describe a crisis caused by bills that could not be paid or unemployment: migration is then 'forced by the situation'. Debts, in particular, were an obvious compelling factor, if, as often seems to happen, no local strategy is able to provide sufficient income to pay debts back. Debts incurred as a result of business failure, mortgages in Poland or simply everyday living expenses were a common migration motive among the UK interviewees. The sudden unemployment of both parents, or of the second parent where the first was already jobless, is another situation that was often perceived to force migration:

> We had lots of problems with money when my husband lost his job. We had two children and I was just finishing college and we had a problem with money, we had no money, and we don't have parents who can help us financially, no one could help us then. But we did have a car, so we sold the car and he took half that money and went to England, and I had the other half, to survive for a couple of months in Poland. (Ilona, UK)

In a similar situation, Magda left her two small children in Sanok to work in Italy: either she or her husband "had" to go abroad, and she was the one who was offered a job by her sister. Barbara and her husband, interviewed in Bristol, had worked in the same factory some way distant from their Polish village. When wages went down, they could not afford to commute, and both became unemployed. Since unemployment locally was 29%, it was not surprising that Barbara's husband went to England for work.[3] Often, however, it seems that unemployment or business failure of just one parent is enough to trigger what is perceived as forced migration, even if the other parent still works in Poland. In the case of four women interviewed in England, it was the mother's business failure that led to the father migrating. The father had work in Poland, but his wage alone was seen as insufficient to maintain a family.

The sense that migration is forced because there is no local alternative is often enhanced when migration is the last of a string of strategies. The feeling of being forced may not be so much created by the severity of the situation (migration or starvation) but rather by the experience of having worked through the options and arrived at the perception that migration was the only livelihood strategy left. Edyta, for example, had moved to a city in Poland A from her small town in Poland B, to study for a vocational qualification. After college, she and her husband stayed in the city, believing that they could shape a better livelihood than in their small town. Even so, having had two children, Edyta could not get a job. She tried to run her own business, a street kiosk selling bus tickets and other small items. When the business failed, leaving large debts, she was unemployed again and her husband's income was insufficient to meet the family's needs. Hence the couple decided to move to England. In another case mentioned in Chapter Three, Iwona and her husband ran a small business in Warsaw for 10 years, but could never build up enough custom. Eventually they gave up and decided to move to the mountains. They bought and restored an old house in poor repair, and applied for an EU subsidy to open a guest house, only to discover that they did not qualify unless they also began to farm. Since they could not see themselves as farmers, and finding themselves stuck without a livelihood in a tiny village where – according to Iwona – every man of working age was a migrant in Germany, the family decided to go to Bristol.

It is clear, however, that a sense of being forced is not just related to an objective reality, but is also induced by the way migration is discussed in locations such as Sanok and Grajewo. Interviewees, making very general comments about the causes of migration, regularly used the terminology of compulsion, particularly the concept of the 'situation that forced you to migrate'. For example:

> I don't like the fact that people migrate, there are lots of divorces and bad consequences. But in some *situations* a person *has* to migrate. If he has no work in Sanok, and no pay, and he's a father.... (Mieczysława)

> Parting is not at all pleasant, no, leaving your family, but *when you absolutely have to*, when there is no money for everyday life and all the bills, and bills are so huge. Then there is only one decision. To go abroad. (Marta, Grajewo)

Living in this society where – as they saw it – many people were forced to migrate, a number of interviewees seemed worried that at some time in the future their own luck might change. The situation that would force them to migrate might be just around the corner:

> *If the situation forced us*, probably my husband and the rest of us would go. *If there was no other possibility*. You'd have to go. (Dorota, Grajewo, considering the outcome of planned redundancies at her husband's workplace)

> Never say 'never'! Because *anything can happen*.... Who knows what will happen in a year's time, or two, or five? *Perhaps I'll be forced* to go abroad to work. (Edyta, Grajewo)

> I'll probably go [to England] *if the situation forces me*. But for the time being I'd rather not. (Magda, Sanok)

In other cases, interviewees felt that their family and friends were being unrealistic if they tried to resist adopting migration as their new livelihood strategy:

> Anne (asking about Mariola's unemployed brother): Doesn't he want to emigrate?

> Mariola: Not much, but you're *forced* to do certain things in life, so it may turn out that way. (Grajewo)

It is possible that interviewees adopt a discourse of being forced to migrate partly because they are anxious not to appear acquisitive. In particular, it is considered inappropriate for parents to migrate except for really serious reasons. Being forced to migrate is the opposite of migrating for luxuries ('looking for coconuts', in Polish), a motive which was often denied.

> [Parents] migrate for bread, *not for their own pleasure*. (Maria, Grajewo)

> There is a group of people locally, who think the same way as me: I wouldn't go abroad. I would go only if for example one of the children was ill and I didn't have money for their healthcare. Or if I really had nothing to give the children to eat. Or to pay the bills. Or if there really was absolutely no work.... But just to *improve my standard of living, no*. (Kazimiera, Grajewo)

Kazimiera talks about improving her standard of living, but there is a fine line between 'maintaining' and 'improving' it. Maintaining a reasonable standard of living is viewed as 'bread', not 'coconuts' and, for many people, low wages in Poland do not ensure what is felt to be a reasonable standard of living. Hence they talk of being forced to go abroad, since, as suggested in Chapter One, their aspiration is to live 'normally' or to have a 'decent' standard of living. Interviewees from migrant and non-migrant households alike made similar comments about themselves or other people being forced to migrate for a normal/decent existence:

> To live *moderately well*, you *have to* migrate. (Anna, Grajewo, ex–husband migrated)

> If only one parent has a job, and the family wants to have a *decent* standard of living [*żyć na godnych warunkach*], then one parent will *have to* work abroad. (Marta, Sanok)

> In our own country, we should be able to earn at least enough to live on a *decent* level. I'm not talking about luxuries. But we need to be able to buy things. A TV or refrigerator or car is a basic *necessity*. (Małgorzata, Grajewo)

In other words, the interviews confirmed the observations of Kaczmarczyk, Iglicka, Morawska and other scholars of Polish migration that migrant earnings are commonly spent on everyday consumption.[4] In the words of Anita from Grajewo: "The money which people earn abroad and is transferred here, I suspect it's, how do you say, used just to make ends meet, so that the family wouldn't be short of money.... The money is just for everyday living."

However, there are two investments that many people feel forced to make. Kazimiera in Grajewo summed it up when she asserted, "Some migrate to buy themselves housing, others to educate their children." These are the areas where increasing numbers of migrants are spending money, in a range of Polish localities.[5] Both aspirations can be seen as culturally determined.

Housing as an objective for migration

Interviewees conveyed the impression that, to quote Wiesława in Grajewo, "A flat is fundamental." It is rare in Poland (compared with the UK) for single adults to live separately from their parents, and, for many newly married couples obtaining their own housing becomes the central aspiration of the household livelihood strategy. Ewa (UK) made a typical observation: "In Poland, everyone wants to own their own home. So everyone tries to earn money for a home, something which you can't do in Poland, unfortunately." Agnieszka (UK) suggested that "In Poland, you build a house, and it's a home for your whole life long. Because it is *your* home … and that home is your main possession in life."

> Above all, people go abroad to earn money to buy a flat, or to furnish the flat. That's the main thing, that's the basic thing, to have your own place. Later you can get a job anywhere but you know it's your home and you can always come back to it, no one will throw you out. That's the most important thing, to have your own flat. (Grażyna, migrant's wife, Grajewo)

Among Iglicka's sample of Polish people in London (average age 29.5), housing was the most common type of investment goal. Iglicka describes housing as the 'eternal, always longed for, hard-to-attain goal of generations of Poles'.[6]

UK interviewees contrasted Polish views on the need to build a permanent home with what they perceived to be a different British attitude. For example, Andrzej in Bristol asserted that Poles rarely moved in Poland, unlike in England, where people rented flats and kept moving about. In Poland, your home was your life's achievement so you stayed put. Ewa claimed:

> In Poland, people are attached to the place where they grew up. That's why it's so hard for them to move to other towns. In other countries, for example the USA or England, people will move to other towns to find work. But in Poland people really appreciate their family home and they only leave it when they get married and have their own family, and even then they don't often go far away.

The cost of housing in Poland is so high that even comparatively well-off couples who want housing often feel compelled to adopt migration as their livelihood strategy. Joanna and Michał, for example, had run a successful business in Grajewo and they started building a house before the birth of their child. However, they found that they could not keep up with the expenses of building, hence Michał began migrating to London. Among the UK interviewees, Patrycja said: "By village standards my husband's work [as a taxi driver] wasn't badly paid, but overall, in order to live and to build a home of our own, we didn't have any chance, especially since I didn't work." The other three UK interviewees who were in England primarily to build or buy a house in Poland – like Patrycja, all in their late twenties, with small children – had also not been badly off by local standards in Poland.

The perceived compulsion to acquire one's own home is such that even newly-weds may split up immediately after the marriage, so that the husband can work abroad to save money for a house while his bride remains in Poland. For example:

> They got married and the husband went abroad, for about three years, he's been the whole time in England, though he comes back [for holidays], but he's away for six months at a time, quite long. They have a daughter now.... When he started working abroad you could make money faster, it made sense financially, they are buying a house.... He started going abroad right after they graduated and got married. (Halina, Sanok)

Such separations may seem a rather unexpected, even shocking, aspect of the migration culture, but should be understood in the context of what "made sense financially", to quote Halina. According to Teresa in 2007, when the zloty–sterling exchange rate was very favourable to sterling and Polish house prices were lower, it was possible to earn enough to buy a flat by working abroad for just two or three years: flats were not expensive in her small town in Wielkopolska. This was why young husbands or fiancés went abroad. However, as discussed later in Chapter Six, not all young couples tolerate such separations, hence the fact that Patrycja and other young interviewees in her situation were currently living in England with their partners.

Despite, and perhaps because home ownership is such a common migration objective, 'building a house' or 'buying a flat' are slippery concepts. A simple statement that someone migrated to build a house is almost as uninformative as the common assertion that they migrated for 'money'. Motivations are always complex. On closer investigation it often transpires that the acquisition of housing was an afterthought, not the initial motivation for migration. A number of UK interviewees, for example, had thoughts of purchasing housing in Poland, even if the initial stimulus for migration had been bad debts or simply the need to cover everyday living costs. In fact, every interviewee who was not planning to remain in England and who did not have a home of their own in Poland talked about housing as an aspiration.

For young couples who have already acquired housing, furnishing a flat may also then seem a 'necessity':

> The situation was that my husband had to migrate. Because we were very hard up. I have a cousin in Germany and he went there during his

leave to earn some extra money. Obviously there's that time [in a young family's life] when you want to buy something, change something in the house, and you can't afford it. (Edyta, Grajewo)

My husband worked in Germany at the beginning of the 1990s, soon after we were married, after our daughter was born. He went to earn some extra money. We did have a flat, thanks to my parents … but we needed things for the flat. As a nurse I didn't and don't earn much, we just scrape by, so he had to find some extra earnings somewhere, so we could manage somehow. (Barbara, Grajewo)

In the case of older migrants, expeditions abroad to improve housing were not usually presented (by their relatives and neighbours) as forced, but rather as a response to opportunity. People without parental responsibilities, including mothers of adult children, were not criticised if they migrated to earn money for household repairs. Danuta's unemployed neighbour, for example, "had the opportunity [to go to England], her children are there, they have a flat … and she said she would just earn a bit of money, to do some repairs on her flat in Poland, or have a bit saved for a rainy day, to be sure to have enough to pay the bills" (Grajewo, 2008). Felicja discussed the case of a neighbour, a woman with three adult sons, who was temporarily staying with them in England:

She's coming back to Sanok next month because she's earned the money, she's going to put in new windows in the whole flat, they want to do some repairs to their flat. She'll come back to Sanok, do what's needed at home, then go back to England to do some work, then invest the money in her flat here.

Being abroad offers its own opportunities, so plans may change and, even in the case of parents with smaller children, 'necessity' may recede into the background and plans with regard to housing become more 'accumulative'. For example, Teresa's husband, as already mentioned, was by her account 'forced' to go abroad, to pay for medical treatment for his wife and daughter. However, as a result of his travels they had made numerous improvements to the house, which was old and in poor condition, and were the first people on their street to install gas. They also bought the shop on the ground floor of their house so that Teresa had her own independent livelihood and was able to combine work with looking after their youngest child.

Higher education as an objective for migration

For older couples in Poland, the perceived compulsion to migrate may reappear when their children leave school. It is a common assumption that parents of grown-up children may be forced to migrate in order to finance their children's higher education.[7] The scale rather than the nature of the phenomenon is new. For example, Alina explained that her father had left Grajewo to work in the USA around 1989 because "My sister was studying in Łomża, and she had to pay more for a bedsit in Łomża than he earned in a month." Irena (aged 34), one of the few interviewees with higher education, had her parents to thank: when it was time for her to go to university they had both moved from their village in Podlasie to Belgium, and lived there for 15 years, seeing all three of their children through university in Poland. Around the same time, in 1995–96, the practice of parents migrating to support their student children was already common elsewhere in Podlasie.[8] Recently, however, the number of parents migrating to finance higher education has almost certainly increased significantly. As already suggested in Chapter Two, many more Poles today aspire to higher education and although the interviewees in Poland did not have higher education themselves they often desired it for their children. Three quarters of Polish parents share this aspiration.[9] Not only is the cost of living high in the cities, but many students also have to pay tuition fees, so higher education is extremely expensive and simply not affordable for many households. Although students themselves often work abroad to finance their studies in Poland, nonetheless many parents also feel compelled to help.

Since losing her job in Grajewo, Beata had dedicated her life to supporting her children through higher education. In 2008 Beata was 48 and her children were 26, 18 and 14:

> This was why among other reasons it was a good idea for me to go and work abroad a bit, to help my children. We have a daughter ... in her final year at Warsaw University, she's doing English and will be a translator. And the money I earned in the USA went to help her.... I'm very glad I could help her and now I want to help our next child.... After all, I'm a mother. Well, everyone wants their children to have a better life, don't they? I did what I could.

The daughter duly graduated and found a good job as a translator, so the strategy paid off:

> It's good that she has established herself. I'm pleased at the moment. But now it's the turn of the other two children. Now it's my [19-year-old] son's turn ... let him study, and then we'll start thinking about the youngest one. (Beata, 2009, second interview)

Danuta, aged 44, had no previous experience of migration. In 2008, having recently become unemployed, she was toying with the idea of migration:

> If I don't find a job somewhere in Grajewo by this summer, I don't know, I may be forced to work abroad. From the point of view of making some money to help our children get through their five years

at university. It costs a lot. Halls, or a bedsit, as well. And food ... and travel home, and they need a bit of spending money.

When interviewed again in 2009, she had been unemployed for more than a year and both her children were at university. She loved her home, was very attached to her husband and mother and could not imagine herself as a migrant. However, she acknowledged that: "if I'm really forced to go, then, well, I don't know, I'll just have to shut my eyes and jump":

> My husband gets quite a good salary, by Grajewo standards, but the problem is that those children of ours have to study for five years. [laughter] I'm glad they want to study, let them study, but the expense is unbelievable. As my husband says, we must somehow combine forces, I'll have to go abroad, or perhaps with the children, well, just to keep them in the city, it's so expensive to live in the city.

Danuta was in an awkward position because both her children were studying at exactly the same time. However, although this was creating a great strain on household finances, at least the problem would only last five years.

It seems that usually it is only one parent who migrates, but a few interviewees did talk about couples who had migrated together. For example, Lidia, in Wielkopolska, talked about a couple – both manual workers – whose children were students in Poland. The parents had gone to live in Ireland where they did farm work and cleaned in order to support their children's education.

Migration by parents as self-sacrifice

In such situations it is hardly surprising if migration is perceived as an act of self-sacrifice. Beata, for example, encapsulated the idea that parents should sacrifice themselves for their children in her remark, quoted above: "I'm very glad I could help her.... After all, I'm a mother." Elsewhere in the interview, Beata described how unhappy she often was when she was abroad: "I think to myself on occasion: my life is slipping away and here I am abroad all alone and they are in Poland alone without me." Other interviewees also described the self-sacrificing behaviour of family members. Wanda, for example, told how her father had gone to the USA from Grajewo and worked there for years to finance the family and their smallholding, dying young of a heart attack: "He went abroad to give us a better start." Anita, talking about her brother, described his migration as "simply self-sacrifice. My brother has been working abroad for 17 years. He had a good profession, he was a land surveyor ... but he said he couldn't have supported his family, working here in Grajewo." Czesława, explaining her husband's motivation for leaving Sanok and working in England, explained: "You can't keep a family, not so that the children have things a little bit better. He just did it for the children's sake, who else for?" Eliza's mother-in-law in the USA was "there as long as she has the strength to carry on…. Other interviewees made more general comments about the self-sacrificing behaviour of parents in their community. For instance, in Grajewo, Edyta suggested: "Sometimes they have no alternative [but to migrate]…. Parents try to give their children everything they can. They do everything for their children's sake. Not for their own."

Conclusion

Localities with a history of migration acquire 'migration cultures': norms and beliefs concerning why, how and where people should migrate. This culture is complex and in some respects contradictory. Despite the fact that so many people migrate from towns like Sanok and Grajewo, there is a belief that migration is caused by a crisis: 'because the situation forces you'. The apparent paradox – that migration is both common and exceptional – derives from the fact that local livelihoods are often precarious: jobs are insecure and wages are too low to cover more than basic day-to-day living expenses, and many households regularly fall into debt. Olga Shevchenko's comment with regard to Russia in the 1990s applies equally to 21st-century small-town Poland: 'a crisis may be perceived not as an isolated occurrence, but as a routine and unchanging condition'.[10] This state of never-ending crisis is particularly marked in Poland, which lurched from one crisis to another even in the communist period, but there is also a general sense in which livelihoods are more insecure everywhere across post-communist Europe, leading to a feeling that 'the situation which forces you' is lurking round the corner. As illustrated in Chapter Three, when a crisis comes there is often a shortage of alternative local livelihood strategies, and a sense of being 'forced' into migration can be induced when the household has tried several locally available strategies and all have failed. Migration by just one spouse/parent alone in response to such crises is regarded as an unpleasant necessity and an act of self-sacrifice. Such crisis in Grajewo and Sanok is provoked in particular by unemployment (especially for those over the age of 40), debt and the perceived 'need' to purchase a home and pay for higher education for the children. For many households the latter is a new aspiration, and therefore an indication of how migration cultures might evolve over time. Chapters Five and Six continue the theme of the evolution of migration cultures, as new foreign labour markets are opening up and as younger generations are rejecting some of their elders' assumptions.

Notes

[1] Elrick (2008, p 1505).

[2] Horváth (2008, pp 773-4).

[3] Powiatowy Urząd Pracy w Kamiennej Górze (2004).

[4] For example, Iglicka (2008, p 70).

[5] Kaczmarczyk (2008b, p 255).

[6] Iglicka (2008, p 121). The sample was 636 Poles interviewed in autumn 2007.

[7] For a discussion of the same phenomenon in post-communist Russia, see White (2007, 2009b).

[8] Lukowski (1998, p 148).

[9] Gwiazda and Roguska (2008, p 100).

[10] Shevchenko (2009, p 2).

FIVE

Local migration cultures: opportunities and 'pull factors'

If one person has already gone abroad, obviously a second will go, and a third, and so on in turn. (Roza, Grajewo)

He didn't have anybody he could go to in Germany, but in England he had a cousin. That's why he went to her. He didn't have any other country he could go to. (Ilona, UK)

This chapter examines whether migration is so common because people see it as something with which they can experiment. Often the attitude that migration is experimental goes hand in hand with the view of migration as an opportunity. This may seem at odds with the perception that migration is forced, but the paradox can be resolved if the concept of an opportunity which 'cannot' be missed is taken into account. Such opportunism is facilitated by the ease with which unpaid leave can be taken from employers, who often share local opinion that migration is worth experimenting with. Even more importantly, migration is facilitated by the huge migration networks that connect Grajewo and Sanok to Western countries, networks which offer ample evidence to support the theory that networks constitute a major cause of migration flows (see Chapter One). It is not the case that migrants simply use networks as a mechanism for migration, but rather that they are often truly a cause of migration, in the sense that migration would not have occurred without an invitation from an existing migrant. This chapter discusses some of the conventions surrounding such networks. Migrants often persuade others to join them by painting attractive pictures of migration destinations, and a further aspect of a local migration culture is the prevailing images of destination countries, images which partly determine the direction of migration flows. This chapter looks at images of the UK that help attract Polish migrants to the UK, but also at negative images of life abroad which colour perceptions of the UK.

It has been suggested that networks do not explain the current wave of migration from Eastern to Western Europe. The *suddenness* with which Poles adopted the UK and Ireland as migration destinations after 2004 might seem to indicate that networks were not the major determinant of these migration flows, since networks normally take time to build. Okólski has suggested that:

> … three major forces, simultaneous and complementary, underlie the size, dynamics and geographical directions of migrant flows from EU8

to EU15 that took place after May 1st, 2004. These were: migration pressures in some sending countries, labour shortages in some receiving countries and across-EU15 differences in the degree to which labour markets in that area have been opened. The fourth factor, migration networks, appear to be of secondary importance.[1]

However, the evidence from Grajewo and Sanok tends to suggest that networks do constitute a factor of primary importance in explaining recent East–West migration in Europe. This is partly because a sufficient number of migrants already worked in the West before 2004 to form a solid basis for post-2004 networks: the main links were probably Grajewo–Belgium and Sanok–London, but there were many others. Even more important is a factor linked to transnational communications, in other words, the potential for networks to expand much more rapidly today than in previous centuries. At the same time, insofar as there has been a sudden change in the migration culture (regarding preferred destinations) this is also connected to generational change and the youth of many migrants today, as discussed earlier in Chapter Two. Young people today have somewhat different attitudes towards using migration networks.

Migration as a response to opportunity and persuasion

As already mentioned a particular feature of the Polish labour market is that many employers seem ready to grant workers unpaid leave to go abroad, something that helps explain why so much Polish migration is open-ended and experimental. Hence it is not only unemployed people and students who have the opportunity to make temporary forays abroad. The following quotations show how interviewees expected employers to be generous in this regard:

> Usually the employers agree to them taking unpaid leave, because everyone knows here in Grajewo that wages aren't high. (Anna)

> I suspect that even here in the kindergarten, if someone asked the director for unpaid leave, if they explained honestly why they needed it, they would get it…. The director would employ someone temporary. Then the old employee would come back and there would be no problem returning to work….You could get [a temporary replacement] with no problem, even for a few months. There are people queuing up for any job, whatever it pays. (Magda, Sanok)

Among the UK interviewees, Marzena, for example had taken three years unpaid leave from her shoe shop in a medium-sized town in northern Poland:

> So I have somewhere to go back to, if that's what I decide to do…. My boss was accommodating, she agreed. She's a really nice boss. There

were no problems at all. She said 'Just go, see if you can make a better life, you and your husband and family'.

Rafał, also in the UK, had taken three months unpaid leave from his factory in the Katowice conurbation. When he left, he was told he should come back because he might be given a pay rise (a goal for which the workers had been campaigning unsuccessfully for years). As Rafał's story illustrates, rather than being made to feel dispensable by the practice of unpaid leave, some workers are given the sense that they are valued by their employers and would be welcomed back. This gives them a sense of security that feeds into the belief that it is worthwhile experimenting with migration, because return is always possible. On the other hand, not all employers were so flexible. Krystyna's brother-in-law tried to take unpaid leave once too often and was refused. As a result, he gave up his job in north-east Poland in favour of occasional short-term contract work in Germany.

In other cases it is not the employee who makes the first move, but the employer who is obliged to slow production. As a result, employees go on forced unpaid leave, and they take advantage of this opportunity to do temporary work abroad. Teresa, for example, explained that production was usually sluggish in the three factories in her small town in Wielkopolska. Hence employees were often laid off and worked abroad while the factory was idle. Justyna was from another small town in Wielkopolska, where there was only one big employer, a mine that produced salt for de-icing roads and that could afford to lay off workers in the summer. Employees would take up to three months' unpaid leave and go to Germany, Ireland and England; picking blueberries in Sweden had recently become popular.

Opportunity, therefore, is an important part of the migration story. Opportunities can be created by a temporary liberation from work responsibilities in Poland, but of course they can also be pull factors, most importantly, the presence of family and friends abroad. It is the pull effect of these networks which help explain the fact that in locations with high migration it can seem more like a strategy of first than of last resort, particularly for people who do not have responsibility for children and therefore may lack very strong ties binding them to Poland. Aldona, in Sanok, suggested that, "They do try to find a job here but they get discouraged very easily, especially young people." Rosanna, who already had many friends in England, described the behaviour of people in their early twenties in her home town in Wielkopolska: "Most often, if someone doesn't have a job, they immediately think about going abroad.... Usually the first thought is to go abroad."

However, some interviewees felt that not just young people but local people of all ages would 'give it a go' if they had a good opportunity. In Sanok, Agata asserted that people with friends and family abroad were generally not likely to look hard for a local job. Magda, from a large village near Sanok, described how "One person brings over another [from her village to London]. If someone gets an offer of work, they think it over! And off they go. Not many people refuse. Perhaps only graduates, people with very good work, those people wouldn't be tempted." I asked her whether she thought people took the attitude that if you had a good opportunity you should not waste it. She thought this was the case. If someone saw how well their neighbour had done in England and they got a similar chance, "they just go off like a shot, right away". Similarly, in Grajewo, Dagmara asserted that, "Anyone will go if they have some kind of contact and a job." She did not think they needed much persuasion. Danuta said simply "Everyone migrates who can."

Some of the UK interviewees or interviewees' husbands had gone to England in response to invitations. Maria, for example, said that Rafał had often asserted that if the opportunity arose and someone offered him work abroad he would accept. Rafał described how he eventually came to the UK:

> My friend had come to England before I did and he phoned me and said, 'Do you want me to help you? I've got some work for you. Decide, and if you want to, then come, I'll give you help. You can live with me and I'll fix up the job.' I said 'Great.'

Jolanta and her family were also in the UK as a result of an invitation:

> We hadn't really thought about emigrating. But it just happened that my husband's brother phoned and he said, 'You know what, there's a job you could do, come if you like.' And my husband said 'OK!' and off he went.

It seems that some people believe that if you receive an offer from a close relative or a good friend you should take advantage of it, even if this means abandoning a promising livelihood strategy in Poland. For example, Aneta's mother-in-law, an accountant, was able to arrange for her son Dariusz to study accountancy in Poland part time for a reduced fee. Dariusz was running his own haulage company but the family hoped that if he became an accountant in Poland he would make even more money. However, Dariusz abandoned this livelihood strategy when his sister obtained a work placement in London. He took advantage of the opportunity to join her, even though he had to work first as a kitchen porter and then as a cleaner. Cieślińska records that people in small towns and villages in Podlasie who had won the lottery to go to the USA found it hard to turn down the opportunity: 'The lottery here acts in a quite magical fashion ... and the person who has won the lottery seems to have nothing more to say, since fate's gift cannot be rejected'.[2] Of course, not everybody would accept any offer to work abroad. Nonetheless, there is a pool of Poles who are not planning to take any active steps to migrate, but who might well depart abroad if the opportunity presented itself, as indicated in Table 5.1.

The language used to describe networking tends to emphasise the active role of the actual migrant and the passive role of the prospective migrant:

Usually one person collects [*zabiera*] someone else. Mostly a woman invites her best woman friend, or a man his male friend. That's how the chain is formed as one person pulls in [*ściąga*] the next. Later perhaps the brother will invite his sister, or a sister her brother. (Celina, Grajewo)

The way it works, one person goes first, and then other people get pulled along too. So they went to Manchester and later brought over some other people from [Polish city]. They invited them over to be with them in England. (Jagoda, UK)

Table 5.1: Are you currently interested in taking up a job abroad (2007)?

	Poland	Podkarpacie	Podlasie
Currently seeking a job abroad	2.4	4.6	2.1
Intending to search for work abroad	7.4	9.5	9.4
Would be interested in working abroad if I received an offer	8.1	9.7	8.6
Not interested	76.3	69.9	75.0
Currently working abroad	0.7	1.1	0.2
Don't know	5.1	5.1	4.6

Sources: Strzeszewski (2008, p 103); Gwiazda and Roguska (2008, p 101)

As the quotations above suggest, the process is often one of invitation, to which may be added an element of persuasion:

Marianna: My sister came to the UK first and she helped me come here. She knew how hard it was in Poland and she thought it would be better in England.

Anne: Could you say that she persuaded you?

Marianna: Yes, I agree, you could say that.

Anne: It was her idea first?

Marianna: Yes, she suggested the idea, and I thought about it, [and asked] my daughter if she would like to go, and she had no objections.

Of course, it is not the case that every migrant waits for an invitation. To 'pull' or 'bring over' (*ściągnąć*) does not necessarily mean that the initiative comes from the people abroad. They may simply lend money, or pay for tickets for those in Poland to join them abroad, after the would-be migrants themselves asked for help. The people in Poland may be expected to offer something in return, so this is not necessarily a free gift. Sometimes there seems to be a happy coincidence, where a person who wants an invitation is in fact invited. For instance, Celina, describing how her friend in Greece had telephoned inviting Celina to join her, explained: "It was a happy coincidence. She phoned, and I didn't really even stop to think, well, I thought it would be great to see a bit of the world, and I'd see how things turned out." Jagoda said she had not been persuaded by her friends in Frome to come there: it was her own idea. Nonetheless, the reason why she went to these particular friends rather than to others in Ireland was that her friend in Frome offered work and accommodation:

> It was because of my friends [that I came to Frome]. There just happened to be a room to let, the first one that came up, that was just how it happened, by chance. It was my friend here who was the first to say that I could come, that 'there's a room available, there's work, you can come'.

Related to the language of opportunities offered is the discourse of 'temptation'. In Grajewo, Ewa explained why her husband worked in Greece for over two years when their daughter was a toddler: "We were *tempted* by the better earnings. You know, to earn for the flat, and for a car, well, it was *tempting*. Particularly since his brother was there already and his brother brought him over." Grażyna, complaining about the fact that her husband had departed to work abroad that very morning, lamented: "Somehow he was *tempted*. He was *tempted*". In Sanok, Magda complained of the same thing. Her husband, previously careful to migrate only to reliable relatives, had been tempted by an unreliable friend:

> My husband's been working abroad more or less all the time since we got married.... First my dad took him to Germany, we have family in Germany, so. Well, later [sigh] he went to the USA, because his sister is there.... And just now he's been in England. A friend suggested it to him, and off he went. He was *tempted by the opportunity*.... I was amazed, I tried to put him off [bitter chuckle] but he wanted to give it a go....

It is clear that much casual tempting occurs. This results in young people, in particular, trying their luck abroad. Returning to Poland for their summer holidays, the migrants tell their stories to families, friends and neighbours who have stayed behind:

> Young people tell each other stories, persuading their friends to join them, saying 'Come and earn some money, you can buy a car.' That's what they say, sitting outside the block of flats. They sit on the benches and have these conversations. One persuades the other. And lots of young people go off abroad, right after leaving secondary school or university. (Felicja, Sanok)

In one case, a Pole abroad had a business and was recruiting employees, not necessarily close friends, from their home area in Poland:

> They know so many people in London. They come from a little place in Poland … a village really, and later they moved to Suwałki. And they have heaps of friends and family in Poland.... He went to England on his own [in the 1990s], before they got married. He was the one who gathered them all together, all those people he knew.... From Suwałki, and from the village, lots and lots. And they have family, her brother, and her husband's brother and his sisters. And it's all through him, really masses and masses of people they know in London.... They are the kind of people that if someone needs help, if someone wants to come, they help. Later on the person will look after themselves, but as for helping them find a job when they arrive, they do that without making a fuss. After all, the husband works in a firm that does building repairs. The firm belongs to his schoolfriend, who went to England right after leaving school in Poland … and now he has a big company and it's been a success and he recruits everyone he knows to come and work there. (Krystyna, Grajewo)

Zdisława told a similar story of a Polish supermarket in London which recruited from Sanok. The proprietor was an émigré from the post-war generation and when he discovered a long-lost nephew in Sanok he invited him and his wife to work at his supermarket. They in turn invited their friends and neighbours and, according to Zdisława, "all their friends" now lived above the supermarket in London.

To go abroad to strangers is definitely not part of the migration culture in places like Sanok and Grajewo, where many interviewees asserted that they knew no one who had gone abroad this way. Edyta in Grajewo summed up the general opinion when she asserted: "If you go abroad, you must have someone to go to (do kogoś). That's the main thing." Similarly, in England, Bernadeta, from Elbląg, said "In Poland we didn't use to organise things through agencies, we simply migrated on our own [through people we knew]." The opposite of going 'to somebody' is 'going into the unknown' (literally, 'into the dark', w ciemno) and the phrase conveys the fear associated with this situation, a fear which no doubt intensifies the feeling that it is a way of migrating which should not be attempted. The corollary of the culture of being taken abroad by a friend or relative is therefore that, if no one invites you, you do not go. For example, Danuta considered she had no option but to migrate to pay for her children's university studies, but she felt thwarted because she had no relatives or close friends working in Western Europe:

> If my sister or sister-in-law or some cousin was somewhere abroad I'd have gone long ago. It's different, you know, if you go to stay with someone who can find you a flat, or a room, to live, and some sort of

> job. Because if you just arrive at the station and get out of the coach what are you supposed to do? I don't have any family abroad, *so I can't go*. (Danuta, Grajewo)

Considering the nature of migration before 2004, a tradition of migrating to someone you know is unsurprising. To acquire a US visa, Poles often need an invitation from a sponsor and domestic work in countries such as Italy or Belgium is normally arranged informally through friends, mothers or sisters.[3]

Another reason why Poles prefer to use informal networks to migrate is the widespread lack of trust in Poland of formal institutions and organisations. In the communist era, people used informal networks to acquire products and services which state shops and institutions could not or would not provide.[4] Friends and family were trusted much more than official institutions.[5] Since the end of the communist regime, informal networks of friends and family have continued to be important.[6] In January 2008, 72% of Poles believed that 'You should be very careful in relations with other people'. In contrast to their suspicious attitude towards strangers, many Poles trusted acquaintances and friends (88%),[7] colleagues (85%) and neighbours (76%).[8]

Morawska has suggested that the reliance on informal migration networks and the propensity to engage in illegal migration in the period 1989-2004, by perpetuating communist-era habits of bending rules and ignoring official channels, was harmful for democratisation in Poland.[9] Nonetheless, democratisation has at least to some extent been accompanied by greater effectiveness of formal organisations and perhaps even, very recently, by some increase in trust of strangers, if not of politicians. In 2004, only 17% of Poles had felt that 'Generally you can trust most people', but this rose to 26% by 2008.[10] Recruitment agencies are a section of the market economy and the huge number of internet and paper press advertisements for job agencies, as well as individual jobs, suggest that there is a market of Poles who will respond to such advertisements. The manager of a recruitment agency in Trowbridge, which had become well-known in Poland, reported that on Mondays in 2006, after the early morning flight from Kraków landed at Bristol International Airport, people would come directly to the agency with nothing but the address, and queue along the pavement.[11]

Jaźwińska contrasts the provinces, where social networks remain strong, with Warsaw, where formal institutions can take the place of social networks. 'In some regions migration capital has been amassed over decades, in others (such as Warsaw) migration capital is acquired quickly, thanks to easy access to knowledge and information.'[12] A Polish government survey suggests that use of recruitment agencies for migration more than doubled over the years 2004-06, but that the picture was very different in different regions, with registered take-up lowest of all in Podlasie, where Grajewo is located.[13] In the first three months of 2008, only 124 people used the Grajewo County Employment Service to seek employment abroad, either through the European Employment Service (EURES) scheme or as seasonal agricultural workers for vetted companies.[14]

Podlasie is a conservative region with strong migration traditions, but the mistrust of formal agencies can also be explained by the fact that people locally have actually had bad experiences with such agencies, or know people who have. These local negative experiences seem to underscore the truth of media stories, particularly about Italian so-called 'labour camps', where Poles are said to have been treated like slaves. They contribute to enhance suspicion of advertisements and agencies and to confirm people believing that only family and close friends can be trusted to help would-be migrants. However, the practice of using employment agencies was not universally condemned even in Sanok and Grajewo; the few interviewees who knew people who had used agencies successfully were ready to admit that there were good and bad ones, and the more knowledgeable pointed out that it could make sense to use a locally based agency to find a job when you arrived in a foreign country.

As some interviewees also observed, going to stay abroad with a personal acquaintance did not in itself guarantee that all would be well. As Faist observes, 'people occasionally act opportunistically, and then violate trust'.[15] Bogusława, for example (thinking of examples she knew from the USA), pointed out: "People aren't always helpful even when you are abroad. It's a problem. Because it occurs that someone invites you, but then what happens next?!" Grażyna, perhaps remembering her own work on a farm in Germany, observed: "Often someone tells you it's amazing and when you get there it's not like that, it's totally different. It's much worse. Life is full of surprises."

> In the old days, when Poles couldn't work legally in England, people who came back on visits from England gave accounts which were a little bit inaccurate perhaps. I know even among my own friends they used to tell stories about how wonderful it was in England, there was so much money, you could earn money, and save, and so on. And lots of people fell for it. (Rozalia, Sanok)

In the 1990s, people were perhaps more gullible in the face of such persuasion, because they were less well informed about actual conditions in England. Nowadays, when many Poles have access to the internet[16] as well as acquaintances abroad, they should be able to check the truth of stories they hear. Moreover, in high-migration localities many people have already been to the West even if they are currently located in Poland: 51.2% of respondents in the Podkarpacie opinion poll had visited Western countries other than the UK, and 7.7% had been to the UK.

However, it seems often be the case that, even today, with so many friends and relatives abroad and extensive migration experience of their own, potential migrants are not really very well-informed in advance about specific new locations. Like Sylwia, who came to Trowbridge 'knowing about the Queen' but little else, they migrate 'into the unknown' in the sense of being ignorant of many important details about the receiving community. Hence they fill in gaps in their knowledge with certain preconceptions prevalent in the sending society. These images of the West can also be considered to form part of the migration culture, and they are explored in the next section.

Images of life in the West

Some interviewees in Poland seemed to expect that, like the early 20th-century Poles described in Thomas and Znaniecki's classic work, *The Polish peasant in Europe and America*, they would simply move into a Polish community abroad, where they would live in a Polish cocoon and hardly feel as if they were in a foreign country. Eliza (Grajewo), for example, illustrated this claim with examples from her own family. "Mostly [my sister in London] only talks to Poles, there are lots of Poles, my husband was in the States, he says there as well, you don't need English because there are just Poles, Poles and more Poles, Poles everywhere." In Grajewo, interviewees talked about relatives in Bayonne or Greenpoint (suburbs of New York) almost as if they were down the road. Moving to the USA would not disrupt their Grajewan social life:

> In Greenpoint, which is a Polish district, *you feel as if you were back home in Poland....* There are *lots* of people [from Grajewo], lots and lots. (Beata)

> At first she said she was going [to Bayonne] for six months, but those six months turned into five years.... She had some thoughts of coming back, but she says it would be worse here than there. Because there ... she's happy, she has places to go in the evening. *She has lots of Polish women-friends, because there are lots of people there from Grajewo,* so they just ... non-stop meet up with each other. (Celina)

Some parts of the West, therefore, may be viewed as culturally and socially Polish. In economic terms, however, the attraction of the West is, of course, that it is non-Polish. The pull of the West complements the push factors from Poland. Interviewees' complaints about Polish livelihoods chronicled in Chapter Three were often mirrored by their belief that in Western countries migrants enjoyed the reverse situation. For example, Alicja in Grajewo asserted: "In England, a Pole who works even at the most humble job can give his family a decent standard of living. Perhaps they won't have any luxuries, but they won't lack for anything." Eliza, also in Grajewo, commented, "My husband was in the States and he says the only thing he likes about being abroad, that's the luxury of it, you work hard, but you go into a shop and buy whatever you like." Beata said about the West in general: "You work hard, but you have good reason to work." The West was perceived as a place where jobs were available and sufficiently well paid to ensure a 'normal' standard of living. Almost universally, interviewees mentioned that you could earn 'enough' money and that you would not need to watch every penny. Moreover, especially after EU accession, you could find secure and legal work, where you would pay pension contributions and have health insurance, not always attainable objectives on the Polish labour market. In countries such as the UK and Sweden it was felt that the state showed its respect for families by paying decent child benefit and, more generally, children might have a better start in life with more opportunities.

Of course, people also project their own individual fantasies onto the West. Wiesława, for example, saw migration as an opportunity to escape from household drudgery:

> I'm sure it's different [voice warming], it's better, it's a new start for a woman, she has her own money. And definitely more freedom.... My life consists of getting up in the morning, cleaning, cooking, waiting for the children and helping them with their homework. But if you go to work abroad life is completely different. You go to work, there are no children, no housework … more money, and those mothers don't have to cook dinner, they can go to some restaurant.... You just want to try another way of life.

Notwithstanding the pull of the West, however, many interviewees had negative and frightening images of Western countries. The most extreme case was Wincenta, who felt she had little option but to migrate, yet was terrified of doing so. In the course of the interview she justified her reluctance with various horror stories that had happened to her friends: in Germany, you might fall ill from standing in muddy fields with boots full of water; in New York you could get cockroaches in your hair. Sometimes these more nervous potential migrants conflated different countries so that 'abroad' became a single area, and this led to assumptions about the UK based on what they had heard about other places. To a large extent negative images reflected either the backbreaking hard work and insecure lives of undocumented migrants in places like the USA or Belgium, or the poor living conditions of seasonal agricultural workers, particularly in Germany. Linked to this was an image of the West as a place where Poles might be humiliated and regarded as second-class citizens. Conversations and interviews with Poles in England suggested that they expected to confront the stereotype of the 'stupid Pole' among British people, even though this is a US, not a British, stereotype. A common belief among the interviewees – as among the Polish interviewees in other studies – was that certain labour markets were becoming 'saturated', either with Poles (a common assertion about London) or with Ukrainians and other nationalities who were supplanting Poles by undercutting them (for example, in Italy). Such images, although often not based in reality,[17] have an impact on where migrants go, explaining, for example, the increasing trend for Poles in the UK to go outside London.

With regard specifically to migration with children, it can be difficult for parents to find out in advance what life in the UK will be like and to form an impression of how quickly their children will adapt. Of course, there is a lot of contact between Podkarpacie in particular and the UK. As already observed, a third of the respondents had had members of their immediate family in the UK in the course of the previous year; 85 respondents had themselves been to the UK. However, except in locations like Sanok where many families have already migrated, it seems that many parents migrate with children without knowing other Polish families in the UK. Building on ideas raised in the in-depth interviews, the opinion poll sought to find out whether the migration culture in Podkarpacie included beliefs about life for Polish families abroad, and specifically in the UK. Overall, the interviewees had tended to share the opinion that life was 'easier' for families in the UK than in Poland, because families' spending power was greater and to some extent also because of perceptions that mothers had more time to spend with their children. The opinion poll therefore asked respondents 'Do you agree that it's easier for families to live in England[18] than in Poland?': 55.1% did agree (30.1% strongly), but 29.8% had no opinion on the topic; 15.1% disagreed (4.3% strongly). Overall levels of agreement were fairly similar across different groups, with one exception: respondents who had been in the UK were considerably more adamant that life there was easier for families (75.3% agreed, 48.2% strongly).[19] Perhaps the most interesting aspect of the responses was how evenly divided they were between 'strongly agree' and 'no opinion': people either had a definite view (it was easier) or no view at all.

An important aspect of an easy life for parents is happy children. Interviewees in Poland almost always asserted that young children were quick to adapt to life abroad, an opinion that was generally shared by the UK interviewees, whose children had indeed adapted well. In the opinion poll, 100% of respondents who had lived with their children abroad agreed with the statement that 'Young children quickly adapt to life in a new country'. Overall, 81.5% of respondents in the survey agreed, including 61.4% in strong agreement. In all the cross-tabulations, by age, sex and so on, the modal answer was 'strongly agree'. It was interesting that most people felt able to have an opinion on the topic, although so few had actual experience of living with children abroad. Women (82.2%) and men (79.7%) agreed in roughly similar measure; 87.1% of respondents who had been to the UK agreed with the statement.

However, interviewees in both Poland and the UK had mixed feelings about teenagers' ability to adapt. Interviewees in Poland in particular often felt that they would not like to take their teenage children abroad. It was true that many teenagers had studied English at school in Poland. However, interviewees worried that they might find it harder than younger children to form new friendships and to adjust to a different educational system. The opinion poll findings to some extent reflected these doubts, since respondents 'tended to agree' rather than 'strongly agreed' with the assertion that 'Teenagers would quickly adapt to life in England, because they learned English at school' (see Figure 5.1). In general, better-educated and younger respondents tended to be somewhat more doubtful about teenagers' ability to adapt than less well-educated people or those over the age of 49.[20] However, probably the most interesting finding is the extent of the faith that teenagers *would* adapt. This probably links to the fact that, overall, migration with children is very favourably viewed in small-town and rural Podkarpacie, as discussed in the next chapter.

Figure 5.1: Do you agree that teenagers would quickly adapt to life in England, because they learned English at school?

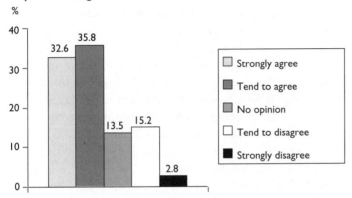

The interviews in Poland often revolved around the topic of how friends' and relatives' children had experienced schooling abroad, usually in the UK or the USA. In particular, there were assertions that children in Polish schools were stretched more academically, but given less encouragement. There have also been some media suggestions that children should not migrate because of 'lower standards' in UK schools, meaning that they would find it impossible to re-enter the Polish school system if they returned. However, the opinion poll revealed that at least in March 2008 three quarters of people had no opinion about whether syllabi in Poland and the UK were similar (see Figure 5.2). It was only those respondents who were younger, better educated, lived in bigger towns, were richer and better-travelled (especially to the UK) who were better informed, in other words, more likely to believe that the systems were different.

Figure 5.2: Do you agree that the school syllabus in England is similar to the Polish syllabus?

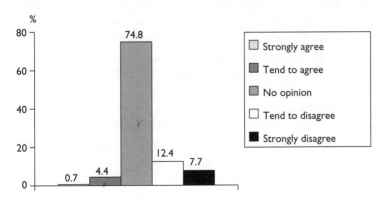

It seems, therefore, that (in March 2008) the migration culture did not include views about whether Polish children might encounter a different system if they went to school in the UK. By contrast, the belief that children adapt quickly to life abroad is part of the migration culture. The opinion poll evidence shows that this was taken for granted by respondents, and the interviewees constantly made the same point. No doubt the widespread assumption that even teenage children might adapt fairly easily to life in the UK is linked to lack of knowledge about the education system, and some parents, it must be assumed, migrate to the UK without thinking about differences between the systems.

The opinion poll also asked about crime, given that this is an issue that receives a lot of coverage in the UK media and concerns many people in the UK. The links between Podkarpacie and London in particular would lead one to suppose that parents considering moving to the UK with their children might have qualms resulting from images of UK cities as being unsafe.[21] Kamila, an interviewee in Poland who lived with her baby in London, had asserted that she did not want to bring him up in London because she was worried about violent youth crime. Angelika, who had returned to Sanok from working in London and still often visited her husband there, had witnessed a knife attack outside a station and did not feel safe, especially with her small daughter. One might have expected more agreement with the assertion that 'English towns are less safe than Polish towns'. However, 'no opinion' was the modal answer for almost all groups. Overall, 44.7% of respondents had no opinion; 26.2% thought English towns were more dangerous, 29.1% that they were safer. The only people with very different views were respondents who had been to the UK: 46.7% of these respondents thought that England was safer than Poland, 28.2% had no opinion and 27.1% believed that English towns were more dangerous. The more sanguine attitude of respondents who had actually been to the UK is surprising, but also in keeping with their optimistic and positive attitudes towards migration, displayed in many other answers to the opinion poll.[22]

Conclusion

This chapter has discussed aspects of the migration cultures which concern pull factors, both in the sense of chain migration – one migrant 'pulling over' the next – and images of foreign countries that attract Poles to migrate. Coexisting with the discourse of 'being forced', as discussed in Chapter Four, is the belief that, just because life is precarious in Poland, potential migrants should take advantage of opportunities to go abroad, if these present themselves. People who are unexpectedly offered the chance to migrate often decide to take it up. Employers connive at this situation by awarding unpaid leave, minimising the risks of experimental migration. Places like Sanok and Grajewo are linked by thousands of transnational migration networks to foreign countries and usually the opportunity to migrate is an invitation from a friend or relative abroad. There are various conventions surrounding such invitations and they are described using a particular terminology. The friend or relative may persuade or 'tempt' the potential migrant, or the latter may fish for an invitation. In either case the language used emphasises the role of the person abroad in 'pulling' or 'taking' the potential migrant out of Poland.

It is often said that 'you have to go abroad *to somebody*' (*do kogoś*). Even people in desperate financial circumstances will not go abroad unless they have a good friend or relative to go to. The migration culture, for many middle-aged residents of Grajewo and Sanok, is that using recruitment agencies or casual acquaintances to migrate counts as going into the unknown and is therefore more risky. There is a prevalent belief that people who use agencies or depend on mere acquaintances will be let down and cheated, and this often seems to happen. However, the culture of going 'to somebody', with its origins in illegal migration to the USA and pre-2004 Western Europe, is beginning to break down, demonstrating how migration cultures evolve over time.

The migration culture also influences migrants' choice of destination. Choice is constrained if migration is only via social networks, although networks do spread to a wide range of countries in Europe and North America. One might suppose that networks promote the spread of detailed information about countries where migrants work and that potential migrants feel that being well-informed about what to expect is an additional reason to follow the beaten track. In fact, people still seem to migrate often having only hazy impressions about their destination. Bauer el al point to the existence of 'herd effects' in migration, where migrants will go to certain destinations without necessarily being well informed in advance, because they assume that so many previous migrants cannot be wrong. They suggest this is as an alternative to network theory for explaining why migrants cluster in particular locations.[23] There is possibly something of a herd effect among young people in Grajewo and Sanok, although it seems that usually some kind of network is also in operation, even if it consists of acquaintances. However, perhaps even those migrants who rely on restricted networks of close friends and relatives do not feel a need to be very well informed. If reliance on networks gives them a sense of having little choice about where to go, this induces a certain fatalism and diminishes the need to research their destination in advance.

Snippets of actual information are backed up by popular images of certain locations. The survey in Podkarpacie tested opinions about a number of images relevant to migration with children to the UK and found: wide agreement that children of all ages would adapt quickly to life abroad; quite a lot of agreement that it was easier for a family to live in the UK than in Poland; little awareness of differences between Polish and UK schools; and little concern about crime in UK cities. The migration culture also includes negative images of life in foreign countries, especially concerning the lives of undocumented workers in the USA and Belgium and seasonal labourers in Germany. However, overall attitudes towards migration are not negative but neutral: as argued in Chapter Two, it is seen as 'normal'. If migration is normal it is therefore possible to use the term 'migration culture' to mean an expected way of doing things. However, migration is more acceptable for some social groups than for others. Both Chapter Four and this chapter have identified some general features of the migration culture. Chapter Six now looks at how norms and expectations regarding migration are applied more specifically to mothers, fathers and children, and how these expectations have been changing in the 21st century.

Notes

[1] Okólski (2007, p 23).

[2] Cieślińska (2008, p 9).

[3] See also Morawska (2001, p 62).

[4] Wedel (1986, pp 94–117).

[5] Bukowski (1996, pp 84–5).

[6] Podgórecki (1994, p 132); Sztompka (1999, p 189); Warzywoda-Kruszyńska and Grotowska-Leder (2006).

[7] The word is *znajomy*, literally an 'acquaintance', but I noticed in the interviews that some Poles seemed to use it as a synonym for an ordinary 'friend' (*kolega*), although not for the very closest of friends.

[8] Wciórka (2008, p [i]).

[9] Morawska (2001, p 70).

[10] Wciórka (2008, p [i]).

[11] Interview with a recruitment agency manager, Trowbridge, 10 July 2007.

[12] Jaźwińska (2001, p 124).

[13] Anon (2008d).

[14] Interview with EURES official, Grajewo County Employment Office, Grajewo, 1 April 2008.

[15] Faist (2000, p 103).

[16] In 2007, 40.1% of Poles had internet access at home (Gwiazda and Roguska, 2008, p 86).

[17] Cook et al (2008, p 28).

[18] The word 'English' rather than 'British' was used in the questions because it is more commonly used than 'British' in colloquial Polish. In retrospect, I regret this decision.

[19] Of those who had had family members in the UK, 62.9% agreed with the statement.

[20] The answer 'strongly disagree' or 'tend to disagree' was chosen by 18% of respondents overall, but by 25.5% of 18- to 24-year-olds, 26.7% of 25-to 34-year-olds, 25.1% of respondents with a higher education and 24.3% of those with a secondary vocational diploma (between grammar school [*lyceum*] leaving certificate and university degree).

[21] There is also crime in Polish cities, of course, and the 2006 Eurostat survey of perceptions of safety in selected European cities suggested that actually more residents of Polish cities were worried about safety in their cities than residents of cities in the UK (Eurostat, 2009,

p 34). However, the issue here is whether residents of small-town and rural Podkarpacie believed UK cities to be unsafe.

[22] Of those who had had family members in the UK, 33.6% disagreed with the statement.

[23] Bauer et al (2002).

SIX

Parental migration with and without children

Livelihoods, as already discussed, have to be culturally appropriate. For example, in Poland it is acceptable for young single men to work abroad to save up for a car, but it is not acceptable for two parents to leave their children to do the same. On the other hand, there are other situations when it does seem to be widely acceptable for parents to leave their children behind in Poland. This chapter considers gender and parental roles as an aspect of the migration culture and of the overall gender culture within which livelihoods are framed. It explores, in turn, opinions about whether it is more appropriate for fathers to migrate than mothers; views on migration by both parents simultaneously, without their children; and levels of support for migration by parents and children together. It also considers migration culture in the sense of how migration should be done, examining the stories of the UK interviewees and how they joined their husbands in the UK. Again the focus here is on gender roles and the extent to which women had an input into the family migration strategy. Finally, the chapter investigates the migration objectives of these particular interviewees: were they predominantly economic or emotional?

Previous chapters have referred to the model of 'incomplete migration' that became popular in the 1990s, particularly in villages and small towns in regions such as Podlasie and Podkarpacie. One parent migrates to Western Europe, but the rest of the family stays in Poland, and the migrant returns home as often as possible. Money earned in the West is almost all spent in Poland. This model can reinforce conventional gender roles if it is the father who migrates. Migration is an act that accentuates his breadwinning role at the expense of his parenting responsibilities. On the other hand, if the mother migrates, this can have the effect of reversing conventional roles within the household.[1] As a number of scholars have argued,[2] women sometimes gain more self-confidence as a result of migration and begin to feel that gender roles should be more equal. Given that Polish women migrants often remain in close contact with their home communities, one might expect these new expectations to shape new patterns of gender relations back in Poland. This would be an example of 'social remittances', to use the phrase coined by Levitt, to refer to 'a local-level, migration-driven form of cultural diffusion'.[3] At the same time, the opinion poll evidence presented in Chapter Two indicates that even non-migrants, especially young Poles, are becoming increasingly supportive of 'partner-like marriages', where roles are more equally shared. Social change in Poland as well as 'social remittances' from the West therefore complement one another in contributing to a situation where rigid gender roles (father = breadwinner, mother = chief parent) are being eroded, at least partially.

Urbańska, following Raijman et al, argues that there are two conditions that allow migrant mothers to reconcile their roles as both parents and migrants. On the one hand, by prioritising their breadwinning role they have to believe that they are acting in the best interests of the family and, on the other, they have to be sure that their children have good quality care from those directly around them, during their absence.[4] Of course, the mothers themselves will retain a care-giving role, but from a distance. Urbańska also cites Pine's research in Podhale (just west of Podkarpacie, an area with a long tradition of migration to the USA), showing that in this particular location the mothers' absences are accepted because hard work and economic responsibility are seen as integral to the maternal role.[5]

Chapter Two argued that attitudes towards migration in high-sending communities were pragmatic, so it would not be surprising if usual gender roles could be abandoned in circumstances where only the mother had the opportunity to migrate. One might also expect to find differences of opinion between different social groups, perhaps with a social remittance effect where people who had spent time in the UK or other countries, which had to some extent moved away from the male breadwinner model, had less conventional views about gender roles. This chapter combines the interview evidence with the findings of the opinion poll used in the research to explore such views about the acceptability of maternal migration.

It is not immediately evident what the alternative, 'parents with children' migration model implies about norms regarding parental and gender roles. If the family decides from the outset to migrate together, this might suggest that both spouses have equal breadwinner roles. Alternatively, if the husband is the pioneer and the wife merely 'trails' after him, it could suggest the opposite. At first glance it seems that these are two quite different types of migration, but I argue that in fact they are more similar than they might at first seem.

Gender roles and parental migration without children

Preferences for migration by fathers rather than mothers

Chapter Three suggested that it is often harder for women than for men to find jobs in Poland. If a wife is unemployed, but her husband works, it would seem logical for only the wife to migrate. As described in Chapter Four, this does in fact happen when children are grown up or in their late teens. Nonetheless, when children are still of an age to be dependent on their parents, it is generally expected that the wife should stay in Poland, to fulfil her mothering role. The husband, on the other hand, because of his role as the family's chief or only breadwinner, will do any migration that needs to be done. The fact that migration is often for the purpose of building the family home enhances the assumption that this is a masculine activity.[6]

The opinion poll in Podkarpacie asked separately about smaller and teenage children, because it was felt that respondents might have different expectations about the roles of mothers and fathers at different stages of their children's lives. As Figure 6.1 illustrates, 63.9% of the respondents, a clear majority, agreed that 'If one parent in the family works abroad temporarily, it's better for the children if the father migrates, not the mother, even when the children are teenagers'; 13.9% had no opinion and only 22.2% disagreed.

Figure 6.1: 'If one parent in the family works abroad temporarily, it's better for the children if the father migrates, not the mother, even when the children are teenagers'

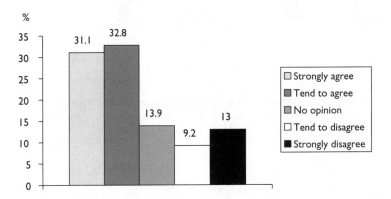

However, different groups of people had different views on the matter. It was noteworthy, for example, that men were much less likely to agree strongly that the father should migrate, and more likely to disagree or not to have an opinion (see Figure 6.2).

Parents of children under 20 and people in the age bracket 25-49 (obviously overlapping categories) were particularly likely to agree that the father should migrate (see Figure 6.3). People who had been to Western countries other than the UK – 51.2% of the total sample – were also especially likely to feel that fathers should migrate. On the other hand, people under 25 or who had been to the UK (in the sample, generally not overlapping categories)[7] were particularly likely to disagree.

The contrast between people who had visited the UK and those who had been to other destinations is interesting. It could be that the middle-aged respondents who had been to Western countries other than the UK were typically doing highly gendered work such as building in Germany or Scandinavia or domestic work in Italy or Greece. By contrast, the UK group had worked in a less gendered labour market and had picked up new ideas about gender roles. This would accord with Siara's conclusions from her analysis of UK-based Poles' opinions about gender roles, as expressed on internet forums.[8] Such ideas, originating in the UK, might spread among the youngest generation even in Poland, hence the support of the under-25s. This would be an example of social remittances. Intuitively, however, it

Figure 6.2: 'If one parent in the family works abroad temporarily, it's better for the children if the father migrates, not the mother, even when the children are teenagers'

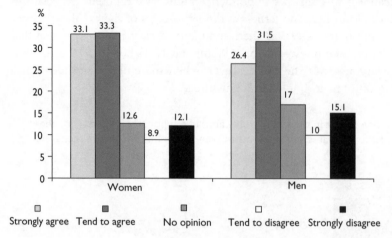

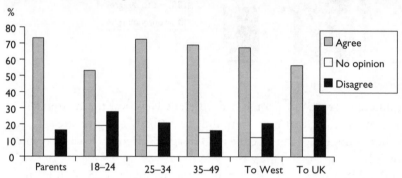

Figure 6.3: 'If one parent in the family works abroad temporarily, it's better for the children if the father migrates, not the mother, even when the children are teenagers'

would seem much more probable that there is an interchange of influences, rather than a direct West–East transfer. Experience of being in the UK surely merely reinforces a less rigid view of gender roles which, as discussed in Chapter Two, is already becoming common among Polish young people and has roots in post-communist Polish social change (under the general influence of globalisation).

There was more general agreement with the assertion that 'Mothers of small children should not leave their children and husbands to work abroad'; 85.3% of respondents agreed, only 4.8% had no opinion, and a mere 9.9% disagreed. All groups agreed with the statement. For example, among the respondents who had been to the UK, 80% agreed that mothers should not leave small children compared with only 56.5% agreeing that they should not leave teenagers. Interviewees often expressed very conventional views about gender roles to back up their views that fathers should migrate in preference to mothers. For example, Ewa, in Grajewo, could not imagine herself migrating and leaving her teenage child in Poland. The mother "spent more time with a child" than the father and the mother was also responsible for keeping house. "Perhaps I am wrong, but that is definitely the normal pattern." Zofia, in Wielkopolska, who had younger children, stated her opinion that husbands should migrate because they were the main family breadwinners and that women should look after the home. I suggested that it could also be the other way round, but Zofia, her female assistant and her female customer – we were talking in her hairdressing salon – laughed at this suggestion. Interviewees of various ages, although in particular slightly older ones, made similar comments, including women whose husbands migrated and those who did not. A woman's place was in the home and not on the coach to London.

It was noteworthy, however, that statements about conventional gender roles were not normally made by mothers who had actually in the past left their children to work abroad. In Sanok, Janina mused:

> If it's all the same, which parent should go, then it's probably better if the children are with their mother. Although it's not better, you can't just say that it's better. Because the children probably suffer just as much, whichever parent goes.

Particularly in migrant households, there was much concern about children missing their fathers (discussed later in this chapter), and this clearly has an impact on how people conceptualise gender roles: the father's absence makes everyone in the family realise that he is a parent as well as a breadwinner and that conventional gender roles are not the only guide as to who in the family should migrate. Even where quite traditional views are held on gender roles, these too can back up the idea that fathers should not be absent from the family home. Several interviewees expressed the idea that fathers have special parenting duties that a mother cannot replace. Joanna, whose husband worked abroad while she stayed in Poland with their baby son, felt that:

> A child grows up differently if they are only with their mother, or their father, it's different if both parents are there. Each of the parents has a different role. Perhaps the mother is more delicate, and the father is firmer.

Mieczysława, whose husband was considering migrating, asserted:

> Children must have both parents at home. Even if the mother mostly brings up the children, obviously the father must keep an eye on them – so they're in awe, not really afraid as such, not so they'd be scared of him, but someone has to keep discipline. So they know they can't do anything they like. They need a mother, too, to cuddle the children, and children confide in their mothers more, they have more contact with them. It's always been that way, that's how it is.

Reasons why maternal migration without children is considered acceptable

In practice, there were situations where it was simply more feasible for the mother to migrate, and most interviewees seemed to accept that this did need to happen. Previous chapters have mentioned that unemployed women with older, especially adult, children, often migrate, but there were also households where mothers of younger children worked abroad. For example, Lidia, from Wielkopolska, worked two months a year on a farm in Germany, despite having children aged two and 12; her husband was disabled. Lidia seemed to have no problem with the fact that in their family she was the migrant: this was the only possible arrangement. A crucial factor, as mentioned in the introduction to this chapter, was whether the children had good care in Poland, even though the mother was abroad:

> My husband works in the chipboard factory, my parents-in-law live downstairs, so I didn't worry at all about the children, because the children had very good care. That was why I could afford to work a little bit abroad. (Beata, Grajewo)

Migration by lone mothers obviously constitutes a somewhat separate category. It was striking that most interviewees who discussed this theme adopted a pragmatic and indeed sympathetic attitude towards lone mothers' migration strategies. Interviewees, whether or not they personally had migrated, leaving their children, generally accepted that a lone mother's breadwinner role could transcend her parenting role if she had someone who could take good care of the children in her absence:

> We are always taught that a mother should be with her child, always. But perhaps some people don't understand what a problem it is if you don't have money. You have nothing to live on. Because that's how it actually is.... If a lone mother leaves her child for example with the grandmother it really must be an extreme situation. To go abroad. And it's really hard there, to work and send money back to Poland. (Eliza, Grajewo)

> Anne: What do people think if a lone mother migrates, leaving her children in Poland?

> Magda (Sanok): They're not wild about it. Although, I don't know, you always have to hear both sides. If she's in a really hard situation, well she's forced, then you can't criticise her, can you? That she left her child. Perhaps it will be better, it's self-sacrificing on her part, to go, isn't it? I don't think you should criticise her, 'Oh so-and-so left her child' and so on. That's not how it is. She isn't doing it for herself, only for the child.

Anne: But do other people have the same opinion?

Magda: Some people think differently, they say she's wrong, but others think the way I do. I think most people agree with me.

The opinion poll findings confirm Magda's impression. Respondents were asked whether they felt that lone mothers should risk emigration, if they planned, eventually, to reunite with their children abroad. 55.1% agreed that 'For lone mothers, migration is often a sensible escape route from a difficult financial situation; afterwards, they can bring their children to be with them and start a new life abroad'. Responses for men and women were nearly identical and in general there were similar levels of agreement among all groups. Consistent with the expectation that younger people might have more liberal views, younger respondents were more likely to endorse migration by single parents – 63.5% of 18- to 35-year-olds agreed, compared with only 53.2% aged 36-91, and there were more 'don't knows' in the older group.[9]

Three of the UK interviewees were lone mothers. One came with her child, to live with her sister and mother, while the other two originally left their children with their own mothers in Poland and collected them later. In all three cases the women fell in love after they arrived in the UK, set up households with their children and new partners, and seemed happy about their migration decision. In Poland, Justyna, when interviewed, was planning to work in England and then bring over her child and perhaps also her mother, but in this case her strategy did not work out and she returned to Poland after a few months.

Not all lone mothers (or other women) felt that it would be better for children of lone mothers to eventually join them abroad. Perhaps it would be better for the lone mother to work temporarily abroad, leaving her children with her own mother, especially if the child, lone mother and grandmother already lived in one household, as often seems to occur.

If they don't have work in Grajewo, lone mothers have to go abroad.... But I don't know if I'd risk taking my children abroad. (Anna, lone mother)

If they don't have work they decide to go abroad. My cousin too. She's a single mum and she spent a year working in the States. But she was in a comfortable situation because her parents looked after her child, her mother, so the child was definitely well looked after and she could feel comfortable about it and earn some extra money, she needed to because she is a lone parent.... But to go with your child is also a problem, because abroad.... I think here in Grajewo it would be easier to find someone you trusted to look after the child. (Barbara)

Not only were interviewees ready to accept that lone mothers could migrate, but they also agreed that sometimes mothers could join fathers abroad, leaving their children in Poland. Ilona's husband, for example, had gone to Bath, but since the family was desperately short of money and Ilona was sitting at home unemployed in Poland, "we had a talk with our mums and said Adaś and Natalka were still really little, and could I leave them with their grandmothers for a couple of months. Well, our mothers agreed. Adaś stayed with my mother-in-law and my mother had Natalka". In Sanok, Iwona had left her children to work with her husband in London; she too left the children with grandparents:

> I went to work in London twice after our children started school in Poland. I was living in Poland, my husband was still working in England, so during the summer holidays two years in a row I went to be with him and left the children with their grandparents. When term started again, I returned home.

Eliza, in Grajewo, described a pattern of behaviour that was also mentioned by other interviewees, where the mother joined the father in order to earn money more quickly:

> They often go abroad as couples. For example the children are left with the grandmother, the grandparents. While they are still strong enough. They say, 'If we go together, we're young, we'll earn more and we'll come home faster.' That's their thinking. They say what one person would earn in two years they will earn in one year, the same amount. That's how it is. Sometimes they go together and then for example the mother comes back and the father stays.... That's often how it is. That's how it sometimes happens. While the grandparents are fairly strong and fit.

Such parents could, however, be condemned if they seemed to be neglecting their children:

> For example I know some people who have been in Ireland three years and left their small children [with grandparents] and I don't know when it's going to end. There's always some reason why it's too soon to return. First the flat, then a car, then something else, then a car again, and there's a kind of chain. They never say: 'That's enough! We need to come home, that's sufficient.' Originally they meant to come back and collect the children, but later they stopped talking about it. They keep putting it off.... The children could have been there three years already ... little children pick up the language quickly.... The children are already calling the granny 'Mum'. It's not a very nice situation. (Magda, Sanok)

Overall, one third of the UK interviewees (both single and married) had left their children for short periods, either on previous trips to work abroad or while they were making arrangements for the children to come to the UK. Five interviewees in Poland had done the same. The women who had migrated without their children were often regretful, but did not usually blame themselves, which might testify, again, to the fact that such migration is seen as being 'normal'. Janina, in Sanok, was unusual in expressing a feeling of guilt:

> It's hard to explain to little children why Mummy isn't there, or Daddy, and I think children are damaged by those separations. I left my children too, although my husband was at home, and my mother-in-law, and my father-in-law, but all the same. It's a difficult thing, and when I think about that time when I had to go and work abroad and not be with my children I do have pangs of conscience. That I left my children.

Migration with children

Levels of support

One might suppose that people would prefer children to stay in Poland, even if one of their parents migrated. After all, migration is usually seen as a temporary strategy, not one that would warrant uprooting children. At least until recently, there were still places in Poland where it was assumed to be better for children to remain behind: the local migration culture had not yet embraced the idea of migration with children. Krystyna, for example, described the shock in a small village near Suwałki when her friend invited a local family to relocate to London:

> So off he went, and after about four months, six at most, not longer than six months, his wife followed after. Everyone in the village thought they were mad, that they simply wouldn't be able to cope, after all, she wouldn't be working and they had two small children.... They reproached them and said he should have gone on his own, or perhaps she could have left the children with their grandmother.

Ewa, in Bath, knew no one except her own family who had migrated with children from her home village in south-east Poland, which had very high rates of migration overall. Usually men migrated, leaving their wives and children. Ewa explained this by referring to culture:

> I think that in Poland we have a custom, perhaps it's in our mentality, that the husband is the head of the household and has to provide for the family. And the wife's job is bringing up the children.

Monika, in Bristol, said that her friends, who had all stayed behind in her home town near Poznań, "are amazed that I went abroad, with so many children and not knowing the language, that I took such a step!" Barbara, a mother of four, commented on how several years ago even Polish migrants in England had been surprised by family migration:

> When we first came [to Bristol in 2005] there were really very few children, when we went to church you very rarely saw a child, and as for four children all at once! Some people couldn't understand how a family like that could migrate!

A contributor to an internet discussion forum linked to a Podkarpacie newspaper suggested in April 2008 that villagers in particular were still wedded to the model of single-parent migration:

> Mostly it's ignorant peasants [*wieśniaki*] who leave their children with grandparents in Poland. People from towns took their children abroad long ago, because bringing up a child eg in the UK is much cheaper and easier than in Poland, but you just have to convince yourself to give it a go.[10]

Interviewees in Grajewo and Sanok almost without exception felt that family migration was a better option than leaving some of the family behind in Poland. Danuta, in Grajewo, expressed the general opinion when she asserted: "I think it's better if they're abroad as a whole family, husband, wife and child, not that one parent should be abroad and the other in Poland. Really." The reasons for this belief – which seems to represent a sea-change in the migration culture – are discussed in Chapter Seven. The next section of this chapter investigates the extent to which opinion poll respondents agreed with the interviewees. It turned out that respondents overwhelmingly supported migration with children over the former model of one-parent migration, at least with regard to children's well-being – 85.5% of respondents agreed that it was better for a small child (under 12 years old) to migrate with both parents, rather than staying in Poland without one parent (see Figure 6.4). Groups particularly likely to agree with this statement included people who had been to the UK (94.1%), those aged 18-24 (91.5%) or those who had had higher education (90.1%). The great majority (78.1%) also agreed that 'It's better for teenage children to go abroad with both parents, rather than staying in Poland without one parent' (see Figure 6.5). Most enthusiastic, once again, were people who had been in the UK (89.4% agreement). With one exception,[11] over 50% among every category of respondent – men/women, different age groups, different income groups, etc – agreed 'strongly' with both statements. These findings suggest that there might be a social remittance effect – since the ex-UK respondents particularly agreed with the statement – but that there are likely also to be causes indigenous to Poland, given that agreement was so widespread.

Figure 6.4: 'It's better for children under 12 years old to go abroad with both parents, rather than staying in Poland without one parent'

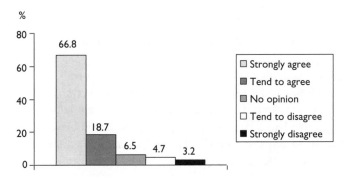

Figure 6.5: 'It's better for teenage children to go abroad with both parents, rather than staying in Poland without one parent'

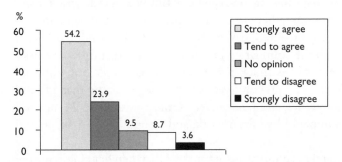

The opinion poll also asked more generally about migration with children, not in relation to the good of the children, but as an experiment. This was because interviewees in the UK often seemed to perceive their migration as experimental, frequently believing at the outset that they could return to Poland without too much trouble if things did not work out. Risks were reduced by the fact that the husband almost always came first, to prepare the way, before the wife and children decided to join him. Nonetheless, letting the chief breadwinner depart on such an uncertain venture was a risky strategy for a family to adopt. The relative youth of most of the UK mothers perhaps helps explain their bravery: most were in their late twenties when they came to England in the years 2005-08, although some were older.[12]

I simply wanted *to see if it was possible* to live a different way. (Renata)

> We became convinced it would be worth *having a go, just to see*, perhaps we could at least improve our work situation. (Bożena)

> We decided to move here. Or rather, we didn't think we would move for good, that we would live here for ever, *we just wanted to give it a go*. For at least a year. (Hanna)

> I *took a risk*, but you know, I *could always have gone back*. (Izabela)

> My husband saw going to England as a way out of the situation. I wasn't happy, at our age [mid-thirties], to start again, and change everything. My husband said 'I have the opportunity, let's go, we have somewhere to return to' (because we had a flat, not one we bought, because we couldn't afford one, but from the council). He said, *'If it doesn't work out, we'll come back.'* I said *'OK, give it a go.'* (Edyta)

In Poland, interviewees who were hoping to migrate with their children took a similar line. In Grajewo, Dorota, for example, said philosophically: "It may be good, it may be bad, that's the way everywhere. But you *have to give it a go*." Another interviewee was hoping her elder child (aged nine) would be invited by her ex-mother-in-law to go to the USA, with her former husband; she herself hoped to follow after with the younger child. She recognised that this was a risky strategy: "Overall, sometimes I wonder how it will actually work out, but – *it's worth taking a risk*, isn't it?" The previous year she had been hoping that a friend from England would invite her, and made a very similar comment: "*I would risk it*. I could take a year's unpaid leave from work, and I could take a risk, go and see if I liked it there."

Emilia (Ełk) was definitely planning to work in the UK when her children were a little older and would then try settling there with the whole family. She asserted:

> You can, you can definitely return to Poland!…. If someone has gone abroad, they can come back anytime…. We'd like to settle in England but if things didn't work out we'd buy a flat in Poland.

Since so many interviewees made comments of this type, and given that other researchers have also commented on the experimental quality of much migration from contemporary Poland,[13] it seemed worth trying to determine if approval of experimental migration with children was a feature of the migration culture. The question asked was 'If one parent has a good job offer, or has already found a good job in Western Europe, it's worthwhile for the whole family to try emigrating (they can return if it doesn't work out)' (see Figure 6.6). Although obviously open to criticism on technical grounds – as two statements rolled into one – the question seemed appropriate because it conveyed the essential background assumption behind experimental migration: the feasibility of return. Perhaps rather surprisingly, there was high level of support for this assertion: 76.4% of respondents agreed.

Figure 6.6: 'If one parent has a good job offer, or has already found a good job in Western Europe, it's worthwhile for the whole family to try emigrating (they can return if it doesn't work out)'

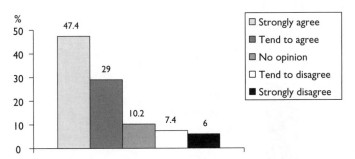

People who had been to the UK were especially likely to agree (85.9%), but so were people who had been elsewhere in the West (79.5%), as well as respondents with higher education (83.4%). With regard to age, the under-25s were both more enthusiastic (85.1%) and the most firmly decided (only 3.2% had no opinion). The middle age group contained the most waverers (13.9% did not know). The over-60s were more likely than other groups to disagree, but even here those disagreeing were in a small minority (see Figure 6.7).

Figure 6.7: 'If one parent has a good job offer, or has already found a good job in Western Europe, it's worthwhile for the whole family to try emigrating (they can return if it doesn't work out)'

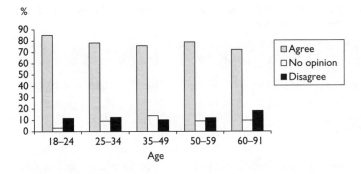

Non-migrant interviewees sometimes said that parents who took their children abroad were particularly brave; sometimes they also claimed that women were more afraid of migrating than men. The answers to the question about whether it was worth experimenting with family migration indicate that people in Podkarpacie considered that the benefits of family migration outweighed any such fears. However, as a check, the survey also included a question that solicited participants' own emotions and highlighted the negative side of migrating as a family. Participants were invited to express their views about the assertion that it was 'frightening' to move abroad with children: 32% of respondents agreed that it was frightening, but a majority, 56.6%, denied fear (see Figure 6.8)

Figure 6.8: 'It's frightening to move with children to another country and I find it hard to understand parents who decide to do this'

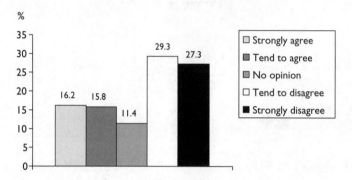

Poorer and less well-educated respondents were particularly likely to feel afraid, but there was little evidence[14] that women were more scared than men. The generational differences were clearly displayed, with younger respondents adopting a braver attitude, although the very youngest group was less confident about family migration than those aged 25-34. Moreover, even the oldest group was evenly divided between those who agreed and those who disagreed with the assertion (see Table 6.1).

Table 6.1: 'It's frightening to move with children to another country and I find it hard to understand parents who decide to do this'

	Aged 60-91	Aged 50-59	Aged 35-49	Aged 25-34	Aged 18-24
Agree/strongly agree	43.0	37.4	25.8	15.8	20.2
No opinion	13.9	10.7	10.3	9.2	10.6
Disagree/strongly disagree	43.0	51.9	63.9	75.0	69.1

Although their responses were little different from those of the male respondents, it is worth looking in more detail at the responses of women in particular, since so often it is up to the women to decide whether to take their children abroad. As in the case of the overall sample, it was women in the younger and better educated groups, whom one would expect to be more confident, who were most likely to disagree that taking children abroad was frightening (see Table 6.2).

Table 6.2: 'It's frightening to move with children to another country and I find it hard to understand parents who decide to do this' (women's responses, %)

	Agree	No opinion	Disagree
All women	33.4	10.3	56.3
Aged 18-24	16.1	8.9	75.0
Aged 25-49	25.7	9.0	65.3
Aged 50-91	41.5	11.5	47.0
Higher education	19.0	71.0	73.8
At least secondary education	37.3	11.1	51.5
Up to secondary education	46.5	11.5	42.0
Mother of child under 20	26.1	9.6	64.3
Without university degree + mother of child under 20	29.9	10.7	59.4
Had been in UK	14.3	12.5	73.2

Given this level of support for migration with children, it is not surprising that 39.1% of respondents thought 'quite a lot' of families had gone abroad from their local area. This included 45.7% of respondents in the south-east of Podkarpacie and 59.5% of respondents from Sanok.[15] Conversely, only 37.6% of respondents in the west of Podkarpacie felt that 'quite a lot' of families had departed. Although this is only the vaguest of measures, it seems possible, although impossible to prove, that opinions do in fact reflect real differences in the rate of family migration between different locations.

A fashion for migration with children could in itself be a cause of migration and, in a migration culture where migration with children was becoming well established, it would not be surprising to encounter social pressure to migrate in this way. As already suggested, the evidence is that extensive migration with children is quite a new phenomenon. Nonetheless, pressure is exerted in individual cases. For example, Celina in Grajewo described how she had been trying to persuade her friend to take her children and join her husband abroad. "I tell her 'He's there, and you're here. Your marriage is practically falling apart. It's gradually disintegrating'. Because that's how it is. . . . And I say, 'If you're a family, you should stick together'." Elżbieta lived in Suwałki with her children while her husband worked in England: she said that in Suwałki it was becoming more common for whole families to migrate and that many of her friends were asking why she did not go to be with her husband.

To test the unlikely but hypothetically possible scenario that many parents experienced such social pressure to migrate with children, the opinion poll included the statement 'In my locality you can notice a certain social pressure on family members left behind to go and join the husband or wife who is already working abroad'. It was unsurprising to find many people with 'no opinion' about this idea, which may never have occurred to them before: 21.9% had no opinion, 56.3% of respondents felt that there was no such pressure and only

21.7% agreed that pressure existed. The poorest (30.2%), least well-educated (25.5%) and youngest respondents (28%) were most likely to agree that there was pressure on families to migrate, but the youngest respondents were also most likely to disagree.[16]

Conventions surrounding family reunification

Perhaps it is too early to speak of a migration culture with regard to how migration with children 'should be done'. Nonetheless, certain patterns can be observed. Iwona, for example, comparing her own family's pre-EU accession experience of migrating to London with young families leaving Sanok today, commented:

> We're in the EU, we are legal now. And younger people today are braver, I think. Everything happens more quickly today. The husband goes off first, soon afterwards the wife visits him to see if she likes the conditions there, then right after that the children start school [in London] and mum starts work.

Several interviewees in Poland asserted that wives were sometimes pioneers, and occasionally they cited examples. However, the pattern described by Iwona, where the husband goes first, seems to be much more common. None of the married mothers interviewed in the UK had been a 'pioneer'. As Iwona also observes, family reunification can be quite rapid today. Among the 25 wives interviewed in the UK who had joined their husbands, the average time between his arrival and hers was about 11 months, but three fifths of the interviewees had waited less than this to join their husbands. The longer waits were almost exclusively in families where the husband had left Poland soon after EU accession, in 2004 or 2005.

Almost always, as Iwona suggests, one parent goes abroad first, while the other remains in Poland with the children. The decision to bring over the second spouse and the children is taken at different stages in different families. In about two fifths of the UK sample, the husband and wife agreed from the beginning that the husband would go first, but that the family would probably reunite in England once he had found a job and somewhere for them to live. In a few cases the couple were more unsure: they knew they wanted to be together, but it seemed equally likely that the husband would come home as that the family would reunite in England. The third scenario was that the wife and children did not expect to move to England; however, circumstances then changed. About half the UK interviewees fell into this category and in Poland I was told many stories of similar couples.

An important part of the process is often the wife's holidays in England. It may seem surprising that money is spent on holidays, if the husband intends to save money as quickly as possible. Nonetheless, such holidays are common, suggesting that the wife has a role to play in the household migration strategy. She is not expected simply to sit at home in Poland and wait for remittances. Holidays can be important for making the wife feel at home in England and positively disposed towards moving there in the future. For example, Monika was in Bristol visiting her husband when their baby fell ill. Despite not speaking much English, they went to the doctor's surgery, where they met and were interpreted for by another Polish mother. She and Monika became friends, so when Monika later settled in Bristol she already had a good friend waiting for her, as well as experience of using the NHS.

The holiday may be used by the wife to reconnoitre, with thoughts of moving to the UK herself. Naturally some wives set off with firmer intentions than others. A number of interviewees talked about such inspection visits as if they were standard practice. "We usually do," said Elżbieta, describing a friend's visit; she herself had visited her husband in England, not liked what she saw, and returned with her children to north-east Poland. The fact that in most families the wife apparently has a veto on family reunification is evidence of her power within the family and the existence of 'partner–like relations' between spouses. Hanna, for example, seemed to have come to the UK with a clearly defined power of veto. As she reported: "I came for a visit, for two weeks, I liked it and I found work and stayed a month…. I got to know my way round and discovered the town was perfectly all right…. We could move here with the children and feel safe." Similarly, Maria said "I would come to see how I'd feel, whether I'd adapt. The children stayed with my mother [in Poland]. For two months. I realised it was fine, everything was OK, I liked it…. I went round looking at various schools with a friend who spoke good English." Celina (Grajewo) described the case of a friend who had taken her children to England to join her husband:

> She had it in her plans already. First she went out to see him. He went first, then a month later she went to stay with him, because she wanted to see what life was like there, whether it was worth her leaving everything in Poland and going to England. She was there for a month and she said the way of life simply suited her better than in Grajewo. So she left everything in Grajewo, she locked up the house, packed, took the children, went through the official procedures, and off they went.

Angelika, who had returned to Sanok from living in London, was dismissive of inspection visits: she said they were all very well, but usually the wife just went shopping and had a nice holiday and did not see the whole reality. Consequently, the wife might agree too readily to make the move abroad. Conversely, however, other interviews suggested that the inspection visit could even be off-putting: some wives were shocked by their husbands' squalid and cramped living conditions in the UK.

Sometimes a holiday is simply a holiday, but even so, some element of 'inspection' is inevitable, and this may lead to unexpected outcomes. Marek, for example, invited Barbara to come on holiday to England, but things did not go according to his plans:

> Barbara: He came to England in December 2004 and I came in April, with our little girl.

> Marek: I didn't want to stay.... But my wife wanted to come and have a look. She came to have a look ... and then she said she wasn't going back to Poland! Well, what could I do?

> Barbara: I liked it.

Dorota and her daughter had also been on a summer holiday, visiting Dorota's husband in Bristol. In this case it was their 10-year-old daughter who unexpectedly announced that she did not want to go back to Poland that autumn. Dorota herself did not really want to stay in England, but she gave in to the child.

Not all wives pay an inspection visit, or even take a holiday in England, particularly if the family's strategy from the beginning is that they will probably relocate abroad. One interviewee had a very good friend with a family in Scotland, and said that the information provided by this friend had been sufficient to persuade her that it was worth taking her children to the UK, even without a prior visit. In just a few[17] families the husband made the decision that the family would reunify in England and his wife felt she had no opportunity to veto the decision.

> I had no plans to come to England. It was just him who was supposed to be here. But he came home to Poland for Easter, bought me a ticket, and said 'OK, you're coming!'... I'd said I'd come just for a bit, to see what it was like, because of course I hadn't been to England before. But in the end, I don't know, it was him who decided!... He said he wouldn't stay there on his own, and that I had to come, and that was the end of it! [laughter]

One of the lone mothers interviewed in the UK had not made an inspection visit, but since she was coming to be with her sister and mother this was perhaps considered unnecessary. The other two had tested the water in the sense of leaving their children with their own mothers and spending an initial period working in England alone:

> I really just came to England somehow to have a look, to see what it was like. To be here a month or two and see if there was work, and so on. And I got that job in the bakery and I worked one month, two, three, and it was good. So I said 'I'm staying'. And I stayed. (Jagoda)

Economic versus emotional reasons for family reunification

As already stated, about half the UK interviewees, together with many friends and relatives of interviewees in Poland, had originally planned for the husband to work alone in the UK, and only later decided that the wife and children would follow after. Each family has its own mix of reasons for changing its strategy, but some common trends can be observed. Although the husband's initial migration motive was always economic, it does not follow that wives and children joined him for economic reasons. Sometimes they did, of course, have economic motives. Three interviewees in Poland thought that the expense of maintaining two separate households encouraged couples to reunite abroad, although my impression was that this belief was not widespread. After all, the normal, apparently economically viable model was the dual location household, with the husband earning abroad and the wife and children living in Poland. Other interviewees mentioned the opposite situation, where the husband did unexpectedly well abroad, and it seemed a waste not to bring over his family. Karolina, for example, told the story of a friend's husband who went from Ełk to Iceland and began earning eight times his Polish wage. Despite his original intention to return, the family changed their plans and the wife and child went to live in Iceland.

Only four interviewees who had actually gone to England with their families mentioned economic motives, and in all cases these were intertwined with emotional ones. Gabriela, for example, originally said that she joined her husband because they missed each other so much. She later mentioned a financial cause: her husband returned to visit Poland every month to see Gabriela and their baby, and the expense of this was one reason why she quickly joined him. In Bożena's account, financial and emotional reasons were interwoven, but emotions were paramount:

> The main reason was because he missed us so much. There he was on his own, and we've been married for 13, nearly 14 years, and had always been together. We helped each other all those years, and also he missed the children. Besides, running two separate households was too expensive.

Monika felt that she probably would not have come to England had she kept her job in Poland, but when she lost it the opportunity arose to reunite her three sons with their father:

> I had good work in Poland, quite well paid and it never occurred to me that I would go to England.... I was manager of a shop. I think that if my boss hadn't gone bankrupt, well I don't know how things would have turned out for us.... And then I got pregnant and that changed everything!... I got pregnant, so that's how it turned out, and we decided I'd come to Bristol with the children.... [The three boys]

needed their father! Well, that's how I looked at it.... It was obvious they needed their father.

Iwona and her husband both left their children to work in London. At separate points in the interview, different motives emerged: how she had missed her children, the emotional impact of the parents' absence on the children and the fact that and they could afford to live in London with their children:

> My husband took me to central London, well, those shops, and all those sights, I was really impressed, I liked it, it was so nice. But then I began to feel that longing to be with children. I began to miss the children so much that I didn't want to have the money I was earning, nothing, I just wanted to go home. Well, later, there I was, coming and going [between Sanok and London] and we had to make up our minds. Either I would come back to Sanok or we would all go to London. So during the summer holidays I set off, we set off [to London], with the children, and we intended to stay.

Elsewhere she stated:

> It's better [for a child as well as their mother to be abroad with the father], too. A child can get *un-used* to their father. When my husband came back after a year our daughter didn't recognise him. She was small, only two. I had told her and showed her on photos that this was Daddy. But she was so small. It was scary. And when I went for three months and came home she didn't want to come to me, only to her grandmother. I wept, it was horrible. That kind of life is really unpleasant. A family should be together.

Finally, she also mentioned a financial reason for reunification:

> When I was in London just with my husband we began to plan to bring over the children.... It was really worthwhile financially to be there ... and we could afford whatever we wanted, so then we thought of bringing over the children....You can earn good money on a building site. We weren't poor when we were in England.

However, it was unusual for the UK interviewees to mention economic reasons for family reunification, even in tandem with emotional ones. Emotional causes prevailed.

> Rafał suggested he could stay in England for five years and then return. I said, 'Oh no,' I said. 'Either I come and see if I like it and then come to live here with the children, or you stay till the end of the year and

then come back to Poland.' If you have children, that life apart, even though we lived with my parents in the same house, but it's not the same thing. You can't open up to anyone, I can talk to my parents about anything, but sometimes we argue, I'd phone Rafał, cry, get upset, you do miss the other person. I said, 'Either we struggle, together, in Poland, or else we struggle together in England.' But you must be together, all the time. Really. It's very important to be together. A marriage, and we've been married 14 years, so it's already quite a long time! (Maria)

The UK interviewees often mentioned how much their husbands had missed the children, and vice versa. For example:

Later, when we saw that our son was really missing his father, and that separation was quite difficult, we decided that all the same I would come to England [with the son].... It was because of the child that we decided we would come to be with my husband in England, just for the child. Because of our son, so he had contact with his father. Because a child does need both his mother and his father. (Patrycja)

He was terribly lonely, he was in England on his own, he went away and when he came back to Poland [for a visit] our daughter had grown so much, little children change so fast, and he wasn't there to see it. 'Oh no [he said]. Let's be all together.' (Malwina)

He wanted to come to England to be with his dad. Whenever his dad phoned he'd burst into tears, ask why he'd left them for so long, why did he go so far. He'd go to the park and tell everyone he was going to England and instead of being called Maciek he wanted to be called Anglik [the English boy]. (Edyta)

In other cases, the interviewees stressed how hard separation had been for all the family. For example:

I was at home with the children for 18 months. It was too long. We had to decide, one way or the other. Because you can't live your life at a distance. I was miserable, and obviously the children, well, children need their father, don't they?... It wasn't very nice. We used to talk on the phone every day, but all the problems, everything fell on me. After all, the children, the house.... He was having a rough time, too, because he was working and at the same time thinking about us and what was happening at home. I would tell him about some problem and he couldn't help. (Marzena)

> When one person is in England and the other person in Poland, it's very hard to live apart. So we decided to be together.... My husband went first, and was here one month, then I went for two months. Then we returned to collect the children.... It was quite hard for us to be without them. (Ilona)

Although these are very personal accounts, they are not out of place in a discussion of migration culture. Their very similarity is evidence that there are some common structural factors, despite the fact that the UK interviewees came from towns and villages all over Poland. Interviewees in Sanok and Grajewo made similar comments about their own friends and relatives who had migrated as families and a number of UK interviewees, even as far back as 2006, made the observation that many other Polish families felt the same way as they did and were not prepared to tolerate separation. In 2009, despite the recession, interviewees asserted that families were still reuniting, for this reason. Sylwia, for example, claimed that more and more families were arriving in 2009. "There are lots of examples of families who want to be together. Because that separation, for a year, or two years, is too long, and they want to be together." Jagoda also asserted that people were still coming to England for the same reason. "There is a man who works in the pizza restaurant here, he's been here about two years, and his wife and children were in Poland, and in the end they couldn't stand it any more, and she's just come to be with him and work in England."

What, then, has happened to the self-sacrificing ethos of the 1990s 'incomplete migrant'? It could be that attitudes towards migration change within families when men are in England, and wives visit them there: this might be linked to a prevailing culture among migrants *abroad*. In other words, there is a social remittance effect. Fathers see that other Poles (particularly childless people) invite their boyfriends and girlfriends or spouses to join them; there is no legal obstacle, so they decide to do the same. This may be a part of the story, but the migration culture among Poles in the UK is of course not created entirely in the UK, but also in Poland. As already argued, it would be most accurate to think of Polish society stretching from Poland westwards across Europe, with ideas circulating in all directions. With specific reference to high migration locations in Poland – if Grajewo and Podkarpacie are typical – it seems that there are places in Poland where there are very powerful local reasons to abandon the old model of one-parent migration. Chapter Seven explores these reasons, seeking to explain why so many respondents from Podkarpacie believed that it was in the best interests of children to be abroad with both parents, rather than be left in Poland without one of them.

Conclusion

Basic assumptions about the gendering of migration among the interviewees and respondents tended to be conservative. If just one parent had to migrate, this was usually seen as the father's role. However, since overall attitudes to migration are pragmatic, assumptions about gender roles can be set aside in certain situations. In particular, migration by lone mothers is often condoned and other mothers also migrate alone, depending on the circumstances. Younger people and respondents who had been in the UK appeared to be more flexible than other respondents about gender roles. They tended to feel that it was not necessarily preferable for fathers of teenage children to migrate rather than mothers. This could testify both to young people's more egalitarian approach to gender roles (as illustrated in Polish national opinion polls) and to the effect of social remittances in the form of ideas about equal parenting roles, adopted from the UK.

However, the Podkarpacie opinion poll also suggested that migration by fathers alone was viewed even by people with strong ideas about gender roles as a necessary evil, not an optimum livelihood strategy. There was overwhelming support for migration by the whole family, including children. This was viewed as much preferable to children being left in Poland with only one parent. Family migration was even seen to be a worthwhile experiment (testimony to the widespread belief in contemporary Poland that migration can be 'given a go' because return is easy). Migration with children is most definitely a break with recent practice, given the prevalence of incomplete migration in the 1990s, so this is evidence that in some regards the migration culture can change quickly.

The usual pattern for post-2004 family migration – to countries where it is legal – is for the husband to go first, then to be joined quite soon, probably usually within a year, by the rest of his family. Among the UK interviewees, some couples had hoped from the beginning that the whole family would go abroad; others were keeping family reunion open as a possibility; and in the remaining households family reunion was unexpected, occurring more for emotional rather than economic reasons. The old model of the 'self-sacrificing' parent is rejected in favour of satisfying the emotional needs of the entire nuclear family, recognising that fathers and children miss one another and that both parents have important parenting roles.

The process of reunion is negotiated among family members and often depends on an inspection visit and on the the extent to which wife and/or children are open to persuasion. Wives normally have a veto on family reunion, a veto that often seems to be used, judging by the stories of interviewees in Poland. Hence, although at first glance the pattern of male migration followed by family reunion seems to indicate the prevalence of traditional gender roles (and a reverse from the pre-2004 situation where increasing numbers of women migrated independently), wives who follow after their husbands should not be seen as passive, trailing wives, but rather as active participants in framing the household livelihood strategy.[18]

Notes

[1] See, for example, Pinnawala's article on how gender relations are 'turned upside down' (Pinnawala, 2008, p 440) in Sri Lankan households as a result of female migration. However, although women may assume the role of chief provider, with associated power and status, men do not always take on housework and childcare. These may devolve not to

the husband but to other female relatives and/or older siblings. See, for example, Parreñas (2005, pp 331-2), writing about the Philippines.

[2] See, for example, Levitt (1998, p 934); Zontini (2004); Triandafyllidou (2006); Coyle (2007a).

[3] Levitt (1998, p 926).

[4] Urbańska (2009, p78), citing Raijman, S., Schammar-Gesser, S. and Kemp, A. (2003) 'International migration, domestic work, and care work: undocumented Latina migrants in Israel', *Gender and Society*, no 5. On lone women migrants and their family roles, see, for example, Parreñas (2005), Zontini (2004).

[5] Urbańska (2009, p 84), citing Pine, F. (2007) 'Góralskie wesele. Pokrewieństwo, płeć kulturowa i praca na terenach wiejskich socjalistycznej i postsocjalistycznej Polski', in A. Kościańska and R.E. Hryciuk (eds) *Gender. Perspektywa antropologiczna*, Warsaw: Warsaw University, p 83).

[6] Datta (2008, p 521) writes of 'a home for themselves in the future – which would reinforce their role as head of household'.

[7] There were only 15 18- to 24-year-old respondents who had been to the UK.

[8] Siara (2009).

[9] Age bands were not used for this calculation; instead, each year group was considered individually. (The normal age bands were 25-34 and 35-49.)

[10] Response to Jakubowski (2008).

[11] The only exception was the small group of 28 respondents who had actually lived with their children abroad, where some of them had perhaps had bad experiences, prompting their return. A total of 64.3% of these parents did agree that it was better for teenagers to move abroad, but of these, but only 21.4% 'strongly agreed', 21.4% 'disagreed' and 3.6% 'strongly disagreed'.

[12] The youngest was about 21 when she arrived and the oldest was 39.

[13] See Eade et al's comments (2006, p 11) on the 'strategy of intentional unpredictability'.

[14] A total of 46.9% of women and 46.1% of men aged 50-91 agreed, as did 24.3% of women and 18.5% of men aged 18-49.

[15] Twenty-two of 37 respondents.

[16] Geographical variables seemed particularly worth considering, given that different places have different migration patterns. There were slight differences in different sub-regions and between villages and differently sized towns. However, the mean scores are similar across the region.

[17] This was apparently the case for three interviewees, although the wives' assertions that they had 'no' choice should, perhaps, not be taken too literally.

[18] For similar conclusions, with regard to Polish women in London, see Ryan et al (2009, p 67).

SEVEN

The emotional impact of migration on communities in Poland

The children miss their parents. They long for them. There are heaps of children who live just with their mum, or dad, if mum's abroad. Definitely. How they talk! 'Oh, my dad's coming home soon, he's coming home today, maybe three days' time.' That's what they say, they miss them so much and they get all worked up in advance, dear oh dear.... 'Dad's coming, mum's coming, they'll bring me a present,' and a bit later, tears. 'Mum's going away already, dad's going away!' Heaps of children say things like that in my class. Dad, or mum. They're little children, under six, and they tell you everything. (Czesława, kindergarten worker, Sanok)

Sanok is a half-town. (Iwona)

It has been asserted that 'Whenever we look at life, we look at networks',[1] and much of this book is concerned with the ties that connect families and people, often across international borders. It is therefore helpful to understand the world in terms of social networks. On the other hand, it is also important to remember the gaps.[2] Sometimes, being in Grajewo or Sanok, it is the gaps that seem more evident:

There was a time when everyone on this street had a relative abroad.... Down from us the neighbour's daughter is in England, she has a granddaughter, they got married and are in England.... Over here's my aunt, who's in the USA, and over there's a neighbour who's also in the USA.... [The houses] are empty.... People just come back here for holidays. (Maria, Grajewo)

Lots of people from our block of flats have gone abroad. Upstairs there's a neighbour in England, there are three families in the USA, their flats are empty, because they've gone away as whole families, or the father is in the USA, and that lady who passed us on the stairs, her husband is in the USA, and her son is abroad, too, so there are really heaps of people, heaps of people living abroad.... And upstairs there's a family where the mother and father work abroad, and they have a girl of about 15, and a boy of 18. And they come to visit their children every three months. (Kazimiera, Grajewo)

While other chapters looked at networks and ties, this chapter discusses gaps and broken links, and how this negative impact of migration influences Polish opinion about migration by whole families. The main section begins with analysis of Polish media coverage of the plight of children left by their migrant parents. This is the most widely discussed aspect of suffering caused by separation. Media preoccupation with the topic sometimes seems to overshadow other consequences of migration, but these can also be acute. The chapter briefly discusses the situation of parents whose children have gone abroad, of schools that have lost students and of friends who have lost friends, of all ages. However, the most important factor promoting whole family migration is the geographical separation between spouses that frequently leads to emotional distancing and even divorce.

Before embarking on a discussion of the suffering caused by parting, it is worth noting the opposite side of the coin. Migration can bring greater autonomy: distancing is not always unwelcome. Alicja, in Grajewo, commented that "some people are pulled towards their families, others towards freedom". For very young people, migration is probably often a kind of holiday, an escape from their parents, from studying and from everyday reality, especially if they live in a small town or village with few leisure opportunities. For young parents, it can be an escape from sharing housing: for example, an interviewee in the UK said that she left Poland "for a better life. In Poland I lived with my mother in one flat, the three of us, and I wanted to get away from my mum!" For slightly older people, it can be an escape from unhappy marriages, as vividly conveyed in Maria Guzik's stories, based on real life, of Polish women working in Italy.[3] Nonetheless, although migration can to some extent be a welcome escape, the suffering caused by parting was a theme that recurred again and again in the interviews.

Does suffering matter? The 'incomplete', self-sacrificing migrant puts up with suffering: it is a by-product of this particular livelihood strategy. On the other hand, Chapter Six argued that livelihood strategies and associated norms are changing in Poland – self-sacrifice is going out of fashion. Interviewees who had migrated to England with their children were not prepared to tolerate prolonged separation. Given the extent of migration with children since 2004, it would not be surprising to find that their opinions were widely shared in Poland.

There are two possible ways of interpreting the connection between migration by parents without their children ('incomplete migration') and migration with children. It could be that incomplete migration is still seen as an acceptable strategy for destinations to which it is hard to bring a family. It is only because the opportunity has arisen for parents to settle legally with their families in the UK, Ireland and Sweden, and more recently other West European countries, that they have started to do so. The other possibility is that there is a conscious rejection of incomplete migration in the communities where it has been prevalent since the early 1990s. This chapter explores this hypothesis, examining the nature and depth of concern in places like Grajewo and Sanok, as in Podkarpacie more generally, about family breakdown and children's problems caused by incomplete migration.

At the outset, it is worth pointing out that separation of family members caused by migration is nothing new in Grajewo or Sanok. Because of emigration to the USA in the 1970s and 1980s even older interviewees had often experienced long periods of separation from parents and siblings. In a newspaper article about migration from Grajewo's neighbouring town, Mońki, Agnieszka Domanowska (2008) describes what young people remember from the mass migrations of the 1980s: 'brightly coloured chocolate wrappers, clothes, and the fact that Mum and Dad had to part'.[4] Many migrants in the USA are stuck there because they are working illegally, and visa applications on the part of their family left in Poland are often refused. For example, Alina, aged 49, in Grajewo, had not seen her father for 19 years and had been refused a US visa. Eliza, from Grajewo, had been married for about 15 years and knew her mother-in-law only from telephone conversations:

> I've never set eyes on my mother-in-law. She went to the States before I met my husband. It was only just recently that she met my daughter, her granddaughter, when my daughter was there on holiday. That's the charm of the situation. She married off her two sons, but she wasn't at either wedding. It's so sad. But that's life. Thanks to her being in the States her children had their weddings. Otherwise they couldn't have afforded them.

Migration by just one parent to places such as Belgium and the USA does sometimes result in family reunification, but it can be a long time before the reunification occurs. In Grajewo, such long separations were considered normal. For example, Maria mentioned how her sister had moved to the USA, leaving a one-year-old daughter in Grajewo. Only "five to seven" years later had she been able to bring the child to the USA.

Anne: But how sad!

Maria [very calmly]: Her grandmother looked after her.

The 'problem' of 'euro-orphans'

Since Poland's accession to the EU, journalists, scholars and officials have identified a group of children they label 'euro-orphans' (*eurosieroty*) and who are said to represent a serious social problem.[5] My opinion poll in Podkarpacie testified to concern about the plight of children whose parents worked abroad. Respondents were asked to comment on the statement that 'In my locality you can notice certain problems connected with parental migration: the children left in Poland have psychological and behavioural problems'. Overall, 68.6% agreed (see Figure 7.1). The only group with substantial levels of disagreement was the very youngest: 34% of 18- to 24-year-olds disagreed with the statement, although a majority – 57.4% – agreed.[6]

Figure 7.1: 'Children left in Poland have psychological and behavioural problems'

%

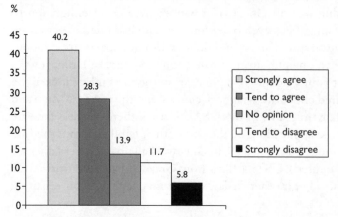

The issue has numerous dimensions, and it is worth exploring in detail both the nature of the 'problem' and potential 'solutions'.

First, what is a 'euro-orphan'? As used in much of the media, the reference is simply to children who live in Poland but one or both of whose parents work (often temporarily) in Western Europe, and who suffer emotionally as a result of migration. Hence the 'orphaning' is by no means complete and the term 'orphan' is used to highlight the children's feeling of being abandoned. This is not the only definition of the term, however. For example, Iglicka suggests that the media use the term 'euro-orphans' to describe 'children left in orphanages as a result of their parents or one of their parents going to work abroad'.[7] If some media can appear to conflate all children whose parents work abroad with children in residential care as a result of EU migration, this suggests irresponsible sensationalism and/or the pursuit of a political agenda. As an example of the orphanage genre, an article by Magdalena Przybyła, 'Mum abroad, child in orphanage', mentioned briefly in passing that some migrants' children were cared for by family members, but gave the strong impression that the norm was for lone mothers to put their children in orphanages. The article was illustrated with a large cartoon showing a mother, carrying a suitcase, running away from a little girl sitting and weeping beside a wall labelled 'Children's Home'. In four out of five cases, Przybyła asserts, the mothers abandon their children in the children's home and never come back for them.[8]

In fact, only 285 migrants' children were placed in residential care in 2007 in the whole of Poland.[9] The interviewees also suggested that placing children in children's homes was an uncommon occurrence. Only one interviewee, Alicja, a Sanok kindergarten employee, mentioned personally knowing someone who had left a child in a children's home: this was a former kindergarten parent. The mother did not completely lose touch and sometimes she took the daughter to Italy. Nonetheless, the child "had problems" and "felt the situation painfully". Alicja said, however, that this was very unusual and that normally children were left with grandparents.

Other articles imply that 'euro-orphans' are children *both* of whose parents have gone abroad. Hugo-Bader, for example, writing in *Gazeta Wyborcza* in 2007 about a case where both parents had migrated and the son had ended up in psychiatric home, asserted:

> No one knows how many Polish grandmothers have to look after their grandchildren, because their children have gone to work abroad, but without doubt this is a significant social phenomenon. Thousands of grandparents, aunties and friends are given children to look after and cannot cope.[10]

Another article, in January 2008, claimed that 'more and more often, fathers and mothers [from eastern Poland] decide to go abroad together' and also mentioned children being left with grandparents.[11] Referring specifically to villages in the Sanok district, an April 2008 article suggested that 'in many families, the real guardians are older siblings, often minors'.[12]

The interview evidence, however, suggests that children with both parents abroad are in a small minority. Of course, given the scale, informality and temporary quality of so much Polish mobility, it is impossible to chart the extent of double parental absence with any accuracy. Walczak's 2008 study of nearly 4,000 Polish school students led him to calculate that, over the last three years, anywhere between 3,000 and 16,000 Polish children had probably experienced both their parents being abroad simultaneously.[13] Walczak estimated that in the whole of Poland there were between 53,000 and 100,000 children with parents working abroad, including seasonal migrants.[14] As Walczak observes, the length of time parents are away is important when considering whether their children can be said to be 'orphaned'.[15] In his study, the average length of parental absence abroad was seven months for fathers and five months for mothers.[16] Walczak does not provide statistics for how long both parents were away together, but, as already mentioned in Chapter Six, among the interviewees for this research, dual parental absences were always short. The use of the term 'orphan' for children whose parents are absent so briefly therefore seems particularly inappropriate.

Whether or not both parents are working abroad, parental migration often implies a greater caring role for grandparents remaining in Poland, and this is often identified as part of the 'euro-orphan problem'. The Podkarpacie survey invited comment on the statement 'In my locality you can notice certain problems connected with parental migration: grandparents looking after migrants' children have too many responsibilities'. Of all the statements on the impact of parental migration, this one prompted the greatest agreement: 76.4%. Only the richest and youngest respondents did not view the overburdening of grandparents as a local problem.

Obviously, how 'euro-orphan' is defined has a direct bearing on estimates of how many children are affected. When trying to assess the scale of the phenomenon, it is also important to bear in mind that estimates for Poland as a whole are not informative about migration from particular localities. There is considerable differentiation even within a single region. One article about the Sanok area asserted that in some villages 'one hundred per cent of children are euro-orphans';[17] a second article about Podkarpacie stated that in some villages over half of the children were being brought up by just one parent;[18] an article about a third village in Podkarpacie quoted a teacher who said that 10% of her pupils were affected.[19] The interviews in Sanok, particularly with women who lived in nearby villages, suggested that it was entirely probable that there are places where half or more of households contain a migrant parent, but also confirmed that even in Podkarpacie one village may vary greatly from another. Podkarpacie, of course, has particularly high levels of migration.

Schutta suggests that the situation is becoming more problematic in the sense that the trend is for the number of 'euro-orphans' to increase. 'There's more and more talk in Poland about parents abandoning their children to work abroad, because what were just isolated examples before are now turning into a social problem.'[20] It could be disputed, however, that this is a 'new' problem. It seems likely that the media pays more attention to the problem of parents migrating only now that migration touches all of Polish society, rather than mainly the 'transition losers', as in the 1990s.

Not all media coverage is entirely one-sided. A group of articles in *Gazeta Wyborcza* in May 2008, for example, identified the positive as well as negative impacts of parents working abroad. For example, in one family the mother was less stressed because she could afford to be a housewife in Poland, and in another, the father, on his return, paid more attention to his children than he used to do when he worked in Poland.[21] In other cases, journalists highlight the fact that parents who are labour migrants have gainful employment:

> 'It's hard to say whether the benefits outweigh the costs of labour migration, it's worth researching,' suggests Judge Jacek Ignaczewski of the family court in Olsztyn. 'I know from my work as a judge. Olsztyn was a region of collective farms. It's poor, people feel they have no future. They're stressed, they drink and behave aggressively. What's better for a child, a drunken father or his occasional absence, because he's gone to work abroad?'[22]

However, it is much more common for the media to identify 'problems' caused by parental absence. There are four categories of 'problem'. For schools and administrators, it is inconvenient not to be able to contact a designated guardian in case of emergency, or to know whether children are supposed to be at school in Poland or whether they have gone abroad. For children, the potential problems are emotional and psychological; relatively minor behavioural problems, such as cheekiness, truanting, not handing in homework or doing it carelessly; and more serious behavioural problems such as drinking, drug taking and stealing. Walczak's study found that the problems were mostly emotional and psychological, or relatively minor behavioural problems. There was no evidence that serious problems such as drug use and theft were really more common among children of migrants. However, it was true that some migrants' children spent less time at home than other children and therefore adults were less able to monitor their behaviour.[23]

Father Bogdan Stańkowski, a local schoolteacher, began his study of local migrants' families in Podhale (just west of Podkarpacie)[24] in the expectation that families would be seriously damaged by migration and that parents would lose their authority over their children. However, the evidence convinced him otherwise:

> Parents report that they do not have difficulties getting on with their children. Moreover, we did not confirm the hypothesis that systematic and long-term labour migration weakens ties between parents and children and consequently interferes with the parents' ability to bring up their children.[25]

A large survey, conducted in late 2007 by the Instytut Europejski of the Fundacja Prawo Europejskie (FPE), came to more alarming conclusions, however:

> Children find it hard to bear the separation and, though they have parents, they feel like orphans. Stress and suffering manifest themselves in various ways. They get on worse at school, they play truant, they get addicted to things. In extreme cases they are aggressive and get into trouble with the police.[26]

However, since the sample in the FPE report was children known to social workers[27] (who conducted the research) it was hardly surprising if evidence of social problems emerged, and disturbing that conclusions were drawn from the research about all children of migrants.

Indeed, press articles often seem to assume that 'euro–orphans' come from the poorest and most dysfunctional families. Articles feature children who have always been unwanted and un-loved, and families where one or both parents drink.[28] There is also sometimes an implication that these are the very poorest people in society. For example, an article from Podlasie painted a picture of starving families unable to cope with their sudden influx of wealth:

> 'Usually emigration affects families who can't make ends meet. So, at first, the family members who stayed in Poland are thrilled to have some money. At last, they have something to eat', [sic] says Anna Zieniewicz, head of the children's home in Krasne. 'Then the family gets richer, so the grandmother begins to give the children money.... At first the children buy chocolate, then as they get older they go into the shop and ask for wine, beer and cigarettes. The grandmother loses control over her charge, the teenager begins to steal and sometimes commit

more serious crimes. The child gets a criminal record and ends up in the children's home.'[29]

In extreme cases, children end up in psychiatric homes[30] or even committing suicide.[31]

Who, therefore, is to blame? The anonymous author(s) of the article just cited assert, significantly (if inaccurately) that nowadays the mothers go away as often as the fathers. Przybyła, as discussed earlier, blames lone mothers in particular. In a wide-ranging analysis of the impact of migration to Belgium on the town of Siemiatycze, the conservative *Nasz Dziennik* quoted a priest who blamed 'moral poverty' and acquisitiveness.[32] As suggested in Chapter Two, this is also the impression given by other articles in the newspaper and by politicians who share similar views. In 2007, for example, Andrzej Mańka, a parliamentary deputy from the League of Polish Families, said that 'A stable family is a precondition for a well-functioning state. That's why we have to do everything to counter this large wave of emigration.'[33]

However, the public, in response to media articles published on the internet, often distance themselves from what they see as the accusing and/or sensationalist tone of such articles. For example:

> Migration had nothing to do with the matter. It just underlined that he'd been abandoned. Olaf was abandoned before, unloved.... There are plenty of children like that in 'ordinary' families where no one has ever migrated.[34]

> In a normal family it wouldn't have turned out like that. I know a case where a woman went abroad to work and left her children with her parents. It was linked to school, so the children could finish the school year in Poland. Those little children just waited until it was time to go to Mummy and didn't think about getting depressed or developing any behavioural problems.[35]

Interviewees in Grajewo and Sanok often reflected on the emotional impact for children of being separated from their parents, and the possibility that their behaviour might suffer as a result. For example, two interviewees described schoolfriends of their own children whose behaviour they believed had deteriorated as a result of parental absence. In Grajewo, Mariola tried to keep her son apart from one of his friends because she saw the friend as a bad influence:

> My son has a friend and the father has been migrating for about six years and says he's doing well. For example they bought a new car. I can see that the 15-year-old daughter is still on speaking terms with her mother but the son somehow isn't really. He's a year older than my own son and I try to keep them apart.... It seems to me that he

has too much freedom and he does whatever he likes. I don't know how he's getting on at school, but my son says things aren't good. And the company he keeps!

However, my interviewees in Sanok and (particularly) Grajewo were not disposed to dramatise the 'euro-orphan problem'. On the whole, the unhappiness of children (irrespective of which parent was abroad) was a topic that came up in interviews more often than suggestions that children might behave very badly as a result of missing their parents. Of course, the Sanok interviewees were often kindergarten workers, so they had a special kind contact with very small children who were more likely to express their misery by tears rather than by 'deviant' behaviour:

> There are lots of children in the kindergarten where one parent is abroad. The father, or the mother. Obviously those children want to be close to someone, they need it, even if it's the mother who stays in Sanok ... she's often too busy to have time for the child. So those children often want to be close to someone at kindergarten. They spend eight hours here, half the day, so. You can see that those children are more, well, they want to be close. To sit and have a cuddle, sit on your knees, they just want attention. (Jadwiga)

The deputy head of a Grajewo primary school[36] said that they did not have any problems with migrants' children (aged 6-14) behaving badly, but that you could tell that the children were often unhappy because of their parents' absence. Even in the case of older children, it was apparent that interviewees in both towns did not think of migrants' children as 'deviants'. Halina, for example, after reflecting on whether migrants' children behaved worse than others, commented: "Things like that don't happen here in Grajewo. There are lots of parents abroad, my daughters' classmates' parents. They're normal people."

The interviewees clearly thought of themselves and their friends as normal, respectable people. As suggested in Chapter Six, parental migration was perceived in Sanok and Grajewo to be a normal livelihood strategy. Some interviewees referred disparagingly to people living off benefits and alcoholics as 'pathological families', but this was seen to be a separate, marginalised social group, and they were usually mentioned because the speaker thought that they were precisely the families who would *not* migrate. Kazimiera, for example, when asked whether there was a 'problem' with children whose parents had migrated from Grajewo, replied: "I haven't noticed anything like that. We have more problems with pathological families. Where parents are actually present, but they drink or just don't pay any attention to their children, they just live for their own pleasure."

Insofar as interviewees were more worried about the impact of migration on older rather than on younger children, their concerns seemed to be mostly about teenagers' need for guidance of a kind that could not be provided at a distance. Even with reference to adolescent children whose parents were both in Poland, they quite often mentioned that they 'needed to keep an eye' on teenagers (*trzeba pilnować*). These attitudes help explain why there was such a high level of support for the view that teenagers would be better off abroad, with both parents, than in Poland without one parent:

> I think that at least until the child gets through that rebellious period, 12, 13, 15, in my opinion the mother, well, if it's a boy, the father too, but if there are girls then the mother, she at least should be at home. She ought to be at home.... Children don't have that support, if their parents migrate. They lack care, not just meals or things being clean, but the kind of care when someone is keeping an eye. Perhaps the child is having difficulties, perhaps he or she isn't coping. (Kazimiera, Sanok)

> That's perhaps the most difficult age, when children need most attention. You have to give them a bit of support, shout at them a bit sometimes, and guide them, and give them advice. (Beata, Grajewo)

As so often in their comments on migration in general, interviewees often pointed out that it was hard to generalise: there were well-functioning families and others which were less so. In Grajewo, Danuta, for example, said that: "It's a question of how the children are brought up. If the mother knows how to keep the children in line…" In Sanok, Jadwiga emphasised that parents did their best: "Of course every parent wants to bring up their child perfectly but it doesn't always work out. I think that there isn't such a big problem [with bad behaviour by migrants' children]."

Absent neighbours and friends

> Many, many people I know have left. To the point where I don't have anyone to drink beer with, or go to the cinema. They do say they are going to return – some time – but they sound less and less sure about it. (Internet forum participant, 2006)[37]

Many interviewees mentioned that they kept in touch with absent friends by using the social networking site *Nasza Klasa*, which links together old schoolfriends. However, there are some activities (such as drinking beer and going to the cinema together) that cannot be done when friends are thousands of kilometres distant. The younger the interviewee, in high migration locations, the more likely they were to have many friends abroad. Jolanta (aged 27, from Grajewo) said sadly "I really don't have many friends any more. Because so many have gone abroad." Ewa (UK, aged 28) was from a village in Podkarpacie. She said that "lots" of her primary and middle school friends had migrated and was more specific about her particular friends from secondary school: "Many are abroad, about five girls in the USA, others in Ireland and Denmark, and I have one other schoolfriend in England, in London." Celina, aged 33, from Grajewo, said "Almost all my women-friends have gone abroad.... I think 80% are abroad. Our class has a page on *Nasza Klasa* and almost everyone is abroad. Very few have stayed in Poland."

Even among slightly older interviewees in Grajewo and Sanok there were cases of individuals who had lost many friends. Dagmara (Grajewo, aged 39) had discovered from *Nasza Klasa* that "half" her classmates were abroad: she named the USA, Canada, Belgium, Iceland, Spain and Sweden. Magda (Sanok, aged 39) said that "very many" of her schoolfriends were living abroad, most in England, but also in Ireland and Scotland. Among the mothers of older secondary school pupils, many had acquaintances who were abroad 'temporarily'. These were women who had gone to work as carers and cleaners, leaving their husbands behind in Poland. For example, Małgorzata, aged 51, said that many of her friends had left Poland; most had gone to Italy but some also to Germany. Anna, aged 48, also said that many people she knew now worked abroad, at least on a temporary basis.

Where families have migrated abroad with children, children left in Poland have to come to terms with the loss of their schoolfriends – although the author of a recent Poland-wide survey noted that, in the opinions of teachers, the schoolmates of departing pupils tended to accept their departure phlegmatically, as part of the routine of normal life.[38] Of course, children in different parts of Poland are more or less likely to have friends who have migrated. In Sanok, 50 children who could have been expected to be at Primary School 1 in September 2008 had actually left to go abroad during their school career (with 10 departing in summer 2008).[39] Thirty-six had left from Primary School 2.[40] Seven children had left just in summer 2008 from Primary School 3.[41]

Absent adult children

Older people who remain in Grajewo and Sanok often suffer because their adult children have migrated abroad. It is true that new technologies and cheap international transport make certain forms of 'care giving at a distance' more feasible than they used to be, and a number of recent studies have shown how this has an impact on relationships between middle-aged migrants and their parents who have remained in their home country.[42] However, it is always important to remember that transnationalism has its limitations. As in the case of migrant parents caring for their children from a distance, adult migrants cannot provide many important aspects of care for their own parents if they are not physically present. Poland is a society where it is still uncommon for older people to live in residential homes and there is a strong expectation that families will be directly involved in the care of older parents.

The 'care gap' becomes acute when women migrate.[43] A Polish newspaper article, revealingly titled 'A million Polish women have left the country', asserted that 'Poland faces an exceptionally difficult challenge with regard to care for older people. Already today there are villages in Silesia and Mazury where the only inhabitants are aging parents, with no one to take care of them'.[44] Many late middle-aged Polish women are working abroad, looking after other people's older relatives in countries such as Italy, or caring for their own grandchildren in countries such as the UK. In some cases they combine these tasks with caring for relatives at home: in Grajewo, for example, Marta described how her six aunts, all migrants, took it in turns to come home and look after Marta's grandmother. In other cases, interviewees were under the impression that older people were being neglected. Luiza, a nurse who worked with older people in the Grajewo hospital, pointed out "You can see all sorts of cases, in the hospital. There are patients for example who say 'I have five children and they're all abroad and I have practically nobody here in Grajewo'." The situation is exacerbated by the fact that it seems to be quite common for *all* the adult children in a single family to migrate.[45] Halina described the poignant case of a male neighbour: "The girl went first, then she brought over two of her brothers, the third boy's here in Sanok, he's studying, but says he's going to migrate as well. And their mother went over [to England] to be with her children, and so they all live in England, except the dad…. Sometimes they come to visit the dad for Christmas or Easter."

Impact of migration on marriages

The opinion poll asked for views about the statement 'In my locality you can notice certain problems connected with parental migration: there are more lone-parent and broken families'. Although not commanding quite the same levels of support as the companion questions about the impact on children and grandparents, this statement also found widespread agreement: 60% of respondents agreed, 12.6% had no opinion and 27.4% disagreed. The most common response was strong agreement (36.2%), although women were much more likely to strongly agree than men (39.3% compared with 28.3%). Respondents who had been in the UK or had family members in the UK were particularly likely to agree or strongly agree with the assertion (67.1% and 65.9%, compared with the average of 60%), suggesting that personal experience about the fragility of marriages under the strain of migration informed the responses. The only group with very high levels of disagreement was the 18- to 24-year-olds, of whom nearly half, a striking 48.9%, disagreed or disagreed strongly, compared with the average 27.4%. Once again, as we have seen in the case of the impact of migration on grandparents and children, the very youngest adults seem to be less worried about the potential negative effects of migration.

Interviewees in Poland whose husbands had migrated did not always feel that their marriages had suffered as a result of migration, but they did report on how hard they (and their husbands) had found it to be parted. Their comments echoed those of the UK interviewees, reported in Chapter Six. I interviewed Grażyna in 2008 the day her husband had gone to Sweden for the first time and she was worrying about how she would cope. Practical and emotional difficulties intertwined in her account:

When it happens that I have a night shift and my mother-in-law has a night shift I don't know what I'll do. I'll have to take the boys with me. And in the morning they can go to school, after work. I was joking with my friend at work, 'You know, I don't have anyone to leave the boys with, perhaps I'll bring them with me, they can pack cheese'.... It's hard if something goes wrong with the house, or someone is ill, it's easier when there are two of you....The worst thing is being apart, if you have a family, each person will miss the other, won't they?... For example in my situation. If I'm left alone with the children. And their dad always played football with them, or took them on outings to places.

A year later:

He'll come back for Easter. I don't know how I'll survive until then, I really don't want him abroad any more, I miss him so much....It's hard for me here. It's hard for me all on my own. I have to do everything on my own. [The heating had failed recently, and it was snowing at the time] ... and it's a tragedy, when the house is cold. It's different when there's a man in the house, isn't it? He'll know what to do.... Oh, and you really have to keep an eye on the children. And they are boys ... they are always getting into fights.They obey their father more than me.

Czesława described how miserable she and her husband had been when he spent two years working in England and then a year in Germany:

He was so homesick, it was horrible. So was our son, and so was I – all just the same. And you know, since we have a detached house [several kilometres outside Sanok], it's a bit scary to be there on your own, and the other thing was, well, just missing each other....He gets so homesick, he'd phone up all the time, whenever he thought of something, probably we spent so much on phone calls that it wasn't worth him going in the first place....

Iwona focused more on her own sense of loneliness:

I was here in Sanok alone with my children and now I sometimes think about ... all those lost years. It's OK during the week, you take the children to school, then there's dinner, a walk, somehow the day goes by. But what about the weekend? I was all alone. My friends had their husbands and I was all alone. I would go for a walk on my own and feel sad. I was always really sad. Sometimes I even cried.Why did I have to live like this? The best years of my youth and I had to be alone. If the situation happened again, I'd never agree. I'd rather go to England than stay in Sanok.

Some interviewees did report a sense of distancing: they were unnerved by how easy it was to become unused to one's spouse, in their absence. For example:

It is hard [to be apart] but still, you can get used to it. You know? [sounding embarrassed]. It's hard for a week, and then you get into a rhythm, you get up at five or six, do everything, take your child to school and go to work, so you get into a rhythm.... Later it's hard, when your husband returns. [laughter] It's hard, because my daughter has her own favourite dishes, quick ones, and my husband likes his meals different. (Grajewo)

He phones home every day ... but, you know, all the same, you lose something. You don't have that contact with the person you were close to and something goes.... When we don't see each other for three or four months at a time – that how often he's in Poland – we simply lose the habit of being with each another. It's different when I'm here on my own and I don't have to cook meals.... But when my husband comes back I have to adapt to the fact that he's at home. (Grajewo)

Four interviewees had been abandoned by their husbands who had gone to work abroad. Anna's account of what had gone wrong hinted at the gradual distancing which had accompanied the disputes between her husband and herself over where the family should live, and – as already suggested in Chapter Six – at the importance of 'being open to persuasion' as a characteristic of family members invited to join migrants abroad:

In the case of families, usually just one of the parents goes abroad. And ... it isn't such a wonderful marriage any more. And then, if the person who stayed at home wants the family to keep together, they have to make concessions.... I know from my own experience, since my ex-husband used to work abroad a lot. He went on his own, when the children were small. Well, you know how it is. I didn't like it very much. But he made several attempts to persuade me to join him ... because he liked it there. And I think that in situations like that if the second party decides to go, lets themselves be persuaded, then the whole family will go. And if not, it can turn out badly, because from what I see people often set up new families.

Other interviewees had close relatives or friends whose marriages had weakened as a result of the one of the spouses migrating. In Sanok, Elwira, for example, described the fate of a friend whose husband had been working abroad for the entire duration of their marriage:

> Those whole 10 years they've just seen each other at Christmas, Easter and in the summer holidays she goes there for a month. That's all. Off she goes, but after 10 years of marriage she goes and doesn't feel like a wife. They hardly know each other. She has her life in Poland. He has his life in England.... She says to me 'We do talk during the first week and it's like being on honeymoon again. But then he has to go back to work, he's tired, and I just sit around feeling useless. Of course, I clean and cook for him. But we have nothing to talk about.... And I can't wait to get back to Poland.'

Celina's friend had also been separated from her husband for several years:

> He comes back here for a week at a time. And what happens? First he goes round his friends. Then they have some parties, because obviously, when someone comes back from abroad, in Grajewo we have a custom that you have a bit to drink. So he doesn't even have time for his wife. And she says that when he comes back she finds him irritating, because it seems she's not used to his ways anymore.

More rarely, interviewees described the plight of husbands, rather than wives, who had been left behind in Poland. In Grajewo, Bożena explained how her husband's sister had worked in Italy, when her children were already independent. She was away for a year at a time and:

> ... her marriage fell to pieces. Her husband felt terribly abandoned. His wife had gone away, and he didn't go to work himself, he couldn't bear to work, she had done him a terrible wrong. And he found himself another woman. He did come home after two years, but all the same.

Interviewees felt able to generalise about the whole community and tended to conclude, like the Podkarpacie opinion poll respondents, that marriages were threatened by migration:

> Lots of people I know have gone abroad, and when they come back, it's hard for the couple to get used to each other again. They have got into different habits. The wife is used to not having her husband around, having money, not having so much responsibility. She's free to come and go as she likes. But when the husband comes back, or the wife comes back, then there are family responsibilities and it's hard to get used to it. (Mieczysława, Sanok)

In Grajewo, interviewees could point to a long local history of marriages ruined by migration. Luiza, for example, said she knew people who had gone to the USA in the late 1980s and 1990s, leaving their spouses and children in Grajewo. "And those families rarely survived such a long absence by one of the parties. The families fell apart. And the children suffered the most." Other interviewees commented on more recent examples, for instance: "The last I heard was that the father had gone away and not returned. He found himself a woman over there.... I think that's the main reason why marriages break up here in Grajewo" (Mariola).

Chain migration has its own dynamic and once parents have separated the family can disintegrate still further:

> There are examples like this. A husband goes off abroad and abandons his wife. And then later the wife leaves [the children] with an aunt or their grandmother, and for example goes off to Italy or England to earn some money. It's a catastrophe. (Eliza, Grajewo)

> My friend has been going to Belgium for about 20 years and she's been settled there for 10. She took her son to be with her, he got married in Belgium, he went to live in Belgium and there they are. In fact she went because her aunt was there and some cousin simply invited her to come too.... She didn't actually split up from her husband but you couldn't say it was a marriage. He began to drink quite a lot and then he died. (Danuta, Grajewo)

Migration strategies in response to fears about the effects of separation

Migration strategies are clearly framed in response to concerns about the impact of migration, both on relations between parents and their children, and between spouses. Of course, if migration is constrained by visa regulations there can be a limit on migrants' freedom of choice: either they stay abroad and risk their family, or they come home. Czesława, in Sanok, explained why her husband had not outstayed his six months' US tourist visa: "If you go for two years, it's obvious what the consequences are. The family falls apart at once." In the case of contemporary migration to Western Europe, people seem to have more freedom of choice about how or whether to migrate and return. There are various ways in which their strategies can be affected by concerns about separations within the family.

Sometimes migration plans can be abandoned because of fears for the impact on the family. In Sanok, Mieczysława, for example, was trying to stop her husband migrating:

> My husband may be going to work in Sweden for six months.... But six months is a long time, it's a long time for children. Our son is only

17.... We have well brought-up children and it would be a shame to waste that good upbringing. And sometimes [young] people don't know how to say no.

Marta, in Grajewo, was married to someone with a very good job and her sons were about to become students in Poland. If anyone in the family migrated, it could only be her. She had been seriously considering migration as a livelihood strategy after she became unemployed. However, she was put off by a friend's example:

I thought it would be nice to go to my brother, to England [voice warming], or perhaps to Italy, women do go from Grajewo to Italy, but that is, it means that often the family suffers [sadly] and just recently I had an example because my old colleague went to England. Her husband went later.... They'd been apart for just one year and all at once they got divorced. He found some woman there.... Those are the results of migration, aren't they? If you go, you must go together. Together. A family must be together.

Sometimes a migrant returns to Poland because of concerns about the children. Anita's husband had stopped migrating from Grajewo when their son reached adolescence:

My husband used to work abroad when our son was between the ages of 10 and 12.... Then the children got a bit older and we began to have new problems. And we decided that the most important thing was the children and to bring them up properly. After all, a child needs both parents. As a mother I couldn't completely substitute for their father.... It's true that while he was working abroad we were a bit better off. But we think that the most important thing in life is not money, it's the family. That's why he hasn't worked abroad for five years.

Sometimes migration is confined only to certain months of the year, because of childcare commitments. Beata, in Grajewo, said that she was glad that she could be at home for most of the academic year, when she needed to keep an eye on her mid-teenage daughter. She migrated only in the summer, when the daughter was safely at summer camp or with relatives.

Most often, however, interviewees said that the best way to avoid the problem of children suffering from migration was for everyone to migrate together:

You can see a problem here in Poland, we call them euro-orphans. People are talking about it a lot and it's true, you can see a lot of children are left in Poland ... with their grandparents. If they go abroad with their parents it's a different matter. Perhaps it's hard for them to adapt at first, but children usually adapt fast, and so I think it's better that if someone has really decided to go for a longer period, they should take their children. It's definitely best for the children. (Rozalia, Sanok)

Reflecting on the dangers of migration for married couples (rather than children), interviewees tended to express support for the second party migrating rather than the first coming home. Marta, for example, criticised her sister-in-law for not joining her brother in London:

> He thought that he would stay in London, bring his wife over to be with him, that's what he wanted to do. But his wife has just been to London to visit, with the child, and she says she doesn't like it.... In Ełk she's used to living near her mother, near her parents, she's been near her mother all her life, they live in the same building.... My brother said, 'If you don't want to emigrate we won't, since we can't live separately or our marriage will fall apart.'

A few UK interviewees, reflecting on why they had decided to join their husbands, also mentioned that in situations like their own, where spouses lived separately, marriages could fall apart. Marzena, for example, commented "It's no life when you're separated. Marriages in that situation fall apart.... From what you hear, there are so many divorces as a result of migration, because couples are separated." On the other hand, some interviewees abandoned the idea of family reunification abroad because they thought the experience of being abroad would in itself put too much strain on relations between the spouses. Janina, who had been working in Italy alone, had also been visited there by her family, and

> We were thinking about whether to be together as a family. To emigrate to Italy and be there with the children. But my husband didn't want to very much. He somehow couldn't see himself living there. It was different to go for a short period. After that, he could return home, where he felt safe, he felt in charge, he was where he belonged. [Being in] Italy did not really suit him.... He's a homelover, he prefers to stay at home.

There is clearly considerable potential for tension within marriages when couples live abroad and where gender roles are reversed in the way Janina describes. This theme also emerges in the next chapter, about the experiences of couples living in England.

Conclusion

'Mutual welfare' has been described as the 'fundamental raison d'être' of transnational families.[46] The truth of this assertion was copiously illustrated in the course of the research, despite the fact that there are many unhappy families whose members are glad to escape from living together. Before 2004, it was often assumed that a family's welfare was best served by the migration of one parent alone. Today, this is increasingly being questioned, as indicated in Chapter Six. Individual families can come to this conclusion as a result of their personal experience of separation: this happened to many of the UK interviewees. However, as illustrated in this chapter, in places like Sanok and Grajewo, from which many parents migrate alone, there is also a collective opinion about the unpleasantness of family separations. Separation is a way of life in such towns. Parents and grandparents are parted from adult children and grandchildren (whom they may expect to depend on for care); neighbours lose neighbours; schools lose students; and people of all ages are parted from their friends. As indicated by the interviews and also by the Podkarpacie survey, many local people believe that marriages are endangered by migration. They tell tales, for example, of families falling apart because the wife refused to join her husband in migration, and knowing about such examples contributes to other wives' decisions to join their husbands abroad. The emotional pain of children whose parents work abroad is also well understood, and there are concerns that their behaviour and schoolwork suffer as a result of such separation. Interviewees often felt strongly that teenagers needed to be 'kept an eye on'.

Media articles about children of migrant parents – who are given the emotive label 'euro-orphans' – suggest even more extreme consequences of parental migration, such as drug addiction, crime, mental health problems and suicide. However, the comments made by the interviewees (like those of many internet commentators on articles about 'euro-orphans') suggest that the media may be over-dramatising the situation and, furthermore, that many ordinary Poles do not agree that migrant parents are 'to blame'. The mothers interviewed in Poland believed that parents who migrated alone were 'normal people'. However, they were felt to be taking a risk by migrating without their spouses and children and, as already suggested, there was widespread agreement that the welfare of the family would be much better served if everyone migrated together. Network theory, in migration studies, suggests that migrants migrate because of nets. They also migrate because of gaps.

Notes

[1] Capra, F. (1996) *The web of life*, London: HarperCollins, p 82, cited in Urry (2003, p 159).

[2] On the suffering caused to families by migration, see, for example, Guzik (2005); Parreñas (2005); Pratt (2009); Zontini (2004).

[3] Guzik (2005).

[4] Domanowska (2008)

[5] I have not been able to establish when the term 'euro-orphan' was coined, but it is sometimes described as a 'neologism' in recent works. I suspect it dates from after 2004, although of course the phenomenon existed before then. A sociological study published in Podkarpacie in 2002 identified the problem, but did not use the term (Malinowski

and Szczepańska, 2002, p 161). A 'euro-orphan' bibliography compiled by the Kołłątaj Education Regional Library (Kraków) mentions one book on the phenomenon (not using the label) published in 1998, but all other entries date from 2005 or later (Eurosieroty: Zestawienie bibliograficzne, Anon 2008b). An anonymous bibliography published at www.pcekamgora.org/files/20081013161641.doc lists several pre-2004 works, the earliest published in 1992, but again without use of the term 'euro-orphan'.

[6] There were particularly high levels of agreement among inhabitants of the northern and western sub-regions (north 75.2% and west 78.2% respectively) that had above average levels of respondents who had actually been to Western countries other than the UK. Women were more likely to agree than men (70.4% versus 64.0%) and agreement levels decreased with size of town; villagers were least likely of all to agree with the statement (64.6% agreed).

[7] Iglicka (2008, p 68).

[8] Przybyła (2007).

[9] Walczak (2009, p 159).

[10] Hugo–Bader (2007)

[11] Szlachetka (2008).

[12] Jakubowski (2008).

[13] The research was conducted among schoolteachers all over Poland as well as among 3,893 school students aged 9-18. See Walczak (2009, pp 154, 159).

[14] Personal communication from B. Walczak, 27 January 2010.

[15] Walczak (2008, p 1).

[16] Walczak (2009, p 156).

[17] Jakubowski (2008).

[18] Anon (2007b).

[19] Anon (2008c).

[20] Schutta (2007).

[21] Wodecka et al (2008).

[22] Kozerawska (2008a).

[23] Walczak (2008, p 2; 2009, p 164).

[24] Stańkowski taught in Czarny Dunajec, which, he claimed, 'breaks all the records', given that 'half' the village lived in America (p 244) (Stańkowski, 2006).

[25] Stańkowski (2006, p 259). Stańkowski's data set was 103 written questionnaires.

[26] Kozerawska (2008b).

[27] FPE (2008, p 3).

[28] For example, Hugo–Bader (2007); Schutta (2007); Winnicka (2007).

[29] Anon (2007a).

[30] Hugo–Bader (2007).

[31] Sądej (2007a).

[32] Wasek (2007).

[33] Sądej (2007b).

[34] http://forum.gazeta.pl/forum/w,902,70771180.html

[35] http://forum.gazeta.pl/forum/w,902,70771180.html

[36] Interviewed on 27 March 2008.

[37] http://forum.demokraci.pl/topic.php?id=1928

[38] Walczak (2008, p 2).

[39] Information from school administrator, 10 and 17 September 2008: 27/50 and 4/10 had gone to the UK. The school had 664 pupils, not including the 50 who had left at some point during their school career but were still of an age to return to the primary school should they come back.

[40] Information from school administrator, 12 September 2008: 580 children remained in the school.

[41] Information from school administrator, 15 September 2008: 5/7 had gone to the UK, 397 children remained.

[42] For example, Baldock (2000); Ackers (2004); Baldassar (2007).

[43] Coyle (2007b, p 8).

[44] asz PAP (2007).

[45] Vullnetari and King (2008, p 163) discuss a similar situation in Albania.

[46] Bryceson and Vuorela (2002, p 7).

Integration into British society

If you have money you like everything, even the rain. (Izabela, Bath)

If it weren't for the language barrier, I'd be a happy person! (Edyta, Bath)

Chapter Eight and Chapter Nine are complementary. This chapter explores integration in the sense of making links with British people and learning how to operate in British society, and examines the interviewees' own perceptions about the most important 'indicators of integration', those aspects of inclusion which would particularly encourage them to remain in England. Chapter Nine looks at possibilities for maintaining Polishness in England and for making a 'home' abroad. The success or otherwise of both aspects of integration help determine families' decisions about how long to stay in the UK. However, such integration does not take place in a closed box. Transnational networks, joining England and Poland, remain strong. The networking described in previous chapters usually goes on working when the Polish family is abroad and this can enhance the return migration potential of each individual and household, as discussed later in Chapter Ten.

The first part of this chapter addresses interviewees' sense of connectedness to the particular towns and region where they lived in the UK, and their feeling of having 'arrived' where they wanted to make a home. Ways in which those local communities were adapting to the presence of Polish migrants are also briefly discussed. Integration, as argued in Chapter One, is best seen as a two-way process in which the receiving community has an active role to play in the inclusion of new migrants. This chapter looks at interactions between interviewees and the rest of the local community, their friendships and everyday encounters with non-Poles.

Other research on Central and East European migrants has suggested that a sense of temporariness may impede deeper integration, for example doing voluntary work locally or becoming involved in local politics, but that nonetheless there is often a sufficient level of engagement for the metaphors of 'segregated' or 'parallel lives' to be misleading. 'Sheer proximity between different groups may sometimes lead to positive encounters. This counters arguments about "parallel communities".'[1] As this chapter will show, in the course of trying to shape livelihoods in the UK Polish parents were not trying to become British but they were definitely attempting to integrate to a sufficient extent to feel comfortable in their new surroundings. Shaping a livelihood, as already argued, is only possible if there is an understanding of how things are done locally, and if migrants are able to create successful livelihoods in the receiving community this could be considered an indicator of 'sufficient' integration.

I argue that English language is the most fundamental attribute of integration, and various facets of interviewees' experiences and requirements are explored. Although studies of Polish migrants to the UK tend to emphasise the good language skills of Polish graduates, among the interviewees, who did not have higher education, poor English was the main factor inhibiting integration. The rest of the chapter looks at employment and schools – the areas that probably have the most direct bearing on whether or not families stay, and for how long. With regard to employment, I particularly focus on cleaning, since this was the most common occupation among the interviewees. Employment in low-status, typical migrant jobs would seem to promote social exclusion rather than integration, but reality is more complex: some workplaces offer more opportunities than others for encounters with non-Poles, and satisfaction levels are also related to comparisons made with alternatives. Polish women cleaning in the UK may compare their position favourably against being unemployed in Poland, or earning a Polish wage, or being a kitchen porter in the UK.

In keeping with the argument of earlier chapters, I suggest that the interests of children were often the main focus of the household's livelihood strategies: the factor that most clearly seemed to anchor the families in the UK was their children's successful integration. A recent study of A8 migrants found that 60% of families intended to stay in the UK permanently[2] and, although most of the interviewees would not make such definite claims, nonetheless the experience of being with school-age children in the UK clearly did constitute a very powerful reason to remain.

Housing is not considered within this chapter because it is more relevant to Chapter Nine. However, with reference to integration in the sense of feeling connected to one's local neighbourhood, it is worth noting that almost all the interviewees lived in private rented accommodation. Markova and Black, in their study of Central and East Europeans in London and Brighton, found that 'those who were in private rented accommodation were less likely to say they felt they belonged to their neighbourhood, or to have participated in community activities, compared to those in council accommodation or owner-occupiers'.[3] When contracts have to be renewed every six months, migrants can find themselves frequently moving house, and this obviously has an impact on how connected they feel to their local area.

Integration and segregation

Chapter One introduced the fourfold acculturation model, identifying possible outcomes of migration. The first outcome, 'assimilation', is not an option for the parents in this sample, at least in the short to medium term. Without higher education, Polish migrants are unlikely to possess the English language skills to become indistinguishable from British-born people. The second outcome, 'marginalisation', would imply losing Polishness as well as not acquiring a British identity. This, too, seems unlikely, except perhaps for migrants who are 'marginalised' in other respects: because they are homeless, for example. Polish families are generally not in this situation; they have many opportunities to maintain their sense of Polish identity in the UK, and have reasons to do so.

The remaining two outcomes are 'integration' and 'separation': in both cases, migrants retain some or many of their original ethnic attributes. These are therefore the outcomes most likely to be experienced by interviewees participating in the research. The term 'segregation'[4] is used because it is probably more familiar to readers and less ambiguous than 'separation'. As mentioned in Chapter One, a single migrant can have more than one acculturation outcome, and it seemed most helpful to think of a spectrum of interviewees, with some more 'integrated' and others more 'segregated'. At the same time, integration, as defined for example in the Home Office *Indicators of integration*, takes place on a community level and is about including migrants in the receiving society on an equal footing, with equal rights to housing, jobs, education and other public services.[5]

Integration can be conceptualised as that happy outcome where migrants choose how much Polishness to keep and how much Britishness to acquire, but have sufficient knowledge of how to operate in British society in order to feel 'at home' and to make adequate livelihoods, as well to access services they need. Among all the interviewees, Dominika seemed closest to this outcome: she claimed to feel 'at home' in Bath, and she had learned English to the point where she did not sense a 'language barrier'. Overall, she had a feeling of progress and personal self-development: she was learning to drive and she was hoping, in a few years, to obtain a professional qualification, building on the studies she had abandoned in Poland. Better integrated interviewees like Dominika had made many 'social connections' (to quote the Home Office *Indicators of integration*).[6] These were contacts with non-Poles who could help them with advice and information, as well as friendships, and, in Dominika's case, a boyfriend.

'Segregation' is where Polishness is retained, but migrants are not really able to operate in the receiving society, lack social connections of all kinds with non-Poles and cannot make adequate, independent livelihoods outside of the Polish community. They are socially excluded in numerous respects. Within the sample, there were four or five interviewees who seemed to be quite 'segregated': highly dependent on their husbands, and, in most cases, unemployed and with poor language skills. Gabriela, aged 26, was apparently the most segregated of all. She had originally tried to persuade her husband not to come to England, but he had gone anyway, and persuaded her to join him. She had stayed at home with her small child ever since their arrival. Hoping for another child, she was not seeking a job or even very aware of how to look for one. She had attended only a handful of English lessons and had no English friends. She was not even registered with a doctor. Gabriela did have a few Polish friends, mostly friends of her husband's; she watched Polish television, cooked Polish-style food (bought from German shops) and was in touch via the internet with her large family in Poland. She did not seem unhappy, just very focused on her family and home.

As suggested in Chapter One, integration is not just an outcome, but also a sequence of events and experiences. Integration can be seen as a natural process, experienced by migrants of all nationalities, away from the segregation that often marks the lives of new arrivals and towards a feeling of being 'at home'.

> It was really hard at first. My daughter cried a lot, the first month she was crying, I was crying, I used to walk the streets and think 'What am I doing here? I want to go home!'... [My husband] was working seven days a week, all hours. He showed me the way to the school just once and said [next time] I'd have to find it myself. I said 'Cool'. (Katarzyna)

> I've changed a little bit [in the 15 months since first interviewed]. I'm more cheerful, smiley, I don't have those days when I feel depressed. I do miss my home and family but not the way I used to do. You get used to being here, you start to make a home in the place where you are. I don't feel I'm still searching to find a place of my own, my own nest. I think this is my home. Perhaps not forever, but a home.... We have settled in a bit, here in Trowbridge. (Sylwia, second interview)

However, it should not be assumed that there is necessarily a clear line of progress towards integration:

> [In Poland] I worked in different places.... And then I came to England and sat at home! It was hard to get used to it.... At first I felt so homesick for Poland. I cried for the first two weeks. And I phoned back to Poland every day. I wanted to go home. But later, bit by bit. And now, the worst thing is, when I'm in England, everything is fine. But when I go to Poland and know I've got to come back to England, I feel exactly the same as I did before! It's best not to visit Poland. Just stay in England. (Malwina)

Integration in the sense of becoming more connected to England is often an experience of starts and stops. There could even be reversals, when, for example, interviewees such as Agnieszka gave up their paid jobs because they had a child:

> To know English you have to be with English people. I knew more at the beginning than I do now.... Now I have no contact with English, only Polish. Except from in shops or at the doctor, places like that of course. But when you work it's quite different.

A sense of being abroad only temporarily can deter a migrant from making ties to the receiving society, so there is a circular causation. In a virtuous circle, more integration makes the migrant more securely lodged in UK society and less likely to go back to the place of origin; this leads to greater commitment and still more involvement. However, a vicious circle can also ensue where poor integration and increasing thoughts of return reinforce one another. By using the labels 'virtuous' and 'vicious' I am not implying that it is 'good' to be in the UK rather than Poland, simply that when virtuous circles are formed the individual is usually a happier person.

Integration is also played out within the household. Individuals, depending on their employment status, language knowledge and so forth, can become locked into their own virtuous or vicious integration circles which can be the same as or different to those of spouses or children. Gender roles can be altered depending on the different integration experiences of the spouses. As Triandafyllidou observes, 'Clearly the migration experience contributes in both material and emotional ways in changing the role of women in their families and their own understanding of who they are and what they want to achieve in their lives'.[7] Women may either identify more with traditional womanly roles – for example, if they had a paid job in Poland but are housewives in the UK – or there may be a more equal distribution of roles than was the case in Poland. At the same time, an individual's own integration path is partly dependent on the integration experiences of family members. Less integrated members may not need to integrate quickly if they can rely on more integrated family members, but they may also be spurred towards greater integration by the desire not to be dependent on spouses and children. There will also be arguments that reflect different degrees of integration. Parents for example, may prefer to take holidays in Poland while their children become increasingly reluctant to do so. Eventually, family members may argue about whether or not to return for good.

Integration into the non-Polish community

> Agnieszka: Here is my home, this is where I live.
>
> Anne: Do you mean this particular building?
>
> Agnieszka: No, I mean here in Bath.

This chapter and Chapter Nine look specifically at families in Bath, Bristol and Trowbridge, as well as a family in Frome. The towns and cities are close to one another geographically, but vary in other respects. Appendix 3 contains some relevant statistics from the 2001 Census. For Polish families moving into these towns important features included the fact that, for example, in 2009 there was a shortage of school places in Bristol. Bristol had council housing, unlike Bath and Trowbridge, and one interviewee in Bristol had secured a council house. Interviewees in Bath and Trowbridge were on waiting lists for social housing.

Bristol has a very diverse economy; Bath is a world-famous tourist attraction, with 7.3% of the population employed in hotels and catering; Trowbridge and Frome are small industrial centres with about a fifth of the population employed in manufacturing. Bath is more middle class than the other towns, has a higher proportion of students and retired people and is generally more expensive: for example, rents are higher and there are no cheap German supermarkets selling Polish-style food.

Bristol is more multi-ethnic than the other locations. Black Caribbeans formed the largest ethnic minority at the 2001 Census, but there were also substantial numbers of Pakistanis, Indians and Somalis.[8] Bath has more non-white British inhabitants than most towns locally, although the city conveys a very 'English' appearance to the casual visitor. Unlike Bristol, where streets are lined with minority ethnic businesses,[9] there are few such businesses, even in the suburbs. Bath's non-British residents are more visible to Poles working as cleaners at the hospital or universities or attending language classes at the City of Bath College.[10] Frome (97% white British) and Trowbridge (95%) are more typical of the south-west census region and Poles moving into these towns after 2004 were the largest minority ethnic group.

In just a handful of cases, interviewees or their family members – usually bus drivers – had chosen their specific destination towns:

> It had to be a small town, a tourist centre. London was completely out, I'd never want to live there, nor would my father, and he chose a small place where life was quieter. (Agnieszka)

> At first we wanted to go to Weston-[super-Mare][11] but after two weeks they rang offering Bath. It was hard but we decided on Bath and he packed his suitcase. [Weston] because it's a nice town, nice environs, the sea....We'd had enough of being in a noisy city [in Poland] and we wanted to go to a smaller town where it would be peaceful. (Edyta)

Even though most interviewees, unlike Edyta and Agnieszka, had arrived in particular towns by chance or through personal connections, the particular characteristics of different towns had an impact on their integration and plans to stay:

> The friend brought over his sister-in-law and the sister-in-law brought him over and he brought over [my husband]. Well, but Bath is very beautiful, isn't it? The problem is, it's expensive. But if you plan to be here for a while, you want to be here, well, I don't know. We're staying here, because it's beautiful. I wouldn't like to live in the Manchester area, it's horrible there and you're afraid to be out on the street. (Katarzyna)

If they had time, many interviewees made a point of organising family outings at weekends to the surrounding region:

> We've been to Cardiff, to Weymouth, down there, everywhere around Bristol, we've been to all the sights.... Me, my husband and our daughter. Or sometimes with our friends, taking two or three cars.... I want to see things.... In Poland I haven't visited lots of places. This is my chance. (Malwina)

Dorota had been to visit Polish friends in other English cities and they had come to see her in Bristol. She commented:

> We try to [travel in the UK], if the weather is warm. We go somewhere, to the seaside or somewhere, to visit some place.... We've been to Newark, to Wales – my cousin lives there in a tiny place – hell, as usual I can't remember the name.

Not surprisingly, given the spelling of many British place names, interviewees found them hard to pronounce and even to remember, but nonetheless they conveyed the impression of 'mapping' out their new home region. This can be seen as one aspect of integration. On the other hand, they were behaving like tourists, which could enhance their sense of being foreigners abroad.

Interviewees almost always denied that they would consider moving to a different place in the UK. In part this was simply because they seemed content where they were:

> I like Bath. It's a beautiful town, old. It's like [my city in Poland].... And the countryside around is nice. I really like it and I can't imagine moving to another town. (Jolanta)

> I like this estate [in Bristol], I like the street. And I like the house. I feel good, and safe, it's really nice here. The neighbours are quiet. You feel good here. (Dorota)

New livelihood opportunities could in theory be opened up by moving from a small town with a limited range of livelihoods to a city. Even Bath might be classed as 'small', compared with Bristol or London, with their much more diverse economies. Mirroring the attitudes of small-town interviewees in Poland, the UK interviewees usually said they did not want to move to a city. In particular they did not like the idea of moving to London, on various grounds: it was described as being dangerous, noisy and expensive. As discussed in Chapter Three, small-town or village identities partly influenced migration plans:

He didn't like London at all, because it's too big…. If he he'd been
sent to work in a city he wouldn't have lasted out. He would have
gone back to Poland at once. But Bath is really quite a pleasant little
town, very pleasant, it isn't big…. We're from a small village. For us,
the quieter the better. Bristol is too noisy. Here is better. (Patrycja)

However, more important than small-town or village identities was the feeling
that, as Sylwia expressed it, "one move is enough". Coming to England, they had
had to find new jobs, a new house, a new school and a new doctor's surgery, and
she was tired of "looking for things" all the time. Ilona also asserted that if they
remained in England they would stay where they were:

We know this town. I don't like to change the whole time. I don't like
to change my job, the place I live. For me it's a very big problem….
I'm adapting here and it would be really hard for me to change later
to a new place and new people. That would be very stressful for me.
I wouldn't like to change.

Barbara had in fact moved early after arriving in England, from a small town to
nearby Bristol, so her sons could go to more suitable schools. She did not want
to move anywhere else: "I like it here." Overall, therefore, interviewees gave the
impression that they were beginning to feel settled in their English towns or city
suburbs. For a family, uprooting was something that could only be done once.

As Chapter One discussed, 'integration', seen on a societal level – as the
integration of whole migrant groups into British society – implies that the receiving
country also reaches out and adapts to the needs of the migrants. The creation of
'sustainable communities' is government policy and this involves 'the promotion
of a stronger sense of community along with greater community involvement,
particularly in disadvantaged urban neighbourhoods'.[12] In Trowbridge, the West
Wiltshire-Elbląg Twinning Association has a particular role to play in reaching
out to new Polish migrants and educating non-Polish residents about Poland
and Polish culture. Bristol City Council has published a booklet in Polish titled
'Witamy w Bristolu' ('Welcome to Bristol').[13] Polish community organisations
are enrolled as partners by local councils, the police force and NHS (see Chapter
Nine). On the level of day-to-day encounters in the local community, Polish
migrants can also notice that they are being made welcome. If interviewees seemed
to identify with their local area in the UK, it was partly because they had found
out how to access local services, and they appreciated it when institutions such as
doctors' surgeries offered interpreters, banks and shops employed Polish staff and
schools had Polish teaching assistants. Interviewees, particularly in Bristol, tended
to comment on the extent of such services, which had sometimes expanded just
over the period during which they had been in England:

You can go there [a Catholic school in Bristol] any time and talk to
them. And the headteacher is Polish so you can talk to her in Polish.
And there is another Polish-speaking teacher. There were more teachers
there at the beginning to help the children. And they used to have
extra English lessons. They didn't go to all the classes, just to English.
They did take care of the children. To give them that extra help. I
can't complain. (Monika)

Nonetheless, there remained circumstances in which interviewees either needed,
or preferred to rely on, friends or family:

[At the doctor's, language] is not a problem because an interpreter
will come. You just have to say at the health centre that you need an
interpreter and they'll fix one up. But if it's some little problem my
daughter can know about she comes with me....We have a friend who
knows English very well because she worked in USA before coming
to England. In the bank you have to be very precise, she comes with
us, or with my husband, and helps us. Although in many banks they
employ Poles. (Dorota, Bristol, 2009)

Interviewees felt glad when non-Poles showed knowledge and appreciation of
Polish culture. Several interviewees, in different towns, were pleased to point out
that not only did supermarkets and corner shops sell Polish food,[14] but also that
non-Polish people shopped in Polish delicatessens and appreciated the quality of
Polish products. In both Bristol and Bath, Polish groups have cooked meals to
which they have invited the surrounding non-Polish community.[15] Interviewees
had British acquaintances who had gone on holiday to Poland, usually to Kraków.
Feeling that the give and take is not always in the same direction, that sometimes
British people are *your* guests, and becoming a bit more 'Polish', is an important
part of the integration story.

When Alicja, in Grajewo, went to work as a nanny in Belgium, with its long
established Polish community, she found that her Belgian employer and children
all knew some Polish because they had had many Polish nannies over the years.
Poles in the UK cannot hope to find many British people who speak Polish. I
have been told several times that people in Bath and Bristol are prone to apologise
to Poles for this failing, saying "Your English is better than my Polish." However,
some interviewees had met non-Polish people who spoke Polish and these rare
occasions stuck in their memories. Maria's husband pointed out that the British
salesperson in the television shop knew at least one word of Polish: if someone
came in asking for a 'pilot', it was a Pole in search of a remote control. Also in
Bristol, Wanda commented:

For example my husband's manager speaks very good Polish....Because
lots of Poles work for that company. So that's why he wants to learn!

He wants to know what the workers are saying! It's nice that English
people try to reach out to us.

Although many interviewees commented on the cheerfulness and kindness
of British people in public places, only seven out of 30 said they actually had
British friends (*koleżanki*).[16] These included two of the three lone mothers, who
had both made a very determined effort to learn English and to reach out to
local people. For example, they had friends among British mothers they had met
in the school playground, unlike some of the other interviewees who were too
inhibited by the quality of their English to take advantage of this opportunity
(see later). Like Spencer et al in their study of A8 migrants' 'lives beyond the
workplace', I found that the length of time spent in the UK did not seem to
have much bearing on whether or not interviewees had English friends; more
important was their confidence in speaking English, a quality which often went
hand in hand with having an outgoing personality.[17] However, Katarzyna, the
one woman who mentioned having a good English friend, had met her when
she still spoke very little English. Obviously there is an element of luck, as, for
example, when interviewees had friendly neighbours with whom they had begun
to socialise, or who they could ask for advice. A few interviewees also knew Polish
people with English partners.

Most of the interviewees had good Polish friends in England, so this cushioned
them against the loneliness that they might otherwise have felt (see Chapter Nine).
However, spending time with Poles could also reduce opportunities for mixing
with non-Polish people. Sylwia, for example, reported that there were two or
three separate groups of Polish parents meeting their children from school and
these groups of friends would stand together while they waited. "The English
parents smile at us but don't try to get into conversation. They just say 'hello',
but they keep a distance."

Describing such situations, Polish interviewees sometimes mentioned wondering
whether or not British people really wanted to be friends. Ewa, for example, said:
"We only know English people from our workplaces. But not so as to be friends
with them." She and her husband discussed whether their English colleagues did
not want to be friends with Poles, but had decided that their overall impression
was that British people were generally not prejudiced against foreigners. Jagoda
was not sure about her English next-door neighbour:

I feel timid about saying anything to her. She's, so. I think she doesn't
want to talk to Poles.... That's my feeling. Or perhaps it's not just
Poles, perhaps she doesn't like foreigners. But I don't know. There's
something she's grumpy about.

Spencer et al (whose survey was conducted in 2004-05) found quite high levels
of scepticism among A8 migrants about whether Britons they met outside work
wanted to make friends with them: 42% of respondents did not know, 33% thought

they did and 24% believed they did not want to be friends.[18] It cannot be ruled out, however, that such expectations are to some extent brought from Poland, rather than resulting from actual encounters in the UK. Several interviewees in Poland – even people who had never been migrants – had the preconception that foreigners would always be treated as second-class citizens. For example, in Grajewo Danuta stated that "I think perhaps migrants are always somehow treated as second-class citizens," just as, for example, Agnieszka in Bath suggested that "I have the impression that English people will never treat us as equals."

Worries about unfriendliness on the part of British people are also well founded in UK reality. A February 2009 article by Wiktor Moszczyński,[19] spokesperson for the Federation of Poles in Great Britain, claimed that there had been at least a 20% increase in racist incidents directed against Poles reported in the British media for 2008, compared with 2007. Blaming stress arising from the economic recession, the article listed 60 separate media headlines referring to clearly racist crimes, for example:

- *This is Plymouth*, 10 April 2008: 'Polish taxi driver needed 12 stitches after attack by two thugs'
- *Wales on line*, 25 May 2008: 'Facebook refuses to act against Facebook group "Get the Poles out of Llanelli" with 148 members'
- *Airdrie & Coatbridge Advertiser*, 10 December 2008: 'Polish brothers attacked with flammable liquid in assault by 10 youths in Airdrie'

Moszczyński observed that 'the spread of new anti-Polish incidents covers all parts of the United Kingdom, namely, England, Wales, Scotland and Northern Ireland'. However, he also commented on the particular problems experienced by Poles in locations which previously had been largely white British in ethnic composition: 'In the more rural areas of the United Kingdom this adjustment had not always been so easy, despite the efforts of local authorities. It is noticeable that *more than 70% of the incidents in the above list have occurred in smaller towns.*'[20]

Trowbridge, for example, is exactly such a town, and in fact three of the articles listed were about Trowbridge:

- 24 March 2008: 'Serious outbreak of anti-Polish graffiti in Trowbridge'
- 20 April 2008: 'Polish delicatessen in Trowbridge suffered criminal damage from racist attack by three teenagers'
- 11 August 2008: 'Polish man bruised by 19-year-old youth in Trowbridge'[21]

I did not try to collect data about racist incidents against Poles. Nonetheless, I had the impression that interviewees were becoming more concerned about racism between 2006 and 2009. For example, in 2006, Eliza, a home help in Bristol, said she heard only good things about Poles from her clients. When they discovered she was Polish they either did not say much or said Poles were 'good' because they came to work, not to scrounge. In June 2007, while I was interviewing the

Polish honorary consul's representative in Trowbridge, she received a telephone call from a local primary school teacher who said that he and his colleagues were concerned because British children had been telling Polish children that their parents did not want them in Trowbridge. This was the first time she had received such a complaint.[22] Also in Trowbridge, in autumn 2007 Sylwia complained of nothing worse than hostile stares from British mothers when she breastfed her baby in the park. This had changed by 2009, however, when she stated: "English people are against Poles." She immediately qualified this assertion by saying that older people in Trowbridge were friendlier and they were used to Poles because of the local post-war émigré community. However, she gave two examples of Poles who had had their cars maliciously damaged, and another instance where British people had repeatedly rung the police with complaints against their Polish neighbours, in the hope of getting them evicted. She did not like her 11-year-old son to walk around town alone because she was afraid of attacks.

None of the interviewees said they had personally suffered racist abuse, still less attacks, but in three of the Bristol families children had been bullied at school for being Polish. In one case the bullying, which took place on the school bus, lasted for months and led to the boy truanting from school. Even small incidents can leave lasting and unpleasant impressions, as Ilona's story illustrates:

> Once I met an old lady on the bus [in Bath], and I was a bit upset, because this English lady ... asked me where I was from ... and said that I was very nice but she really didn't like Poles because they come here and English people don't have jobs....Another time we were on the bus and ... there were two ladies and they said 'What a lovely little girl, what a pretty dress, what beautiful curls', and everything was fine, Natalka and Adaś smiled at them, everything was fine until Natalka spoke to Adaś in Polish and then the two ladies began whispering to each other and staring at us as if we were aliens....There are lots of situations like that, mostly with older people ... and when I go to the shops or I'm on the street I try to stop the children talking to each other....Lots of people are very nice, they smile at you, I'm not saying the majority are hostile, most people are really nice....But more than once we've met people who think Poles are inferior. I try to understand them because I think that in Poland as well lots of people don't like foreigners.

Several other interviewees also said that in their opinion Poles were equally, if not more, racist than British people.[23] This perhaps reflected their wish to be polite to me, as a British interviewer, but probably also links to the fact that they had been mulling over issues to do with 'race' and ethnic difference in the two countries, and imagining themselves in the place of a migrant in Poland. Studies of Central and East European migrants frequently point out that the experience of living in British cities makes people think about such issues in a new way, particularly if they come from countries like Poland which, since the Second World War, have been nearly mono-ethnic.[24] This is particularly the case since they are quite likely to live in parts of the British city where there are high concentrations of minority ethnic groups and to do jobs which are typically taken by migrants. In the research study these comments apply particularly to Bristol, but a number of Bath interviewees also mentioned non-British, including black and Asian friends, colleagues and neighbours. Although a couple of interviewees made racist comments about particular UK locations being preferable to others because they were less racially mixed, all interviewees who commented on their individual first encounters with non-white local people did so in a positive way. Aneta, for example, describing her job as pizza chef for an Iranian asylum seeker who ran a kebab shop opposite their flat, described him as "my first Muslim friend" and emphasised how well they understood each other despite the difference in cultures. Barbara's family had been befriended by a Pakistani landlord:

> Later we moved to be with a Pakistani man who had lots of Polish tenants.…We went to that Pakistani man, he was so nice, really super. We lived there and he helped the boys find a holiday job on a building site. (Barbara, Bristol)

English language

Research among Polish and other A8 migrants has highlighted the importance they attach to learning the English language.[25] Interviewees in both Poland and the UK repeatedly made the comment that language was 'fundamental' and interviewees in Poland almost always raised the topic of language in their discussions about whether they personally would migrate, or not. Poles who went to school under the communist regime (and indeed well into the 1990s) were taught Russian, only occasionally learning another foreign language. The majority of Polish women do not know English: one large recent survey of women of various ages showed that 62% claimed to know no English, and 14% knew only the basics.[26] Interviewees in Poland who had a cluster of reasons for not wanting to migrate and could not envisage themselves as migrants usually emphasised their fear of a 'language barrier' which they had built up in their minds as being a huge and insuperable obstacle. In Grajewo, for instance, Anna explained her reluctance to move by saying: "I'd be terrified, I'm a real panicker and I'd be afraid, in general, especially when it came to the children, well, that they might get ill, or some harm would come to them because I didn't know the language." A typical list of reasons not to go was provided by Urszula (Sanok), aged 45 at the time of the interview. She had four siblings living and working abroad, but claimed:

> I personally would never go. I'm afraid. The language barrier, I'd never leave the children, never. And taking the children with you means tearing them away from their normal surroundings, for me that

would be, well, I don't know. I'm too attached to my family. I had the opportunity, they invited me more than once to join them for a while. I wouldn't go. I don't see myself there. I'd be afraid.

Wincenta, aged 49, was certain that her situation forced her to go abroad, but very reluctant, for all sorts of reasons. Her fear of the language barrier fed into this reluctance. Having looked at her niece's English textbooks, she had persuaded herself that she would never be able to learn the language. "I can't make head or tail of it."

However, some women who did not learn English at school took into account the fact that friends and family abroad were coping linguistically, and this gave them confidence that they too might learn a foreign language. Again, this can be seen as a network effect, where vicarious familiarity with how things are done abroad encourages potential migrants to try their luck:

> I think I would learn English if I had to and I wanted to, don't you think? It's hard at first, of course. My friend who went to England, she didn't know English at first either. But now in fact she speaks it really well. She was forced to learn it. (Jolanta, Grajewo)

The need to know English was emphasised repeatedly by all the UK interviewees. Even Gabriela, described earlier as leading a segregated life, was studying English on her own, showing her toddler BBC children's programmes on the family computer and planning to stay in England at least until the little girl had completed primary school, so that, with excellent English, she would be equipped with a useful life skill. The only interviewees who mentioned a reluctance to learn English did so in the context of their unhappiness after their first arrival. Agnieszka, despite attending a language class, "used to have a terrible aversion to English. The first year I was really depressed about being here and the language annoyed me." Edyta said she could not "mobilise herself" to learn English at first because she was so miserable.

Language knowledge is a good example of an area in which it is possible to have two or more identities: you can come to England as a Polish-speaker, but become an English-speaker as well. On the other hand, one language can of course be favoured over the other. For example, two interviewees had watched English television when they first came to the UK and they agreed that it had been good for their language acquisition; however, they switched entirely to Polish once they had acquired a Polish satellite link.

There are different reasons for considering language to be important. Language is often seen as a tool. The Home Office *Indicators of integration* refer to it as a 'facilitator'.[27] David Blunkett, as Home Secretary, expressed this instrumentalist approach: 'acquiring English is a pre-requisite to social integration, to further education and employment'.[28] This is obviously true, and interviewees did mention the need for language skills in order to get jobs:

> There is definitely a lot of work to be had, but the language [is always required]!... So I stay at home.... I've looked everywhere, there is cleaning work everywhere ... but only if you have English at least to be able to communicate. (Malwina, Bristol)

Language, nevertheless, is much more than an instrument for getting things done. As Alexander et al point out, 'to acquire language is to do more than acquire the ability to communicate; it is to acquire culture'.[29] Even if they did not want to 'become English', and felt, for example, that they wanted to be watching Polish television programmes rather than English ones, interviewees had a sense of needing English language in order to live in England, to understand what was going on around them, to feel in control of their lives and livelihoods. When Edyta, quoted at the start of this chapter, said that she would be happy if it were not for the language barrier, she was referring to a general sense of discomfort that pervaded her life. She liked her job, her children were doing well at school, the family had bought their own house, yet despite these sources of pleasure, it was impossible to feel quite at home.

Learning a language is an unending journey. You can look at it optimistically ('I'm learning more and more' or 'I already know sufficient for my needs') or pessimistically (I'm still a long way from where I want or need to be'). UK interviewees had broken through the first barriers. However, they still sensed barriers all around. It is easy in this situation to become discouraged. For Polish people a particular problem which takes a long time to overcome is pronunciation, especially vowel sounds.[30] As Malwina complained: "The worst thing is pronunciation. You try but it comes out completely different!" Many interviewees were at a stage where they had a working knowledge of written English and quite good at listening comprehension, but nonetheless were often frustrated by their inability to make themselves understood. The importance of being able to converse is a recurring theme in the following discussion.

The youngest interviewees had studied English at school, with differing outcomes: Ilona found it hard to speak at first, but understood "everything" and quickly built up confidence, whereas Malwina, with three years of English at school, and having lived in England for two years, "could not put a sentence together". Some interviewees had taken private classes in Poland before they came, and interviewees in Poland also mentioned future migrants paying for private tuition. It is easy enough to find a small language school or individual teacher in Poland. Some interviewees had also organised extra English tuition specifically for their children before they came. Nonetheless, it was a common experience that learning English in Poland was one thing, but having to use it when they arrived in England was quite another:

> I did go on a language course, but studying a language is one thing, it's another to come to a particular place in England, and when

people start talking fast and with their particular accent and using abbreviations…. (Katarzyna)

I'd had quite a lot of contact with English [in Poland]. But the first time I was in England I really, I just couldn't understand what was being said to me!… Later I began to get used to the accents. (Joanna, Grajewo)

Some women, once in the UK, had adopted a strategy of learning English better first, before they even applied for jobs, but this was only feasible for women whose husbands could support them and who did not have daytime childcare responsibilities. It can be very difficult to acquire English tuition in England and recent shifts in government policy have exacerbated confusion about entitlements to free or subsidised tuition.[31] The problems migrants face accessing a language course suitable for them, or even any course at all, free or at a price they can afford, at a convenient time and place, is a recurrent finding in recent studies.[32] The University of Bath offered free English classes during the working day until autumn 2008 and this made the university an attractive employer in the eyes of local Poles. For mothers of small children, who had the least opportunity to speak English and were perhaps most in need of language tuition, the main barrier seemed to be childcare responsibilities: they needed a crèche to be able to access classes. For many of the interviewees, it was essential to find a beginners' level class, and these were not always available.[33]

However, to be effective, formal language tuition must also be backed up by self-study and conversation practice. Several interviewees complained of lacking time or energy to do homework or even watch English-language television. They usually seemed a little embarrassed to admit that they watched Polish television, since the context was that they had just been complaining about how hard it was to learn English. A number of interviewees, however, were studying systematically, in several cases using computer programmes that gave them a good sense of making progress. Maria addressed her pronunciation problem by singing along while she was listening to music in the car. The most common form of self-study, however, seemed to be helping children do their homework.

Interviewees who were not in paid employment or not doing a job that involved speaking English often lacked speaking practice and felt tongue-tied as a result:

Piotr (factory worker, four years in UK): I can't speak English. Only Polish. That's the way I am. It's hard to learn English. I was in Germany for one year and I picked up German, but somehow I can't manage to learn English.

Monika: But you do know something, you do manage. It's not as if you know absolutely nothing!…

Piotr: Perhaps it's because I've always worked with Poles.

Despite its many difficulties, work in a care home was prized because it offered good opportunities to practise English and some women were pleasantly surprised at how fast they learned, once they were in an English-speaking environment. Dominika, for example, was amazed at how quickly she learned to speak English. She felt that she was forced to do it because she was the first Pole employed at her care home. She had never considered herself to be good at languages at school (where she studied German), but here she had a real incentive to learn. Sylwia and Kinga were also working in care homes. After a few months they were delighted with their progress.

Just being at work, of course, does not guarantee absorption of the language. A number of interviewees (including Sylwia) mentioned that although they could make themselves understood they felt frustrated because they could not have an in-depth conversation on a particular topic. This was why they could not become close to English people, even in situations when it would be natural to chat to them, for example at a lunch break or when waiting to collect a child from school. As Edyta complained: "I don't have any English friends. The main thing is that language barrier. We do talk over lunch but I don't speak so confidently, so fluently as I would like to."

Frustration at perceived lack of progress was an emotion commonly reported among interviewees and their husbands. Even bus drivers (as mentioned, a number of Bath interviewees were married to bus drivers) do not necessarily improve their English beyond a certain point. One driver pointed out that the range of conversations he had with passengers was limited and that if drivers did not associate with English people off the bus they would not make progress. During rest periods at the bus station, Poles tended to stick together.

Nevertheless, husbands usually had a better command of spoken English because of their job and because they had been in the UK longer than their wives, including a period alone when they had had to fend for themselves. Bernadeta, for example, remarked sadly: "My boyfriend [a builder] has more [English] friends because he works with his boss every day, they talk more, and if he's in a shop or somewhere he will talk English to people, but I don't." As Bernadeta's comment implies, women could feel particularly frustrated if they sensed that they were becoming locked into a vicious circle, where their husbands did all the talking and they were always silent. Their speaking confidence could not improve in this situation, and they could only envy their husbands as the latter became increasingly fluent.

Some obviously felt uncomfortable about the dependency their plight induced. Marzena, for example, complained because she did not like being "completely dependent" on her husband after about six months in the UK. Gender roles became ever more distinct as wives became increasingly confirmed in the impression that their husbands were 'naturally' communicative and they were 'naturally' diffident. They were impressed by their husband's self-confidence that had helped them to learn spoken English very quickly. However, by working at home with a dictionary, some wives were able to overcome any sense of inferiority and, instead, to complement their husband's language skills. This was particularly important for Wanda, whose daughter had diabetes, and who had learned the special vocabulary associated with the condition and its management:

> Wanda: He doesn't speak English that well. [He's been in Bristol] two-and-a-half years, but he's always worked with Poles. Although he does have English workmates and when it comes to his specific work – he's a mechanic – he's very good at English. But if it's a hospital for example that's different.
>
> Anne: You're better than him?
>
> Wanda: I have more time. I only work two hours a day so I can sit in front of the laptop and find the words I need. But he works eight and sometimes 10 hours. When he comes home he's tired.

Ewa described a similar case of teamwork:

> We only know everyday language, not medical, or words they use in offices, like in the bank, for example, we have problems. My husband perhaps less, because he's been working here longer and always with English people. So he's more fluent. But we usually go and do things together because together we understand more. I'm better at reading, because for example I've had to translate every piece of information from Iweta's school, and that's how I learned a lot of language. My husband has learned to understand more by listening. So that's how we work together [laughter]: we make a good team.

In other cases, however, there seemed to be some tension between spouses because one was more advanced than the other. For example, where the husband has poorer English, conventional gender roles can seem to be reversed, and this can create an uncomfortable situation. In Poland, Aneta's husband clearly liked to feel in charge. She had given up her part-time studies because he did not like the idea of her being 'cleverer' than he was. In England, however, he had had to acknowledge that she learned the language faster than he did. He had been working as a cleaners' supervisor, but they swapped jobs because he felt he could not cope, and she was much more confident. Ilona's husband, also a cleaner, was frustrated in the UK, partly, it seems, because his English was poor and he was reliant on his wife, creating a vicious circle where he was failing to integrate. Ilona, by contrast, was locked in a virtuous circle: she had 'lots' of friends, including an English one, cleaned in English houses and was confident about her English language and her ability to improve still further. The power shifts within the household were reflected in diverging opinions about whether to go home to Poland:

I would like to stay here in England, because I have a job, and perhaps I could go to college, so I'd have really perfect English, but my husband doesn't want to stay.... He speaks a lot worse English, because he never learned it at school. And always if there is some problem or we need to go to the bank or to some offices it's me who goes and organises everything. But in Poland it was the other way round. In Poland he used to arrange everything. But here, I speak better English than he does.... He really is finding it very hard to learn the language. Some people find languages hard. That's another reason why he doesn't want to stay in England: the language barrier.

Integration and paid employment

Employment can also facilitate integration simply by virtue of providing the opportunity to leave the house and mix with other people. Many interviewees told stories illustrating the very different integration experiences and satisfaction levels of full-time mothers and women in paid employment. For example, Paulina in Sanok contrasted the situations of her sister Anna, with a baby in London, and her friend Ewa:

Anna [my sister] can't go out anywhere. She doesn't have any friends to visit. Her neighbour is Polish, they sit at home together. And they don't have anyone to go and see, anyone to talk to. It's no life for her, abroad.... Ewa [my friend] is working, so she doesn't want to come back to Poland.... She goes out, she has [women] friends, because she works in some restaurant, in the kitchen, and it's good that she mixes with people. When the child was small she sat at home and wanted to return to Poland. Now it's better.

Iwona, who had first worked in London, but then stayed at home after she brought her children to the UK, complained "we sat in that little cell of a flat as if we were in prison"; eventually she went back to Sanok. To some extent such emotions were also experienced by the UK interviewees. Sylwia, for instance, when first interviewed in 2007, complained of feeling isolated and having no friends and little English. Re-interviewed in 2009, she was quick to impart the news that she was working:

I'm very happy. It's better that I work, for financial reasons, but as well I just wanted to go to work. My husband said I should stay at home a bit longer, our little boy's still very small, but I said I just couldn't cope any more with staying at home. I was really suffering, I was just tired out by being at home.

Malwina had only had two temporary jobs since arriving in Bristol two years previously and was at home unemployed. Her daughter was out at school all day. She expressed her frustration:

> [In Poland] I worked in different places, in another shop and then in the one close to our home. I came here and stayed at home! Oh dear, it was so hard to get used to it. I did get used to it in the end … [but] I'd go anywhere, just to have a job.

However, not all women were unhappy to be housewives.[34] Monika, for example, had many Polish friends and said she was not tired of being at home:

> I've plenty to keep me busy. It's not as if I just stay in the house, I like to go out for walks. And our daughter still needs a lot of attention, she may be nearly three, but you need to keep an eye on her and keep her entertained. And think what would happen if I went out to work – all the housework! The day would have to be longer! The gentlemen [sons plus husband] would find themselves with some tasks to do. Everyone would have to do more around the house. But for the moment I'm not complaining.

At the time of interview, 21 women were working and 12 were not;[35] 13 interviewees were cleaners (one also a supervisor), six were care workers, one was a dinner lady and one a self-employed hairdresser. Eight were not working because they had pre-school age children, two were unemployed, two were housewives and part-time students of English. All but two of the interviewees had worked in Poland,[36] but only two (one cleaner and the hairdresser) had worked in their UK occupations. The most common Polish occupations were shop assistant (7) followed by clerical/secretarial (5), self-employed (5), dressmaker (3) and hairdresser (3).[37] Cleaning was therefore by far the most common occupation among the interviewees (13 wives and four husbands), and much of the following discussion will concentrate on cleaning in particular.

Those interviewees in Poland who were most reluctant to migrate were often the happiest in their jobs. By the same token, migrants to the UK had often not enjoyed their jobs in Poland and some said that they and/or their husbands were feeling less stressed and more comfortable because of the 'easier' pace of work in England:

> Doing accounts, because I helped with that. I used to take in goods, pay the drivers. I did almost everything [in the wholesalers] and I know how to do it. But I had no satisfaction because I was treated like a nobody. [In England I just went and did my cleaning.] People weren't ordering me around all the time, 'Do this, do that.' (Katarzyna)

In some cases, feeling less stressed was related to working part time. In Poland, as observed in Chapter Three, fewer people work part time than in the UK, and interviewees sometimes commented on the difference. Barbara, for example, was working just five hours a day as a cleaner and was satisfied, despite the fact that she had four children:

> I go to work, I get my pay, and that is enough for my needs. I'm not short of money. In Poland I used to work as much as 16 hours a day … and still I didn't have enough money…. It's not hard work, I have a contract, I have paid holiday. It's OK….We don't need to send money to Poland, we have enough to live on without doing overtime.

On the other hand, there were cases where couples – especially if they were both cleaners – were working every hour available to make ends meet, and trying to find ways of 'combining' different jobs and earning additionally in different workplaces. In other words, this was exactly the way of life complained about by interviewees in Poland.

Given what was said in Chapter Three about the insecurity of livelihoods in Poland, and the attractions of working for 'solid' employers such as the dairy in Grajewo or the bus factory in Sanok, it is not surprising if Poles in the UK prized jobs with major local employers. In Bath, for example, these included the Royal United Hospital, the University of Bath and First Bus. In general, it was felt to be very desirable to come off agency work and find a steady job with a formal contract, where the employer adhered to all the legal obligations. Paid leave was a particular criterion, since families were anxious to take their children on regular holidays to Poland. They welcomed what they perceived to be inclusion in the regular workforce. If they had jobs in the state sector they often mentioned this as being important (and when one interviewee, who cleaned in a private school, referred to "state work" she was in effect paying a compliment to the school).

Legal and secure employment is not to be taken for granted. As other studies[38] have shown, A8 workers are not always protected from exploitation by their EU member status; workers of any nationality can be vulnerable in sectors such as hospitality. For instance, when she first arrived in Bath, Ilona had worked for less than the minimum wage in a hotel. The hotel had reneged on its promise to pay her a proper wage after a year and after 18 months she gave up and left. Ilona then found a job cleaning at the hospital, which she treasured because it paid reliably.

In 2009, interviewees had a sense of insecurity induced by the economic recession, but still possessed a certain confidence that if you were willing to accept poorly paid jobs and kept your ear to the ground you would be able to find something:

> We have a sense of security – I feel that even if I lost my job here I could find another. Perhaps for the minimum wage and hard work,

like in a hotel, because obviously there is always hotel work. Here if you have work you can make ends meet. (Edyta, Bath, June 2009)

You can find work here, even if it's not very good. (Patrycja, Bath, January 2009)

In Bristol, one interviewee's husband had just changed his job, when interviewed in June 2009; he found the new job through one of his hairdresser wife's customers. The interviewee in Frome, who had been unemployed in January 2009, managed to find work shortly after the interview at the factory where her boyfriend worked. Some interviewees knew people (including their husbands) who had been retained because they were good workers, while British colleagues were made redundant, and this eased their suspicions that non-British workers would be the first to lose their jobs.

Media articles and scholarly articles often focus on the 'deskilling' of highly qualified Poles who come to the UK and do manual jobs such as cleaning. Aneta, working as a recruiter in a Bristol cleaning company, mentioned that many Poles applying to her for cleaning jobs emphasised that in Poland they had been teachers or had higher degrees, and she had to reassure them that there was nothing shameful in cleaning. The interviewees were not highly educated people and often they did not face the dilemmas experienced by migrants switching from intellectual to manual work, or express sentiments about manual work being demeaning. In particular, like their counterparts I interviewed in Poland, many women did not have any problems with cleaning as an occupation. Agnieszka suggested that the comparison was between earning a respectable wage abroad (which by implication made one feel a respected person) and working for pennies in a white-collar job in Poland. "They prefer to clean in England, but for decent money, instead of slaving away in Poland, sitting in an office 12 hours a day, for peanuts."

No women said anything about actually enjoying cleaning as an occupation, but it could be worse (working as a kitchen porter), and it was better than not having a job at all in Poland. If they presented their jobs positively, it may have been partly because they were using their narratives to assert their self-worth. To quote a Brazilian male cleaner from a London survey: 'I had never done a cleaning [job]. But here, you have to give it value, because that is what you have.'[39] However, insofar as they genuinely liked their jobs, the main reason was that they felt comfortable and respected in their working environment and because they had friends at work. For example, Dorota (in Poland a self-employed hairdresser, now a full-time school cleaner, with good colleagues), said: "I'm really happy with my job. It may be cleaning, but it's not bad." Edyta (a clerical worker and running a small business in Poland, now a school cleaner, also with good colleagues) said:

I like going to work…. In Poland I never worked as a cleaner, but here I had no option…. I don't know, because I never worked as a cleaner in Poland, but as I ran a house I had to keep it clean. I'm not scared of any job. I was just sad that my work [as a hotel cleaner] was never appreciated.... Here [in the school] ... they notice if I do my job well.... It's completely different when people say thank you for your work. So it's good.

Other women made similar comments, including one who cleaned private houses and was friendly with her employers.

Nonetheless, other women, who had a further education qualification and/or aspirations to higher education and/or done an office job in Poland could feel frustrated by the fact that they were cleaning in England. On the one hand, they recognised that the pay was better than what they could have earned in a more high-status job in Poland:

I'm a cleaner, unfortunately. But I think that – although it's probably not what I'd choose to do my whole life – all the same, it means I've better prospects for the future than I'd have in Poland. (Ewa)

On the other hand, after a while in England the more ambitious interviewees could begin to feel depressed by the idea that they might have many years of cleaning still to come:

On the whole I'm not at all happy that I'm a cleaner. It wasn't my life's ambition to clean. (Katarzyna)

Earning enough money to be able to go out and buy things, acquiring an identity as a British consumer, was an important aspect of integration. Chapter Four discussed the aspiration to live 'normally': parents in Poland often say that the purpose of migration is to assure children a 'normal' or 'decent' standard of living. Interviewees in England made identical comments. Their jobs were not such that they were earning 'coconuts' (to use a common phrase), but that they had what they needed for everyday life:

It's true we're not rolling in it ['earning coconuts'], because I'm not working ... but compared with Poland it's just much much cheaper. (Agnieszka)

The pound has fallen a lot, and prices have gone up so much that money just slips through your fingers like water. So most people who are here with children have just enough to live on, for a *normal standard of living*. (Katarzyna)

Again and again interviewees highlighted how relaxed they felt about spending money, compared to how they had lived in Poland:

You don't have that problem that you worry, like in Poland, if I bought my child some shoes and a winter jacket I couldn't buy myself any clothes that month. Because I couldn't afford it. It was a choice – me or the children, or my husband, whose turn it was for clothes. But here, prices compared to earnings, everything, food, clothes, they're lower. Even though the bills are colossal, gas, electricity, it's a nightmare, if they weren't so high it would be even better! But food in Poland is almost the same price as here and people earn a third the wages. So it's hard. Here, I don't have to refuse the children things. Well, of course, you shouldn't buy a child everything they ask for, how would they turn out when they grew up! But in general I don't have to worry that I can't afford to buy them fruit juice, or clothes. It's so much easier for us here. It's less stressful. You're not under such pressure. (Maria)

Interviewees also made identical comments to the interviewees in Poland about child benefit, complaining that in Poland it was means tested and that, although they were poor, they had failed to qualify. The state respected families in the UK and made their lives easier. It should be emphasised, however, that interviewees' expectations about how to spend their UK incomes were often extremely modest. Gabriela, for example, enthused that "We can afford to buy any food … we buy whatever we want." However, it transpired that she did all her shopping in the cheapest supermarkets.

Children's integration and schooling

Interviewees made comparisons between themselves and their children, who often quickly arrived at a stage where English was their preferred language for playing, reading or watching television, and they were much more competent than their parents. This could enhance their parents' frustration, although they also felt pride in their children and sometimes depended on them. Iwona described her 18-year-old daughter as her "permanent interpreter" and Monika and her husband claimed to rely on their three teenage sons. Even Sylwia's 10-year-old son was sometimes called on to interpret, for example when the police knocked at the door after neighbours were burgled. However, Sylwia complained that he could abuse his better knowledge of English to play tricks on his parents, for example when they went to a safari park and had an unfortunate misunderstanding with an official who believed there was an animal in their car. Dorota did not try to befriend her daughter's friends' parents, relying on the daughter to communicate: "We exchange polite greetings. I don't know the language well enough to have a specific conversation. If I need to, Sonia will interpret."

Several interviewees commented that their children's good knowledge of English was an important motive for staying in the UK. Taking comfort in this could partly mitigate a sense of frustration on their own account. Bernadeta, for example, explained that she wanted to stay in England largely because "the girls will have a better future. They'll know English well. So it will be easier … [even if they go back to Poland]."

Chapter Four suggested that many Poles living in Poland are not very aware of the actual differences between British and Polish schools, although those who were better informed believed that the academic standard was 'higher' in Poland, that children were made to work a lot harder and that in general the regime was stricter and pupils were given less encouragement. Polish parents in the UK repeatedly stressed such differences between the systems: "two separate worlds", in the words of Bożena. Given this perception, integration of Polish children into the British school system might seem to pose special problems. A recent survey of Polish parents in London showed that some were very critical of British schools.[40] Parents whom I interviewed in the West of England voiced some of the same concerns; in particular, they wanted children at primary schools to have more homework and for there to be more checking that they had really learned the material. Barbara and her husband were distressed because their teenage son, who was outstanding at maths, was not being taught maths at all, apparently because he was so far ahead of the other children in his year group. Another interviewee, although very happy with her son's primary school, was suspicious about what would happen later, saying "Children get a very good start, in English schools, but somehow it gets lost later on."

On the other hand, parents' main emphasis was on positive attributes of the British system. These were not related to academic level but instead had a direct bearing on integration. Teachers were considered to be approachable, children were made to feel valued, their free time was not monopolised by academic work and what they learned often had a practical application:

> It's true [the standard is lower in English schools], but I look at it another way: English people give *us* work, not the other way round. My children are happy, Ola was really unhappy in Poland: she was always in tears and upset and she had much too much homework. (Iwona)

> In England schooling is based on play and practical experience. But in Poland from Class 2 everything has to be memorised. So much homework. It's too much and you don't actually need it in real life. And what Szymon [aged 13] learns here is relevant to real life. That's my impression. (Maria)

> The teachers and the atmosphere are so nice, they organise different events, I'm really thrilled with it. The teachers all know how to be approachable with children. In Poland the headteacher stands on a pedestal and gives orders. (Edyta)

However, often the first few months were so hard for children of all ages that parents could feel conscience-stricken that they had uprooted them. For example,

161

Kinga was seriously thinking about returning to Poland when I first interviewed her, two months after her daughter had begun school in England. Marianna, too, was so upset by her daughter's initial unhappiness that she offered her the opportunity to return:

> At first, when I saw that she was having a really hard time, because of course, the new school, the language, I asked if she wanted to go back to Poland but she said no, it was nice here, she liked it, there were more things to do and school was quite different.... There were times when she was isolated, other children weren't talking to her. But I said 'Don't worry' and I tried to explain that I didn't understand what people said to me, either, and it was hard for us, too ... and somehow gradually she understood.

The nature and quality of integration partly depended on whether there were other Polish children in a child's class. If there were, they could feel more at home to begin with, but it could have a negative effect on their long-term ability to communicate and to make friends with non-Polish children. Parents with more than one child at the same school contrasted their different experiences in this respect:

> The middle one didn't have any Poles in his class when he began school here, in the primary school. He knows English much better than the other two. He was on his own, he was forced to learn English. (Monika)

> Łukasz is in Year 8, he speaks English brilliantly. In Year 7 he was the only Polish child in his class so he was forced to learn English. I wish I could speak like him! (Barbara, contrasting Łukasz's progress with that of her other two sons)

Overall, parents whose children had been in primary schools in the UK for more than a few months tended to emphasise that the children were doing well academically, sometimes backing up that assertion with mention of exam and test results, certificates and prizes awarded and other recognition. They also had non-Polish friends, often including best friends, and Aneta, for example, said that her eight-year-old son was even picking up an "English sense of humour". However, a few interviewees made comments about obstacles to socialising and/or young children's poor integration. When I interviewed Kinga for a second time she was glad because her daughter, who had initially been unhappy in the reception class, was now making friends with other children and had been invited to three birthday parties. Unfortunately, however, Kinga felt reluctant to take Amalia to parties, firstly because Kinga was shy about staying in an English house and having to talk to the other parents, and secondly because of the expense. Patrycja was concerned about her son who had been at nursery followed by primary school for more than a year, but was very shy and had only one friend, another Polish boy. "In classes he doesn't join in and he's too shy to repeat any words in English. He has a problem with the language. It depends on the child."

Bafekr's study of Polish children in Brussels found a distinction between less well-adjusted older and better-adjusted younger children.[41] Interviewees with teenage children sometimes did have the impression that they had found it harder to mix with other children and that to some extent this was connected to their strong friendships back in Poland. Monika and Piotr, for example, agreed that it had been harder for their 13-year-old son than for the younger boys:

> He was the one who most wanted to go back. Somehow things weren't right, we discussed it, and we agreed that when he finished school here, at 18 or whenever, then he could return to Poland. But now it's turned the other way round, now he wants to stay here.... Children often change their minds. Let's see what happens next!

Renata commented:

> My daughters don't seem particularly unhappy. Our elder daughter has a very good friend in Poland and she misses her. But she's made lots of friends in England, Poles, of course.... Those older children have problems with making new friends, and if there's a group, and there is a group of Poles at her school.... At first the English children were interested in the Polish ones, they were a novelty but then they saw the Poles were doing alright in their own little group, and were quite self-contained.

There were also practical reasons limiting older children's ability to socialise, such as the distance travelled to school, where parents had chosen to send their children to Catholic schools that were not very local. Continuing her discussion of her sons' adaptation, Monika commented:

> Most of their friends are Poles, they travel quite a long way to school, and round here there aren't so many of their English friends. Of course if they go out to play football in the park and there are English boys there they will play with them. But they don't have really close English friends.

Conclusion

This chapter has discussed integration in the sense of engaging positively with British society. Although the UK interviewees did not want to "become British", they did want to be able to operate competently in their new surroundings, and feel comfortable about shaping their new livelihoods in the context of a foreign culture. Language knowledge, therefore, was more than a tool to get a job: it was an essential prerequisite for living in the UK. Most interviewees felt frustrated by what they perceived to be their inadequate progress in learning English. Because most were of an age to have studied Russian rather than English at school, they usually came to the UK knowing little or nothing, although some had taken private classes before they left. In England, they tended to work alongside other Poles or alone; others were not in paid employment. They also found it hard to access language classes in the UK. Local classes were often not at the right level or the right time, and the absence of a crèche was also mentioned as an obstacle by several interviewees.

Nonetheless, interviewees who were in paid employment could usually find positive things to say about their jobs, and some were very satisfied. This was partly because it was easier to live on a British wage than a Polish wage, but also because of social aspects of the job: they felt their labour was respected, they had good colleagues and they had at least some contact with British people even if they could not have in-depth conversations with them. In other words, it was the integrative aspects of the job that were particularly important. Women often appreciated being able to work part time, which had not been possible in Poland. The more dissatisfied interviewees were also the more ambitious ones: they could tolerate cleaning as a job for a few years, but they did not want to do it for ever. These women were also the most frustrated about their level of language knowledge, although often they were the interviewees who were taking the most active steps to improve their English.

In general, interviewees felt that British people were pleasant and polite, but they also reported some unpleasant incidents and several children had been bullied at school. There seemed to be a change between 2006, when I did the first interviews, and 2009. By 2009 there was more expectation that British people would be unfriendly. A few interviewees had British friends – sometimes from minority ethnic backgrounds – but many did not have any British friends at all. Because they felt that their language was inadequate for them to become intimate with English speakers, they could be uncertain as to whether this language barrier was the reason why they were not making British friends, or whether in fact their British acquaintances (such as work colleagues or other parents at their children's schools) did not want to be friends with them. If they had not had Polish friends, interviewees could have felt quite lonely in this situation. It was certainly inconvenient at times, when they needed advice or information, not to have built more bridges into the wider community.

Despite such frustrations, most interviewees were beginning to feel at home in their local areas. They knew their way round and could communicate with doctors, teachers and bank staff, sometimes with the help of interpreters. Many families also travelled around the local region, taking their children for day trips to the seaside and other tourist attractions. They had formed an attachment to their towns or neighbourhoods and usually felt they wanted to stay, not move on to another place in the UK, even a city that would offer a more diverse range of livelihoods.

With some exceptions, children had integrated quickly at school and they spoke quite good English and had English friends. The exceptions tended to be older children and/or children who studied alongside other Polish students and had not been completely immersed in English. Parents of children at school usually seemed more anchored in the UK than mothers who were at home with babies and toddlers. The housewives were the most 'segregated' of the interviewees, whatever their level of language knowledge.

Of course, all migrants interact differently with their new surroundings and some people are more flexible than others about adapting to new cultures and shaping new livelihoods. In many households, differences in personality between spouses and between parents and children helped contribute to a situation where different family members were integrating at different speeds, and some wives or husbands felt they had come to a stop. There was a sense that 'vicious' and 'virtuous' integration circles had been created, where, for example, a wife was integrating fast and liaising with British people on behalf of the family, but the husband was mute and depressed. As she spoke more, he spoke less. Most often it was the children who were forging ahead, while the parents had a sense of rather ruefully trailing behind. On the other hand, not all families are divided by the experience of attempting to integrate. There were also many examples of teamwork, where family members clubbed together their various skills, and interviewees gave the impression that their families were working together collaboratively as a result of migration.

It might seem that some of the evidence discussed in this chapter suggests there is a zero-sum game, where gain on one side equals loss on the other. Some Poles are not making connections into the non-Polish community because they belong instead to Polish networks. They can begin to feel permanently segregated. However, having Polish friends, using Polish language and working with fellow Poles is not really the *cause* of such integration problems. The interviewees had plenty of will to make non-Polish friends and to learn English. It was their lack of confidence in speaking English that was the barrier to further integration. In this, they contrasted strongly with more linguistically confident (often more highly educated) Poles in the UK who quickly develop English-speaking networks.[42]

As already argued in Chapter One, transnationalism and integration are perfectly compatible, and other studies have shown that the same personal characteristics, the social skills and confidence which facilitate making friends in the co-ethnic community, can be equally useful in forging networks in the receiving community. 'Migrants who establish strong, trusting relationships with their co-ethnics and who develop the necessary skills, such as language, may be able to adapt these skills to establish more extensive relationships, weak ties, beyond their own ethnic group.'[40] As this quotation suggests, however, language is the crucial extra factor without which social skills in the abstract are useless. Looking at the problem as being the migrant's fault is unhelpful here: integration is also the responsibility of the receiving community and the provision of better access to English language classes is essential.

Some interviewees were pessimistic, others optimistic. The pessimists saw the 'glass half empty': they felt they were not sufficiently integrated and they assessed their language knowledge as poor. The optimists saw the 'glass half full' and were more content with their integration progress, pointing out that in important respects they were achieving what they wanted to do: they had enough English to get by and, if they worked, they were reasonably satisfied with their jobs (especially those who had been unemployed in Poland). Among their own personal 'indicators of integration', first place was occupied by their children's successful adaption to school and life in the UK, and in most cases they felt that this was being achieved.

Notes

[1] Cook et al (2008, p 30).

[2] Garapich (2008a, p 19).

[3] Markova and Black (2007, p 66).

[4] Berry uses 'segregation' to refer to 'separation', but on the level of society at large, rather than individual strategies. See, for example, Berry and Sabatier (2010).

[5] Ager and Strang (2004).

[6] Ager and Strang (2004).

[7] Triandafyllidou (2006, p 237).

[8] CRE (nd).

[9] This led one interviewee to conclude: "Here in Bristol I think English people mostly live on the outskirts. In the centre, the majority are foreigners."

[10] For example, Ewa, a hospital cleaner, commented: "There really are lots of ethnic minorities: from the Philippines, lots from Brazil, Australia, practically from every country in Europe."

[11] A seaside resort near Bristol.

[12] Hudson et al (2007, p 1).

[13] 'Witamy w Bristolu' ['Welcome to Bristol'], at www.bristol.gov.uk

[14] See Rabikowska and Burrell (2009) for a discussion of what Poles in a London survey liked and disliked about supermarkets and corner shops as alternative places to buy Polish food.

[15] The Family Club, based at the Barton Hill Settlement in Bristol, does this annually. See Kowalik-Malcolm (nd) for an account of the Club's activities. Parents at the Polish Saturday School in Bath also cooked a Polish lunch on 3 May 2009, as part of a celebration of Constitution Day. See http://polskaszkolabath.co.uk/aktualnosci.html

[16] A *koleżanka* (male equivalent *kolega*) is more than a friend/acquaintance (*znajoma, znajomy*) but less close than a very good friend (*przyjaciółka, przyjaciel*). In practice different

speakers use the terms differently. Some people reserve *koleżanka* for quite close friends and others seem to use it more loosely (where another speaker would say *znajoma*).

[17] Spencer et al (2007, pp 58-9) found, nevertheless, that one in five of those who were fluent still said that they spent no time with British people, as did 39% of those who described their English as adequate.

[18] Spencer et al (2007, p 62).

[19] Moszczyński (2009).

[20] Ibid.

[21] Ibid.

[22] Interviewed on 25 June 2007.

[23] The 2006 CRONEM (Centre for Research on Nationalism, Ethnicity and Multiculturalism) study of Poles in London asked whether multiculturalism would 'work in Poland' and found that '90% say "Poles are not tolerant" towards others, mainly meaning people from Asian and Black minorities, and that they would not imagine ethnic pluralism in Poland on London's scale' (Garapich, 2006, p 21).

[24] See, for example, Siara's analysis (2009) of internet forum discussions, and Eade et al (2006, p 18), who conclude: 'The experience of London's diversity has resulted in 54% of respondents expressing enthusiastic to positive attitudes towards multiculturalism and treating it as one of the city's main strengths and attractions. At the same time approximately a third of the respondents disagreed and regarded ethnic diversity as abnormal.'

[25] For example, Cook et al (2008, p 41); Spencer at al (2007, pp 54-7).

[26] Zadrożna (2006b).

[27] Ager and Strang (2004, p 3).

[28] Writing in *The Guardian*, 3 September 2003, as quoted in Alexander et al (2007, p 784).

[29] Alexander et al (2007, p 785).

[30] My observation from teaching English to Poles.

[31] This observation is based on comments made at various seminars and meetings I attended during 2007-09, for example, 10 February 2009, 'Supporting Polish and other East European communities' meeting at the Council House, College Green, Bristol.

[32] Spencer et al (2007, p 54); Cook et al (2008, p 41).

[33] See Garapich (2008a, p 66) for similar comments with reference to the London Borough of Hammersmith and Fulham.

[34] Ryan et al (2009, p 68) found the same to be true of some of their interviewees in London.

[35] I have counted out of 33, since 2/3 of the repeat interviewees changed their status between the two interviews (one had a baby and the other began work). One of the hairdressers owned her own business, so she has been counted twice in the list of occupations.

[36] One was a student as well as a mother.

[37] Their husbands' and partners' occupations were bus driver (7), cleaner (4), builder (3), chef (2), mechanic (2) and other manual worker (8). The latter category includes a wide variety of jobs, for example, demolition worker, abattoir cleaner and security guard. The husbands of the repeat interviewees did not change job in the interval, so I have listed each of them only once. I have only counted the husbands/partners who were joined in England by their families, not the men living with interviewees who originally came to England as lone mothers.

[38] For example, Anderson et al (2007).

[39] McIlwaine et al (2006, p 1).

[40] See Sales et al (2008, pp 33-6) for a detailed discussion of 'conflicting expectations' between Polish parents (from a range of educational backgrounds) and British schools.

[41] Bafekr (1999, p 296).

[42] See, for example, Fomina (2009).

[43] Ryan et al (2008, p 676), referring to Cox, E. (2000) 'Diversity and community: conflict and trust?', in E. Vasta (ed) *Citizenship, community and democracy*, Basingstoke: Macmillan, pp 71-90.

NINE

Being Polish in England

Your homeland is where you earn your bread. (Polish proverb)

This chapter, the companion to Chapter Eight, explores aspects of integration linked to constructing Polish identities abroad. It discusses why interviewees led 'Polish' lives, looking at the different choices they made and the different opportunities they possessed. It also explores the outcomes, the extent to which interviewees felt more, or less, at home in the UK, as the result of their engagement in transnational activities.

After some general comments about identity, and specifically Polish identity, the chapter looks in turn at home and community. It begins with a discussion of the physical homes occupied by the Polish families in England and how much the interviewees felt at home in them. Insofar as it was indeed 'home' because the family was finally back together, how much were spouses able to enjoy being at home with their family, rather than being out at work? What are the implications of new working patterns for gender roles within the family?

The chapter continues by exploring selected transnational activities. First, it considers whether people feel at home in England because they can spend time there with their extended family, either by telephone or internet connection to Poland or directly, when relatives are invited to England for visits or for a long-term stay. The chapter then discusses buying and cooking food as an aspect of maintaining Polish cultural identity. For families, an important choice is whether to send their children to Saturday school. For all Poles, there are decisions about how far to socialise with other Polish people and whether to take an active role in building Polish community organisations, including Saturday schools. The final part of the chapter looks at socialising and collaboration among the Polish community, with particular emphasis on the possibilities for forming friendships and finding social support among fellow Poles. Emotional connections with Poles can help mitigate the effects of lacking such connections to the British community.

The chapter links logically to Chapter Ten, about return. Maintaining Polish identity and Polish networks in the UK can, paradoxically, have opposite outcomes for return. Keeping alive Polish identity and maintaining transnational networks – keeping on close terms with friends and family in Poland – would seem to be essential in preparation for eventual return to Poland. At the same time, if Polish migrants can make a sufficiently Polish home in the UK and use transnational networks to alleviate their homesickness, feeling they have integrated sufficiently to shape a satisfactory livelihood, they may prefer to stay in the UK.

Polish identity

Poles are often regarded as possessing a particularly strong sense of national identity[1] and opinion poll data such as the figures in Table 9.1 indicate that Poles do feel a strong sense of attachment to and identification with Poland and the Polish nation. However, very few interviewees in Poland raised the topic of patriotism, suggesting that they did not feel it was relevant in a discussion about who migrated from the local area. This was in keeping with their overall tendency not to see migration issues in national terms,[2] except insofar as they blamed the Polish state for not supporting families adequately. Instead of identifying Polish identity with a particular geographical location, the Polish nation-state, interviewees in both the UK and Poland seemed to regard identity as portable: you could be Polish anywhere in the world. (The proverb 'Your homeland is where you earn your bread' exemplifies this attitude and shows that in some respects Polish transnationalism is nothing new.) If territory is not so important a component of national identity, family and culture, which are portable, become even more significant. Gabriela, one of the Bristol interviewees, arrived in England with her baby, her clothes and a television satellite dish.

Table 9.1: Identification with Polish nation, home area, Poland and Europe (%)

I feel a very strong/strong link, and identify with:	Poland, average	Podkarpacie	Podlasie
My own nation	80.2	76.9	86.0
My town or village	77.1	78.4	80.7
My region	69.6	66.7	77.2
Poland	85.3	83.3	86.1
Europe	63.3	61.7	67.2

Source: Strzeszewski (2008, pp 60-2); Gwiazda and Roguska (2008, pp 61-3)

In general, interviewees in Poland tended not to reflect on Polish identity, even in a cultural sense. Interviewees in the UK more often spontaneously raised the issue of identity: being abroad, they were forced to think about Polish identity quite often in the course of everyday life. On the one hand, their accented English means that they are continually being identified as non-British. On the other hand, they themselves muse about cultural difference. There are multiple reference points arising from observations of how things seem to be done differently in the UK. For example, I overheard an older Polish woman in Bath claim that "You can always spot a Polish baby because it has a pillow in its pram and it wears socks." 'Polish babies wear socks' is a simple example, but many Polish migrants would probably also agree with Patrycja's sentiment that "Poles are family-oriented and they want to be with their relatives, with their parents" or Piotr's observation that "Polish food is nicer."

It is hard to say how much scattered moments of reflection on ethnic difference really add up to an individual gaining an increasingly strong sense of ethnic identity. Insofar as this does in fact happen, migrants can be viewed as undergoing two processes simultaneously. In the case of Poles, they have to sort out what they think about their own personal Polish identity, but also to decide what makes fellow Poles Polish. Class, regional and other differences within the Polish population make it hard to generalise about Polish identity, and migrants in the UK encounter Poles from different backgrounds. On the one hand, it is interesting to meet a diverse range of new people, and many Poles find marriage partners among the Polish migrant community. On the other hand, looking at one's fellow nationals with a critical eye can also lead to a desire to distance oneself from those who are not viewed as a credit to the nation.[3]

> They are not interested in reading, finding things out ... because for these people, England is not a foreign country. I have the impression that these young people bring Poland with them, more than we do. They have to eat Polish sausage, cook Wiener schnitzel, get dressed up and go to church on Sunday, like in Poland. They have to buy the sort of car which is a status symbol in Poland, a Passat or something. (Iwona)

Interviewees like Iwona consciously selected only some components of Polishness and contrasted this openness to other cultures with the perceived cultural insularity of other Poles. In this case, Iwona drew a distinction between herself, in early middle age, and "young people". Her remarks also imply a class dimension, and it was true that Iwona was better educated than some interviewees, although she did not have a university degree. As already suggested, better-educated Poles have more choice about how much to keep up their ties with Poland. Overall, however, the working-class identity of the particular sample created a certain background of uniformity, against which it was easier to notice the role of personal preferences and the particular resources and opportunities available to given households.

Whatever their actual range of transnational activities, the interviewees never suggested that they personally might become 'less' Polish as a result of living in the UK.[4] Even Dominika, perhaps the best integrated of all the interviewees, who spoke excellent English and was living with a non-Pole, asserted "I'll die a Pole": her culture would be with her all her life, even if she did not return to Poland until she retired. Apparently underlying such comments was a sense that being Polish was a birthright. Even if an individual flouted certain 'Polish' conventions, choosing livelihood strategies with many non-Polish components, this did not dilute his or her claim to be 100% Polish.

As often happens in migrant families, parents' sense of being exclusively Polish could contrast with the perceptions of their children. In the interviews, parents occasionally asked their children directly about their ethnic identity, and although some children defined themselves entirely as Polish, it was clear that others were acquiring dual identities:

Mother: Now Julia will tell you if she likes it in England.

Julia (aged 7): In Poland and in England.

Mother: But are you Polish?

Julia: Polish and English [*Polka Angielka*].

Mother: And are your friends English or Polish?

Julia: English, and Polish.

It was impossible to imagine any of the adult interviewees stating that they were "Polish and English".

On an everyday basis, nonetheless, people cannot always be thinking about their ethnic identity. Interviewees often seemed to mix aspects of Polish culture with culture they found in the UK, quite unconsciously. In any case, there is a great deal of overlap between 'Polish' and 'British' so it was not always necessary to categorise everything as being one or the other. As Pierik observes, the '*compartmentalization of culture: the tendency to view cultures as discrete entities with sharp borders*' is an unhelpful fallacy.[5] Poles, as demonstrated in Table 9.1, have a strong sense of being European, and it is important not to forget perceptions of overarching similarities between Poland and the UK.

There was little evidence that, on the whole, the interviewees were practising a deliberate strategy of transnationalism, with a view towards avoiding assimilation.[6] Poles who settled in the UK after the Second World War as exiles cherished certain cultural traditions, for example folk dancing, because these were a way of keeping Poland alive in their memories. Long-established Trowbridge Poles commented that the new migrants were uninterested in participating in the folkdance group attached to the Polish Club. Migrants today who frequently come and go between Poland and the UK and, in the UK, have extensive 'real time' contact with Poland over the internet and telephone lines, can afford to be much more casual about neglecting traditional markers of Polish identity.

Home and housing

Home has a special significance for migrants. Wiles, discussing New Zealanders in London, argues that '*home* and the *idea of home* structure the experience of migration'.[7] 'Home' is constructed by different individuals in many ways, not always linked to physical housing,[8] and it can also have different meanings in different cultures. In Polish, the fact that *dom* means both 'house' and 'home' increases the scope for multiple interpretations. A Polish national opinion survey in 1997 asked the open question 'What does home mean for you?' and found that the largest category, or 32% of answers, could be grouped under the umbrella of 'a safe place', a refuge from the outside world.[9] Definitions of 'home as refuge' are of course commonplace in many societies (although they have been challenged for ignoring the common reality that homes can be sites of oppression).[10] The idea of home as a haven of Polishness emerged as a theme in interviews:

> My neighbour is about 50. But it was easier for her to go to England because her children were there. One daughter, and her son, with his own children.... Well, of course, everything around is English but she has a Polish home. I think that's much better. She goes to work, does her eight hours or whatever ... and it's easier because though all round there are English streets and houses, the place where she actually lives is utterly Polish. (Danuta, Grajewo)

As a reason for watching television in Polish, UK interviewees mentioned the desire to relax in a cosy, familiar setting, after a hard day at work. They simply felt too tired at the end of the working day to make the effort to watch television in English. (Unconsciously, they were also improving their feeling of safety in the UK by watching Polish television to the exclusion of British television and not being well informed about British gory crimes and corrupt politicians. These were identified as Polish problems from which it has been good to escape.) No one said that Polish television was too expensive and this seemed to be a transnational activity that was open to everyone.

Migrants also accumulate objects that remind them of home in their country of origin.[11] However, to some extent this is a luxury of people who are already somewhat settled abroad, unlike the UK interviewees who had not been long in England and were usually living in temporary rented accommodation. As families they had to be economical in their packing, so mementos from home were not perhaps so likely to be included as they might be in the luggage of childless migrants.[12] Often they had rather few possessions on display, apart from children's toys that were international in character. The most noticeable objects in their living rooms were usually the television and the laptop, testifying to a very direct form of transnational activity that perhaps diminished the need for souvenirs from Poland.

The stability of home is an important aspect of feeling safe and this is connected to permanence of housing. The importance for Poles of acquiring a house or flat – and with it a guarantee of stability for the rest of their lives – was discussed in Chapter Four. Poles often arrive in the UK expecting to earn money to purchase a home in Poland, but, like migrants from all countries, their plans can change and they can end up buying a house in the UK. If Poles regard a house once purchased as a home for life, this would seem to be a good indicator of intention to stay. Of the 30 UK interviewees, only two had bought houses in the UK, both in 2008. Both women were married to bus drivers and therefore had a certain financial stability. They were also lucky in their timing. As Edyta observed: "We won the lottery in the sense that we got the mortgage when house prices were falling but you could still get a mortgage … and so it turned out *we have our own house!*"

Both families were busy doing up their new homes and Edyta's family was expecting to stay in Bath, although they kept their flat in Poland. Magdalena, however, was more ambivalent. Although they had sold their house and officially deregistered themselves from Poland, the house in Bath was regarded as an investment rather than as a definite symbol of commitment to England. They might still sell it and return to Poland.

When other interviewees raised the possibility that they might try to buy a house in the UK, the ostensible reason was to avoid throwing money away on rent.

> Malwina: We're also looking for a flat somewhere because we want a garden. It's a quiet street, a nice neighbourhood, but we really want a garden. Just some kind of garden.
>
> Mother-in-law: They don't get much sun here.
>
> Anne: It's quite expensive, isn't it, to rent a flat?
>
> Malwina: It is [expensive to rent], which is why we are thinking about perhaps getting a mortgage, if they'll give us one. Flats have got cheaper so instead of paying someone that £500 we'd just be paying for our *own* house [said very enthusiatically].

As this exchange suggests, the desire to have one's own house (with a sunny garden) could also be an important factor and this would imply feeling more settled, not just saving money.

There is no council housing in Bath or Trowbridge, but in Bristol some interviewees had heard that it was possible to rent from the council and then buy later: this was an alternative route towards possessing one's own home. Polish migrants are eligible to apply for social housing if they have been in registered employment for one year (under the Home Office Worker Registration Scheme) but to date very few actually do live in council or housing association accommodation. Just 0.4% of recorded social housing tenants for 2006-07 were Polish.[13] In the research sample, Dorota lived in a council house. The family had been in Bristol almost three years and had thought of getting a mortgage. However, they were asked for a £25,000 deposit. "Of course we don't have such money, and we're not going to sell our flat in Poland to pay the deposit and then spend 25-30 years paying off the mortgage. I was a bit scared, because it's a risk, you might lose your job." Hearing from friends that they could apply for council housing, they did so, and received their first offer six months later. They turned down the house after being warned by both a friend and a council official that the neighbourhood was not safe for non-white or non-British residents. They then moved into the second house they viewed. Slipping an English word into the conversation, Dorota complained: "As they say, the house was *rubbish*. Well, it wasn't such a disaster, but there was a lot to do." It was hard to feel at home when the house (as I could see) was full of rubble, but overall, thinking about the future, she felt they had made the right decision. Like the two owner-occupiers, they were busy making the place more homely.

The other interviewees were renting privately, and they had a wide range of experience. Being in rented accommodation did not necessarily preclude feeling settled and at home. Immediately after the interviewees arrived, they had often been upset by poor quality rented housing, but they had usually managed to find better places by the time of interview (despite recurring problems such as damp). Like many migrants, Poles often live in cramped quarters, particularly target earners who have come to the UK to save money and go home as soon as possible:

> I was missing Poland, my mum, my dad. I was thinking about home, my flat here in Poland, it may not be so wonderful, but it's got everything we need. And I didn't like the conditions in England.... We lived in the cheapest flats, you know, just a room and a kitchen of some sort ... all of us in one room. Here in Sanok the children have their own rooms, they have their toys, their own space to play. But it was so cramped in London. (Iwona)

The UK interviewees' families avoided sharing with strangers, although in several cases they were sharing small flats or houses with relatives and friends on a semi-permanent basis. Other families, by contrast, had spare beds that were used by short-term visitors. Not surprisingly, these were the families that appeared to be slightly better off than the others, often because the husband had a good job as a mechanic or in the building trade. The main distinction between interviewees, however, seemed to be between the security offered by longer tenancies, particularly if the latter were agreements reached directly with the owner rather than an agency, and housing which was on a six-month contract. Agnieszka, for example, had lived in the UK for five years and was unlucky enough to be currently in her fourth home: she described the family as "wandering from home to home". They liked their house but experience suggested that if you found a place you liked you would have to move on. Renata was living in a house with a garden outside Bath that she described as "very pleasant", but their contract was up for renewal in a few months' time. "Perhaps it will be, perhaps it won't. That's what's nerve-racking, you never know."

Some interviewees had rented their house or flat ever since they arrived, or at least for two or three years. Even though the accommodation was rented, they were beginning to feel that it was more "theirs", to fill it with possessions and to identify with the local neighbourhood. In such cases, if interviewees wanted to move somewhere else, the reason was usually that they were in the same situation as Malwina, quoted earlier: they had practically no garden, or none at all. This was a recurring theme. It was hardly surprising, perhaps, in families with small children, but there also seemed to be a specifically Poland-linked feature: a garden was something interviewees had possessed back in Poland, and it was an essential attribute of 'home'.

Home and family

> I can adapt. For me, it's all the same where I live [in London or Grajewo].... Because even if you have a home in one place, that doesn't stop you setting up a new one somewhere else, does it?... Home is where you are happy and fulfilled and safe.... For me, the family is the main thing, to be together. (Joanna)

Like Joanna, some interviewees made the point that home was where your family was. Whatever the standard of their accommodation, the main point was that, following the family reunification, they were all together again. In practice, however, there was often a sting in the tail: despite all living in the same house, family members might be spending little time together. Some households, as already discussed, contained relatives and friends who could help out with childcare, although often this seemed to be only on an occasional basis. Typically, parents with smaller children seemed to rely on one another for childcare. This meant organising shifts so as to take turns looking after the children, but not seeing much of one another:

> I'm working in a hotel as a housekeeper and somehow we cope. I work in the morning, my husband [a bus driver] works in the afternoon, and our son is at school.... We just meet each other in passing. (Patrycja)

> When I'm at work, it's my husband [who looks after the children], and when my husband's at work, I'm at home, and that's how it is all the time. (Ilona)

One corollary of such arrangements is that the partner doing the night or early morning shifts – often the wife, since husbands tend to have better paid and more inflexible jobs – suffers from chronic tiredness and shortage of sleep, so that even when the family is all together, it is hard to enjoy this time. However, a number of interviewees mentioned that, to compensate, they tried hard to keep Sundays free and the wish to devote at least one day to the family was given as a reason for arranging special family outings to local parks and beaches, as described in Chapter Eight.

Harder to determine is the impact of such arrangements on perceptions of appropriate gender roles. On the one hand, the husband may be doing more childcare than he would have done in Poland. On the other hand, this may not happen if his role is confined to waking the children and taking them to school, whereas the wife spends the afternoon and evening with her children, feeding them dinner and checking their homework. If the wife has a part-time job or does not work, her homemaking role may be even greater than it was in Poland. If she has time to devote to housework, then the home will be more home-like in the material sense and the rest of the family is more likely to feel settled, even if she herself feels frustrated and unsettled as a result of leaving paid employment. A further factor enhancing a sense of being at home in the English home is the arrival of a baby: five of the interviewees had had babies in England (and one had had two).

Previous chapters have mentioned Poles' close ties with their extended families. Interviewees in Poland often mentioned these. For example, in Grajewo Kazimiera explained:

> Our family is very close-knit [*zżyta ze sobą*]. And we really miss each other and even if one sister lives in Białystok and one in Olsztyn, all the same, every Saturday, or once a month, we all get together, or in summer, or for Christmas or Easter, so we can't be anywhere else, or go abroad. People go abroad if they don't have ties like those. If you have that sense of family bonds, I think, you feel fixed to one place. Not necessarily a specific town, but you have to be all together.

However, people do migrate abroad despite feeling very close to their extended families, and UK interviewees made similar comments about bonds with relatives. It was not surprising to find that, however comfortable their new home, and however glad they were to be with their immediate family, interviewees could not feel at home because they were missing their parents, siblings and other relatives left in Poland. All interviewees seemed to keep in close, although not always daily, touch with people in Poland. This occupied a significant part of their already busy lives. As Burrell points out, migrants can spend 'considerable amounts of time' every day telephoning and communicating by internet with people back home.[14] When they first arrived in the UK, some interviewees had never possessed a computer and did not know how to use the internet, but a laptop seemed to be one of the first items which families purchased and by 2008-09 all UK interviewees were using the internet to keep in touch with people in Poland. Nonetheless, not everyone in Poland had internet access, nor did they necessarily have the landline connection needed to receive certain forms of internet communication.[15]

Despite their extensive use of telephones and the internet, interviewees often wanted their close relatives to be physically present. As well as the emotional reasons, they said they would simply feel more secure:

> We're here on our own [couple plus son], without our family, without anyone close to us, so it is hard, all the same. You have no one to ask for help. (Patrycja)

> I'm really scared because if anything happened for example I had to go
> to hospital or my husband did, and someone had to come from Poland,
> well, my mother, both mothers, they don't really want to journey so
> far, they are really scared of it. (Ilona)

Many Polish migrants do invite their own parents to come to the UK, and
grandparents may be happy to go if there is little keeping them in Poland and the
family seems more complete to everyone when they are in the UK. Childcare
problems are often resolved at the same time. Ewa described how her husband's
mother had settled down with them in Bath:

> At the moment my mother-in-law is living with us ... so we don't
> need to worry [about childcare].... You could say she's here the whole
> time, but she often visits Poland. She's just been there for a week....
> She was in the States for a very long time and when we got married
> I hadn't even met her. We only talked on the phone. But we never
> met, face-to-face. And when Iweta was three I went to the States to
> stay with her for six months. And that was when we met.... And after
> we came to Bath she returned from the States to Poland and we went
> to Poland for a holiday, and then she came back with us. I wanted to
> work more hours, I was only working part time. Because of Iweta.
> And with Granny now it's easier.... She cleans private houses, just
> three or four hours a day.

In this family, the grandmother kept a foot in each country, something that had
not been possible when she was a cleaner in the USA. In other cases, grandparents
are clearly still based in Poland, but make lengthy visits to England:

> My dad came last year, stayed for four, five weeks, and he wanted to
> earn a little bit of money, so we had some stuff to do in our house and
> he found a little job somewhere like painting the house, something.
> So he came in May as well, so he earned a little bit of money, four,
> five weeks, and he went back. (Kamila)

In Poland, interviewees' accounts of chain migration often seemed to imply
that as more and more members of extended families reunited abroad, the pull
on the remaining members became irresistible. Halina told the story of some
neighbours who had gone from Sanok to Ireland:

> Right after their wedding the husband went abroad, he spent two years
> there, he used to come to Poland to visit, but two years ago the wife
> and son went out and now they're living in Ireland.... There's also her
> sister, she helps look after the little boy. Their mother also came out
> for a month, and another sister with her daughter, so lots of people

visited her there … and they rent a house with a second brother, and his wife, they went out with their children, so two brothers and their families share a house.

Network theorists would see a kind of determinism here: 'individuals who are related to migrants will, *ceteris paribus*, be more likely to migrate themselves'.[16] However, one can accept that there is a migration logic without abandoning the idea of a household livelihood strategy and believing that individuals and families have freedom of action. Chain migration is not automatic: every link-up has to be discussed within the household concerned and, many factors come into play. Australian immigration law includes the concept of a 'balance of family': if the majority of close relatives are in Australia, this entitles the remainder to come to Australia too.[17] The concept of a 'balance of family' often seemed to be at the back of people's minds when they discussed the topic of whether extended families would reunite abroad. However, the number of relatives in Poland vis-à-vis the foreign country is not the only issue, since potential migrants feel some pulls more strongly than others. Persuadability cannot be taken for granted and stubborn potential migrants can resist even the pull of multiple close relatives abroad. Sylwia described how her parents had visited them for her son's first communion but did not want to move to Trowbridge, even though all three of their children lived there. "They've nothing [sic] to come to in England. In Poland, they have a house, work, animals, trees … their own parents on both sides." Other interviewees also mentioned that their parents were unwilling to reunite with or even visit their children abroad, usually because they were still in paid employment, unwell, said to be worried about travelling or had caring responsibilities towards their own parents in Poland. Since the interviewees were in their twenties to thirties, and the average age of childbirth has been low in Poland until recently, the interviewees' parents were usually middle-aged; hence frailty as a hindrance to relocation was in most cases a problem only anticipated for the future.[18] There were situations, however, where the interviewee or her husband had had a particularly close relationship with a grandparent and the latter, despite being in their late seventies or eighties, had moved to England, while the interviewees' own parents stayed in Poland.

Most often, visits by relatives seemed to be short in length and not for the purposes of settlement or even earning money. Gabriela, for example, said that now they had managed to rent a three-bedroomed house, they would finally be able to have relatives to stay, and as a result they had fixed up a whole timetable of visits: her mother, cousins and in-laws would take it in turn to visit over the summer. Malwina also had space for guests and since, like Gabriela, she did not have a paid job and seemed rather isolated in day-to-day life, she had particular reason to value guests from home:

My sister and her husband have been twice, our friends have been, and now we have Mum. And we invite everybody who wants to come, let

them come and see! They haven't been abroad before, they didn't have
the opportunity, and now they have the chance to come and look.…
They come just for a week or two. To see things, to go shopping.
Clothes, of course. Clothes are cheap [in England]. (Malwina)

However, even when there was not much space in the house and the interviewee
was very busy, there often seemed to be a string of visitors.

Both in Poland and the UK interviewees mentioned their children's
schoolfriends coming for short visits to England. Obviously such visits can help
to make the hosts feel more at home in England: they are no longer the guests,
but the hosts. It was a measure, perhaps, of the fact that some interviewees were
beginning to feel more at home in England than in Poland that they said they
actually preferred people to visit them, rather than going to Poland themselves.
In this case, 'home' was definitely a place identified with the family (or even the
location in the UK) rather than Poland as a country. However, the financial costs
of visits should not be underestimated, and there were interviewees who stressed
that much less mutual visiting occurred than they would have liked.

Food

> Sugar is sugar, flour is flour, oil is oil. (Katarzyna)

> I don't like English food.… I can't make a cake with English flour.
> (Barbara)

Cooking and eating food is an aspect of life in which migrants would seem to
have quite a lot of individual choice about how far to express their ethnic identity.
It can be a consciously chosen method for asserting continuity with the past in
the 'unhomely' conditions of the present.[19] It is usually relatively easy to identify
national dishes as aspects of a specific culture and interviewees often listed 'typical'
Polish dishes, even if they immediately mentioned that they personally never or
only rarely cooked them. (Illustrating the actual complexities of 'national identity',
'typical' Polish dishes mentioned by interviewees were often 'Russian dumplings'
and 'Breton beans'.)[20]

Food is one of the most visible and commercialised aspects of ethnic identity.
Poles are lucky in the sense that it is not difficult to maintain this particular
transnational practice, thanks to the fact that so many Polish food products are
now on sale in the UK. The stocking of Polish foods by major supermarkets and
corner shops alike is one of the most noticeable aspects in which the receiving
society has adapted to the Polish presence. Iwona, quoted earlier in the chapter
for her disparaging comment about young and culturally insular Polish migrants
who "have to eat Polish sausage [and] cook Wiener schnitzel", was the only
interviewee who said she did not feed her family specifically Polish food and

she had not cooked Polish dishes even in Poland. It was notable that most other interviewees said they did cook Polish dishes much of the time. They placed differing emphasis on the importance of acquiring ingredients made in Poland and of not mixing Polish with other cuisines as illustrated in the quotations at the beginning of this section. To Barbara, British flour tasted foreign, but Katarzyna did not feel that there was any real difference.

Agnieszka, at the opposite extreme from Iwona, always cooked Polish dishes. To her, English food products such as cheese and cold meats tasted "completely different" from their Polish equivalents. The family transported cold meat and seasonings from Poland and they bought "staples" such as flour and sauerkraut from the Polish shop, as well as occasional treats of ready meals such as *bigos* (sauerkraut and bacon) or filled dumplings. It should be noted that Agnieszka did not match Iwona's description of the ignorant young Poles: she had dropped out of university just before her final exams and expected to stay in the UK for the foreseeable future. However, she was extremely homesick for Poland and also (like Barbara who could not eat English flour) very centred on her house and child. Katarzyna, by contrast, seemed more flexible and better integrated into British society in a variety of ways. She had a basic level of confidence that meant that she could manage her affairs in the UK, whether on the level of preparing Polish dinners from English ingredients, or in more complicated situations.

Specific circumstances must surely always be important in determining whether people think about eating Polish food: migrants are not constantly thinking about doing transnational things, but from time to time they seem significant. Interviewees spoke of sometimes remembering and wanting some particular food, particularly when they were reminded of Poland and began to miss it. In this case they might make a special trip to the Polish delicatessen. On normal occasions they did not mind compromising and producing hybrid dishes. Marzena, for example, said that although she brought seasonings and some cold meat from Poland to Bath, she would normally buy food in English shops, not necessarily typical 'Polish' products. By using English foods she could make Polish meals that tasted a bit different but were near enough to what she would have cooked in Poland.

Despite the hugely increased availability of Polish products over the past few years, in fact foodstuffs made in Poland are not equally available to everyone. Bath has only one entirely Polish food shop, which opened in 2007, and no big supermarkets with shelves of Polish foods, so interviewees had less opportunity to purchase Polish products than people in Bristol, Frome or Trowbridge. The research sample is only small, but the Bath interviewees did therefore seem to be more likely to compromise.

Different members of the same family could naturally have different attitudes about what they wanted to eat. As Evergeti and Zontini observe, relationships within families evolve during the process of negotiating ethnic identity abroad and the two processes are interlinked.[21] For example, Malwina commented on how her husband's tastes had changed after working with English people for four years:

Sometimes my husband buys takeaways. When my husband first came to England he didn't like chips or mayonnaise. But now he eats chips, he eats mayonnaise, I'm amazed. Things he wouldn't eat and didn't like in Poland, now he eats them in England. Kebabs!

At the same time, however, Malwina was a full-time housewife and she cooked as she had done in Poland, making time-consuming dishes out of fresh ingredients. In families where the wife had left paid employment in Poland to become a housewife in England, this placed a special responsibility on her to (consciously or unconsciously) uphold the family's ethnic identity, even if the husband was the person who seemed more attached to Polish food and the wife was prepared to make some compromises.

Anne: Do you buy Polish food?

Monika: We buy it as well.

Anne: So mostly not?

Monika: Mostly not.

Piotr: We buy Polish meat.

Monika: It depends. If it's macaroni, or tomato puree, or jams, then more often English. Milk is milk.

Anne: But you cook Polish dishes?

Monika: Yes.

Anne: And a real dinner?

Monika: Yes, because you need to. I suppose it depends on the home. I was always taught that dinner should be a big meal. When the boys come back from school and Piotr from work they want something hot to eat. Those ready meals [*fastfoody*], well, we eat them sometimes, but somehow it's not the same....And it's cheaper to cook your own food.

Piotr: And Polish food is nicer. Perhaps English people don't like it, but I've heard that English people buy Polish sausages and cake.

Monika: Sometimes we like to try something different, too.

When interviewees talked about 'English' food, I often wondered what they meant, given that British people eat such a variety of dishes from around the world. Monika's comment makes plain that, to her, English food is the ready meals found on supermarket shelves. Rabikowska and Burrell also report that among their respondents 'English cuisine [was] regarded as unhealthy and over-processed'.[22] This probably explains Barbara's assertion that she cooked Polish food because she "did not like English food". Given that most interviewees had no British friends and did not eat at British houses, they could only form their impressions of normal home cooking from what they saw in the shops or ate in workplace canteens, and from their children's schoolfriends who sometimes asked for chips when faced with *pierogi* (dumplings). Polish food, as defined against its 'opposite', is therefore identified with painstaking home cooking.[23]

> Anne: But could you cook English food?
>
> Agnieszka: Oh, *no*! That's not food for us.... Polish cooking is really delicious.... In Poland there always has to be soup and then a second course. I don't know what people cook for dinner in England. We have a proper dinner every day and you're preparing it from morning onwards.

The Polish community

The phrase 'ethnic community' can be understood in various ways. Used loosely, the term 'community' might just refer to the fact that a sizeable number of Poles live in a certain location abroad. When Hanna came to Trowbridge in 2006, for example, she felt that she was coming into a Polish community. "I didn't see a difference, at the beginning. I felt good because I was surrounded by Poles. I didn't feel I was in a foreign country … and today I still feel the same way." Hanna's sentiment illustrates how even in 2006 there was already a critical mass of Poles in Trowbridge. Since Hanna's husband had been one of a hundred Poles recruited to work in a local meat factory in the summer of 2004 he had a large circle of acquaintances, so it was not surprising that she was able to come to England and feel that she was still in Poland. Trowbridge in fact already had a Polish community consisting of Second World War servicemen and their descendants, with a Polish priest, club and Saturday school, and since 2000 it has been twinned with the city of Elbląg in northern Poland.[24] This twinning arrangement, with the energetic participation of members of the established Polish community, played a role in encouraging the most recent wave of Polish migrants to Trowbridge, although more important was the presence of factories needing migrant labour and recruitment agencies ready to bring in Polish workers. West Wiltshire, the small county of which Trowbridge is the county town, has a particularly high percentage of A8 migrants (estimated at 1.5% of the population), whereas Bath and Bristol are more average (0.5% and 0.7% respectively).[25]

The Polish community in Bath is a new phenomenon, as illustrated by Katarzyna's and Marzena's contrasting experiences on their arrivals in the city in 2006 and 2008:

> It was horrible, really. I wanted to go home, if I could, I'd have gone home at once. A completely different culture, different people. (Katarzyna, Bath, arrived autumn 2006)

> I already knew lots of Polish people because I'd met them when I came on holiday to see my husband....Then last Christmas we had a joint Christmas Eve supper [at the Saturday School] and I met lots of people. And now I'm meeting more and more all the time. I've met lots through the Saturday School. (Marzena, Bath, arrived summer 2008)

Local parents, who see each other at Polish masses and/or are participants in the social networking site *Nasza Klasa*, did already have a sense of which other families lived in Bath. However, with the founding of the Saturday School in autumn 2008 disparate families acquired an institutional collective identity and a sense of 'critical mass'. This was not achieved by a short-lived parent and toddler group (2007–08) that collapsed largely because attendance was so irregular.[26] By contrast, the Saturday School, two years old by summer 2010, created a feeling of continuity. Bristol is like Trowbridge in that it had a Polish community dating back to the 1940s, with a church, Saturday school and club. In recent years the Polish church has been active in trying to help new migrants,[27] and the number of Polish businesses and institutions has expanded. For example, Bristol gained its own Polish website (Polski-Bristol), community radio (Radiowski), a second Saturday school and at least two groups for Polish mothers and small children, as discussed later in the chapter. None of the towns has a 'Polish quarter', although some districts of Bristol have higher proportions of Polish residents than others.[28] All the interviewees and their husbands, if they were employed, were working for non-Polish employers or were self-employed. They were not part of an ethnic business enclave.

However, 'community' is about more than size and the presence of formal institutions. First, it implies a certain commonality. As Garapich observes, 'for the majority of British society, Poles constitute a homogeneous ethnic group',[29] but as Garapich also illustrates, UK Poles are often at pains to point out – to themselves and others – the actual diversity of Polish society in the UK. There is often a sense of distance between the established émigré community and more recently arrived migrants.[30] Moreover, as already suggested, differences in educational background and English language knowledge among the new Polish migrant population also lead to very different experiences of life in the UK.

Used broadly, the term 'community' could imply a quality of relations between Poles, a sense of solidarity. This is not to be taken for granted: émigré communities are always subject to competing tensions and there are many reasons why they should not be cohesive. These include pressure on migrants to assimilate with the receiving society, competition between migrants for jobs and the stressfulness of migration which may make households turn in on themselves and feel they do not have the time or energy for socialising outside their close family networks. On the other hand, there are unifying forces, which do induce a sense of solidarity among migrants. These include a desire for co-ethnic friends when it is hard to find friends in the receiving community, a practical need to share information, the role of certain individuals in the community who actively promote such affirmation by building formal migrant organisations and so forth.

New migrants often have rather limited social capital, in the sense of being able to ask for help from friends, or friends of friends. Hence the importance of solidarity based on shared ethnicity. 'Solidarity goes with weak social ties when individual or collective actors feel closely bound to religious, ethnic, national and other symbolic ties.'[31] Ideally, therefore, sharing a strong sense of Polish identity should encourage community in the wider sense. Migrants should be able to call on fellow Poles for help. If being a migrant often implies the deliberate maintenance of a sense of ethnic identity, the desire to affirm ethnic identity in a collective setting may promote displays of solidarity. A rhetoric of 'helping one's own' can create a sense that the community exists even if individual co-ethnics do not, in practice, always prove to be helpful. It creates expectations about helpfulness to co-ethnic strangers.[32]

The assumption that ethnic communities will display solidarity is one which is often made, yet deeply problematic.[33] Portes and Sensenbrenner suggest that:

> The more distinct a group is in terms of phenotypical or cultural characteristics from the rest of the population, the greater the level of prejudice associated with these traits, and the lower the probability of exit from this situation, then the stronger the sentiments of in-group solidarity among its members and the higher the appropriable social capital based on this solidarity.[34]

Poles in the UK today do not meet these criteria and in fact it is striking that Poles often engage in a rhetoric of not expecting to be helped, summed up in the phrase 'Poles are like wolves to one another' (*Polak Polakowi wilkiem*). This supposed behaviour is frequently mentioned by Polish migrants.[35] A high degree of connectedness to the Polish nation in the abstract – as for example evidenced in the survey data quoted at the beginning of this chapter – coexists with a considerable capacity to criticise fellow Poles. As already mentioned (see Chapter Four), Poles in Poland, like Poles abroad, are also positively mistrustful of Polish strangers, although perhaps they are becoming slightly more trusting in recent years. The CRONEM 2005-06 study of Poles in London found that:

> … criticism of fellow Poles was one of the interviews' most striking features. This criticism is made even more interesting since the

interviews indicated that the vast majority of migrants maintained close ties with Poles in both the UK and Poland and are embedded ... within Polish networks, both socially and economically. This combination of discursive hostility ... and ethnic cooperation became one of the main focuses of our analysis.[36]

The recent history of Polish migration is probably an important factor contributing to the atmosphere of hostility towards fellow Poles abroad, since being illegal is almost bound to exacerbate mistrust of all kinds. Grzymała-Kazłowska, for example, writing about undocumented Polish workers in Brussels in the 1990s, charted a progression from cooperation to competition, as more and more Poles arrived and competed for the available jobs.[37] In Grajewo, Alicja also mentioned her cousin's experience of cut-throat competition among Poles in Belgium (in the early 1990s). In Germany, host to many thousands of Polish seasonal workers, similar phenomena apparently occur. Grażyna, from Grajewo, commented about her own experience working on a German farm: "It was only Poles working there, I couldn't say how many, they kept changing, but there were huge numbers of Poles. And they were very competitive and did each other down.... If someone accepted lower pay than the rest, he would keep his job there." In London, too, before EU accession, Jordan and Düvell[38] uncovered 'unrestrained competition' among Polish workers and a tendency to be positively unhelpful towards one another. Iwona from Sanok told a similar story about her time in London before 2004:

> It's so unpleasant that we Poles don't know how to help one another, like other nationalities. There is so much envy among Poles – one person has a better job, the other one is worse off, but I'm not going to help you, I'd rather you were worse off. I don't know why we are like that. I've noticed other people, Ukrainians and Czechs for example, help each other, for example, if I don't have a job, someone will help me find one. But Poles aren't like that – though perhaps they are more helpful to their own family.

In Sanok, with its pre-2004 tradition of migration to London, such images live on:

> Polish people, sometimes, well, as they say, it can be better to among foreigners. Because a Pole could be out to get you because he says 'you're earning more money and I'm getting worse money and you only just came'. (Grażyna, Sanok)

> When they go abroad, it turns out that Poles are not good-natured people. (Danuta, Sanok)

However, where Poles can work legally and there is less pressure on jobs, perhaps there is sometimes a more relaxed atmosphere and the potential for more actual collaboration (contrary to Portes and Sensenbrenner's suggestion). Garapich suggests that 'it was essentially the lack of freedom of mobility and participation caused by immigration restrictions before enlargement that contributed to Poles' sense of insecurity and led to these "Darwinian" life strategies. Illegality in this period impeded not only their job prospects but also their ability to forge ties'.[39]

My interviewees, who had all arrived after 2004, did not tell stories about cut-throat competition. Nonetheless, they often made suspicious comments about other Poles, perhaps because the image of the rival migrant lives on, but often implying that the problem lay in Poland and even in the Polish national character:

> There is such envy, such jealousy, when someone is successful. Perhaps because it is the same in Poland.... In Poland if your neighbour sees you bought something [he doesn't have], he's so envious, so jealous. [I bought a car recently because I need it to drive to work and when people meet me they say] 'You've got *two* cars?! You must be pretty rich!'

> On the whole I try to keep a distance from other Poles.... Poles are unpleasant.... 'He's bought a car, she's working illegally, how come they could afford this, why do they have that?'

It is embarrassing to see fellow nationals behaving inappropriately abroad and some studies have shown how Poles in the UK and Ireland are embarrassed by Poles who, for example, shout or swear in public. Bobek's work in Dublin suggests that there is a class dimension, as middle-class Poles try to distance themselves from people they regard as uncouth villagers.[40] However, only one of my UK interviewees mentioned feeling this kind of embarrassment. Of course, many interviewees were themselves villagers – although far from uncouth – so snobbishness of this type was not so likely to be a problem.

Most often, criticism of fellow Poles is not about behaviour, but simply a lament that there is not a great deal of collaboration and that Polish migrants split into separate sub-groups rather than forming a coherent community. Perhaps, as Grzymała-Kazłowska observed in the case of Brussels, there is more camaraderie among relatively small groups of newcomers. For example, Hanna's husband reminisced fondly about the hippy-like existence of the pioneers in 2004 and commented that Polish people in Trowbridge were not so nice nowadays (in late 2007). The community in Trowbridge had rapidly become so large that it could not remain united. In Bath, a similar trend could be observed. One interviewee commented that although all the local Poles knew one another, after mass people split up into their little friendship groups. She did not think there was a sense of community, and concluded by generalising about all Poles: "probably Poles all the same don't stick together in the same way as people from other countries".

However, interviews and conversations with local Poles provided many examples of mutual help between members of the Polish community. Places with particularly large concentrations of Poles, for example the bus company or the further education college in Bath, are also centres for information and support. I was often told of instances where bus drivers had helped one another out with advice, particularly in the early days preceding and following family reunification. For example, Patrycja reported that "My husband found out [in advance of our arrival], he asked people he knew who had children what benefits you could get, whether there would be problems finding a flat, things like that." Marzena's husband found a school for their son by asking other fathers he knew at work. Renata, also married to a bus driver, commented: "People say Poles don't help each other but they do in the sense of sharing information. So that's how they find schools." The bus drivers also provided social support: for example, Patrycja said that her husband had been very unhappy after he first arrived, but immediately commented on how he had made friends with lots of Poles. Bristol interviewees told similar stories about being helped by fellow Poles. For example, when, shortly after her arrival, Eliza needed to find a cheap garage, she turned to the parents of the only other Polish child in her son's class at school. Rafał explained that he had found his new job (in 2009) through his wife's hairdressing clients.

Simply having Polish friends and being able to socialise with them is important both for individuals and also for creating a sense that there is a Polish community. Having Polish friends compensates for not having English ones. Friends are especially important when parents and siblings are in Poland. These friends are almost always new ones: it was unusual, among the UK interviewees, to know other families locally before arrival, although the Sanok interviews suggested that it would be different for a Sanok family moving to London.

> Monika: We have quite a circle of Polish friends. When people ask us, Poles, whether we are on our own in Bristol, I say no, we have a group of friends, we meet up. If we were here on our own we wouldn't like to stay here, not for a long time, because sitting at home on your own, well, but if you can meet up with people, have a chat, well, we do have friends.
>
> Anne: Where can you meet people?
>
> Monika: At church, in the shop.
>
> Anne: A Polish one?
>
> Monika: No, or well, yes, there too, but now there are lots of Poles. Lidl is near our house, you hear Polish all the time there. At the playground there are sometimes Polish mothers.

Now there is a critical mass of Poles in each town it becomes possible for people to pick and choose their friends, and to decide how many friends to have: interviewees mentioned having their particular 'circle of friends', some circles naturally being larger than others. Several interviewees also mentioned that they had formed close friendships. These were people with whom they could talk freely, who would never refuse assistance and who could be depended on, for example to help with childcare.

For some interviewees, Saturday schools and toddler groups were a particular source of friends. At the same time, these institutions performed many other functions, maintaining Polish identity and creating a sense of a 'home from home'. Sending a child to a Saturday school requires a certain financial investment (several hundred pounds a year if there is more than one child and/or bus fares).[41] Nonetheless, thousands of Polish parents in the UK choose to send their children to such schools and the number has more than doubled over the years 2004–09, with 90 schools in 2009.[42] Saturday schools teach not only Polish language, but also history, geography, religious studies and music, as well as organising festivals and other cultural activities and entertainment. Some parents may have aspirations to keep their children sufficiently well-informed to be able to integrate back into Polish schools if necessary, and the head of the new Saturday school founded in 2007 in Bristol hoped that his school could facilitate this.[43] My interviewees often seemed to have given up hope that their children would be able to return to school in Poland, but nonetheless made comments about the value of history and geography lessons for maintaining a sense of Polishness. Patrycja, for example, expressed the opinion that "History, or Polish language are basic things, which a child – those are his roots – he should know something about them." For many interviewees the main point of the school was for small children to learn to write in Polish and for older children to not lose contact with the written language, particularly spelling.

In Bath the organisers of the Saturday School (founded in autumn 2008, with about 30 children) have a specific mission to create a sense of Polish community in the town, where previously there had been no Polish community institutions at all. However, this is a community that nestles within the wider community of Bath residents and the school deliberately reaches out to that wider community. The school's aims included 'support for newly arrived parents, but especially help [for] their children who often feel lost and lonely'. The school also 'would like parents to be involved and actively participate in school's activities, so their sense of belonging to the local community will be increased'. Furthermore, 'we want to show to our English friends and neighbours the rich Polish culture and our traditions by organising school events'.[44] Activities during the first year included a communal Christmas Eve dinner, a whole-day festival to celebrate Constitution Day, with a children's concert, Polish dinner, games (for example, to test knowledge of Polish geography), music, a barbecue and other activities, outings to local attractions such as the theatre and safari park, a children's ball and visits by representatives of the NHS and other local services and officials, including the mayor and Fire Brigade.[45] The school has affiliated with the Federation of Poles of Great Britain to form a Bath Polish Association. It is seen as a point of contact by the local authority, police force and so forth, in part precisely because the 'Polish community' in Bath is so amorphous and otherwise hard to contact.

In Bristol, the Polish Family Club has a similar mission both to be Polish and at the same time to promote interaction with the wider local community. To quote the website:

> 'I've got two small boys myself and for a long time I looked for a place where I'd feel relaxed and at home [*jak u siebie*]. Because I didn't find that place, I decided to create it,' says Magda Kowalik-Malcolm, the club's initiator and founder. The meetings are a chance to swap ideas about caring for children and bringing them up, but also to have a rest from everyday routine and to meet new people.

Another page of the website lists the club's additional activities, activities which include collaboration with the local NHS (for example, health promotion and providing information regarding interpreters and complaints procedures against doctors), evening social activities (to give mothers a break) and:

> ... organising multicultural events in collaboration with Barton Hill Settlement [like a Polish House of Culture]. During these events we have the opportunity to represent Polish culture and to learn about the culture and traditions of other peoples.[45]

One of the interviewees who attended the club commented:

> They're really nice people. There's such a friendly atmosphere. Sometimes in Poland there's an atmosphere of mutual envy. Since I've come to England I haven't noticed that. Perhaps it's just the people I know. But the meetings are terrific.

Conclusion

> I feel at home here, relaxed about things.... When we are on holiday we live in our own house in Poland. East West, home's best. Whether it's England or Poland.[46] (Jolanta, Bath)

Jolanta's comments suggest a happy transnational existence, the ability to feel at home in both Poland and England. As this chapter has illustrated, there are indeed many ways in which interviewees successfully kept a foot in both countries. Using 'integration' not as a synonym for 'assimilation' but as a state of combining elements of new and old identities, this chapter has explored aspects of making a Polish home in the UK and constructing a Polish identity in the UK within the context of local Polish communities. Interviewees regularly engaged in 'transnational' activities: doing Polish things in the UK that helped maintain their sense of being Polish. They cooked Polish food, socialised with other Poles, sent their children to Polish supplementary schools (Saturday schools), telephoned back to Poland and so forth. Probably much of the time this was not a deliberate exercise in identity building, but nonetheless the outcome was to reinforce feelings of being '100% Polish'. Reflecting their individual personalities, interviewees expressed their Polish identity in different ways.

However, people are not completely free agents when it comes to choosing how Polish they will be in the UK. Households possess different resources and a shortage of money, time, childcare or transport can all restrict access to transnational activities (just as they can restrict access to engaging with the non-Polish community). Moreover, there were situations in which some interviewees had little choice but to do things the Polish way, as, for example, when their family members expected them to provide Polish food. In particular, many women complained that although they would have liked to have had British friends and to watch English-language television, their limited knowledge of English meant that they spent their leisure time in a Polish-language environment. The outcome of these various constraints was that transnational activities did not necessarily constitute a happy ending and guarantor of settlement.

The chapter has examined different dimensions of homemaking. Feeling at home depends largely on being comfortable in one's physical home, and here the interviewees found themselves in various situations. Almost everyone lived in private rented accommodation, but there was a big difference between people on six-month contracts who could never put down roots, and those who were becoming more settled. Even more importantly, 'home' is being with one's (nuclear) family. The families in the study had reunited precisely in order to achieve this state and in some cases they had done so. Particularly where the wife did not work, or only worked part time, families could spend more time together than they had often done in Poland. The mother's presence at home also guaranteed that there would be a 'proper dinner' and a tidy house. There was a return to traditional gender roles which was to some extent welcome but which, as illustrated in Chapter Eight, could also be frustrating and unsettling. In other cases both spouses were working long hours, often coordinated so that they could share the childcare, with the effect that they met only in passing. In several particularly extreme cases, the couples were also seriously considering return to Poland, and there was a circular causation, since the reason they were prepared to sacrifice their home life was because the arrangement was seen as being quite temporary.

Feeling at home was often also said to encompass being with one's extended family. All the interviewees kept in close contact with relatives back in Poland by telephone and the internet and many families had relatives who came to visit, sometimes for extended periods. Parents and grandparents were living in some households on a temporary, part-time or permanent basis. Since interviewees tended to feel very close emotionally to their extended families, their presence was important to helping interviewees feel at home in England. No doubt, too, a sense of being at home is induced by playing the role of 'host' rather than 'guest'. By the same token, people whose extended families were still in Poland felt less comfortable in their new homes and sometimes quite insecure, wondering what would happen if one spouse fell ill. It was not to be taken for granted that relatives would want to settle in the UK, particularly migrants' parents who were still of working age and had many ties to keep them in Poland. Moreover, there were interviewees who themselves could not afford to travel very often, as discussed in Chapter Ten.

A particularly important transnational activity for many parents was sending their children to Polish Saturday school. As with buying food and having guests, there were financial costs that not everyone could afford, but many parents felt quite strongly that children needed formal tuition in order to acquire or keep intact their knowledge of written Polish. To some parents, history and geography lessons were also important for constructing their children's Polish identities. Saturday schools, like Polish parent and toddler groups, have functions for parents themselves, since they provide opportunities to meet other parents and to organise and participate in events such as Polish days and Polish dinners which keep alive a sense of Polish identity as well as being an opportunity to host members of the non-Polish community. They are also a link to UK service providers, since the NHS and police see them as ways to access the wider Polish community. This is a good example of how transnational activities can combine successfully with integration on the local community level.

Furthermore, the fact that new Polish community organisations are being created and running successfully goes some way towards dispelling Polish expectations that Poles abroad will not help each other, although interviewees in both countries did talk about lack of solidarity between Poles in emigration. There is a difference, however, between lack of solidarity and simple fragmentation, and to some extent complaints about the actual Polish 'communities' in England were less about lack of community spirit and more about the fact that there were disparate sub-groups of local Poles. Looked at more positively, the existence of sub-groups within the community testifies to the fact that by 2009 there was a sufficient number of Poles even in Bath for interviewees to be able to choose their friends. By 2009 (unlike in 2006) they all had Polish friends. Many described having a 'circle of friends' and some had close friends. Friends both provided emotional support and were important sources of information, compensating for interviewees' shortage of ties to the British community. Monika's comment, quoted earlier, that if they did not have friends, they would go home, probably reflects the feelings of many interviewees. Next to their children's happiness and good progress at school, their social lives often seemed to be the most satisfying aspect of being in the UK.

Notes

[1] The actual complexities are well reflected in the title (and content) of Rychard et al (2006) *Poland: One or many?* as well as numerous other works, notably Tadeusz Konwicki's novel *The Polish complex.*

[2] Just six of the 72 interviewees said they would not work abroad because of patriotism. Even these interviewees sometimes sounded embarrassed to make such a connection.

[3] See Garapich (2009). Of course this is far from being a uniquely Polish phenomenon.

[4] A third of UK interviewees were contacted through Saturday schools, which might have meant that they were especially concerned with preserving children's ethnic identity. However, the remaining two thirds expressed similar sentiments.

[5] Pierik (2004, p 524).

[6] An important exception is their desire to maintain their children's proficiency in Polish, as discussed later in this chapter.

[7] Wiles (2008, p 117).

[8] For discussion of 'home', including 'home' as constructed by migrants, see, for example, Blunt and Dowling (2006); Webster (1998); Parutis (2006); Parutis (2009).

[9] Anon (1998, p 3).

[10] Feminist scholars in particular have pointed out that perspectives on home are highly gendered and that conventional images of home as haven reflect masculine expectations. See Blunt and Dowling, (2006, pp 14-21).

[11] See, for example, Tolia-Kelly (2004).

[12] See Rabikowska and Burrell (2009, pp 213-14) for a discussion of luggage brought from Poland.

[13] Robinson (2007, p 105).

[14] Burrell (2008, p 27).

[15] For a discussion of constraints on using electronic communications in the sending countries, see Panagakos and Horst (2006).

[16] Palloni et al (2001, p 1264).

[17] Baldassar (2007).

[18] Cf the West European migrants of varying ages discussed by Ackers (2004). Some of the interviewees worried about caring responsibilities in the long term and, as Chapter Seven argued, the problem of a 'care gap' already exists in Poland.

[19] For more detailed discussion, see Rabikowska and Burrell (2009), especially page 220.

[20] The Polish Family Club in Bristol published a menu of showcase dishes on the occasion of the Polish Dinner it cooked for the local community in 2009: see www.klub-rodzinny.bristol.org.pl/Polski_Klub_Rodzinny_Bristol/Aktualnosci/Entries/2009/6/2_Wielokulturowa_uczta_-_Polski_Obiad.html

[21] Evergeti and Zontini (2006, p 1026).

[22] Rabikowska and Burrell (2009, p 220).

[23] See Smith and Jehlička (2007) for a discussion of attitudes to wholesome food in Poland and the Czech Republic.

[24] Technically, it is the five largest towns of West Wiltshire put together that are twinned with Elbląg, because the latter is a major city, population 126,500. The link came about because Elbląg was twinned with Leer, Trowbridge's twin town in Belgium. See www.trowbridge.gov.uk/towninfo.asp?id=108

[25] Pollard et al (2008, pp 63, 67, 65). *Nasza Klasa* membership also gives an indication of how many Poles live in each location. On 10 September 2009 the figures were Bath 716 and Trowbridge 570. Bristol had too many to list (www.nasza-klasa.pl).

[26] This is normal for such groups, but there was a particularly 'migrant' aspect to the attendance problem, since members went back to Poland for extended holidays, at different times of year, and at least one went back for good. Source: personal observation.

[27] See, for example, Audit Commission (2007).

[28] See Dallas (2007, pp 10-11) for the number of Poles living in different Bristol postcode areas.

[29] Garapich (2008c, p 133).

[30] Garapich (2008c).

[31] Faist (2000, p 110).

[32] For example, Albanian migrants to the UK from former Yugoslavia; see Dahinden (2005, p 197).

[33] See, for example, Goulbourne (2006). For a discussion of Poles in London, see Garapich, various years, and Ryan et al (2008).

[34] Portes and Sensenbrenner (1993, p 1329).

[35] See Toruńczyk-Ruiz (2008) for reflections on this paradox in the context of the Netherlands.

[36] Eade et al (2006, p 15).

[37] Grzymała-Kazłowska (2005).

[38] Jordan and Düvell (2003, pp 11-15).

[39] Garapich (2008b, p 747).

[40] Bobek (2009); Garapich (2006, pp 17-18). The CRONEM project, discussed by Garapich, asked 'You travel on the London Underground and there are some drunken Poles talking loudly and swearing. What do you feel?'.

[41] Bath Saturday School fees in 2008-09 were £5 per morning.

[42] Email communication from Aleksandra Podhorecka, Polska Macierz Szkolna, 28 May 2009. Statistics about enrolments are not collected on a national level. Sales et al (2008)'s study of Polish schoolchildren in London found (p 29) that 'all the parents in the study were keen that their children retained and improved their Polish language'.

[43] Interview with Wojciech Nowak, headteacher of the Bristol Saturday School in Fishponds, 15 September 2007.

[44] Polska Szkola Sobotnia im. Jana Pawla II w Bath, 'Dzień Polski: Polish Day, 3 May 2009' (leaflet).

[45] See http://polskaszkolabath.co.uk/galeria.html for a pictorial record of some of these events.

[46] www.klub-rodzinny.bristol.org.pl/Polski_Klub_Rodzinny_Bristol/Witamy.html

[47] 'Wszędzie dobrze, ale u siebie w domu zawsze najlepiej. Czy tu, czy tam.'

TEN

Return to Poland

You can, you can definitely return to Poland!... If someone has gone abroad, they can come back any time. (Emilia, north-east Poland)

They are forever 'just on their way back', but they never manage to return! (Lidia, Wielkopolska, on friends living with children in Germany)

This book explores factors which help determine Polish families' decisions about how long to stay in the UK, and therefore, by implication, whether and when to return to Poland. Chapters Eight and Nine discussed some of the reasons why such families had integrated, or, alternatively, felt excluded and therefore less settled in England. This chapter considers interviewees' opinions about returns, both to live in Poland and for holidays which help shape thoughts about longer-term or permanent return.

The chapter opens with some general thoughts about return migration and then looks more specifically at the scale and patterns of contemporary return migration to Poland. Discussion then turns to interviewees' perceptions about how many people were returning, and the permanence or otherwise of that return. This is followed by an exploration of how migrants think about the duration of their stay, including the changeability of their plans. Finally, and most importantly, the chapter looks at their perceptions of Poland and of their potential livelihoods in Poland as compared to their actual livelihoods in the UK.

Return and migrant mobility

'In most migration theories ... the assumption is that human beings are inherently sedentary.' The origin country is 'the place where one fits in ... and has an unproblematic culture and individual or collective identity'.[1] Return, therefore, is easily visualised in normative terms, as a good thing, the return to normality. This links to the traditional understanding of return as the completion of the migration process. It can be seen as a happy ending, although, since Cerase's influential 1974 article, scholars have often also noted the phenomenon of the 'return of failure'.[2] The Polish interviews suggested that to some extent these perceptions continue, with migration attempts classified as ending either in success or failure. However, migration scholarship today tends to take the opposite approach. The literature on transnationalism, mentioned in Chapter One, draws attention to frequent travel to and fro as a key aspect of 'the multiplicity of migrants' involvements in both the home and host societies'.[3] 'Thanks to the insights of transnationalism and social network theory, return is no longer viewed as the end of the migration cycle; rather, it constitutes one stage in the migration process.'[4]

One of the purposes of this chapter is to explore the extent to which return is really seen as being no different from the original act of migration. Emigration and return are indeed similar in the sense that migrants, coming back to Poland, often have open-ended plans, thinking that they might quite possibly continue to migrate in the future. There are also similarities regarding what Morawska labels the migrant 'toolkit',[5] conventions about how migration should be done, which are equally applicable in either direction, from or to Poland. Given that the interviewees had been in the UK only a few years, it is highly possible that their migration culture would not have changed very much. At the same time, it is likely that return would be different from the original act of migration in at least two traditional respects. First, King, summarising the findings of the return migration literature, suggests that 'non-economic factors generally weigh more heavily in the return decision than do economic factors, certainly in comparison to their role in the original decision to emigrate'.[6] Second, return must also be different from the original act of migration in the sense that returning migrants are (if only slightly) older and wiser; their experience of acculturation abroad means that they return feeling to some extent 'a different person'. This feeling is often accentuated because of the reception given to return migrants by local people, who do not let them forget their migrant identities.[7] Many studies have illustrated the difficulties faced by return migrants in re-integrating into their origin communities. One of the reasons why this chapter explores the significance of visits home is to identify whether these do indeed offer opportunities for friction between stayers and visitors, and what impact this might have on the visitors' desire to return permanently to Poland.

Scale and patterns of Polish return migration

How long migrants will stay abroad is a topic that naturally fascinates the migrants themselves, their families and friends, as well as policy makers and politicians. It is often an emotive subject, partly because there is a strong normative and political dimension, with many Polish and British commentators assuming that return would be 'better'. Polish internet discussion forums, for example, feature participants in Poland taking the line that Poles belong in Poland because Poland is superior, and that the UK has failed Polish migrants. UK-based participants in such discussions often dispute this interpretation, elaborate on the positive sides of their UK experiences and are highly critical of Poland.[8] Since electronic discussions easily deteriorate into slanging matches, one should perhaps avoid assuming that even the participants themselves always feel so passionately about these issues, but at the same time there is clearly some sense in which they do reflect different sections of public opinion. By contrast, the research interviews, which were always calm and non-confrontational, perhaps had the opposite shortcoming, discouraging the expression of extreme views. Nonetheless, it was surely significant that interviewees in Poland very rarely put forward the viewpoint that return was somehow inherently 'better'. Their matter-of-fact approach to the subject was entirely in keeping with their generally pragmatic understanding of migration as an integral part of everyday life, not something alien and suspect.

Partly because return is an emotive topic, it is common to exaggerate the numbers involved. It is impossible to establish the exact scale of the phenomenon. Records are not kept of individual migrants leaving the UK, but the International Passenger Survey (IPS)[9] indicates that since December 2007 more A8 migrants (from the eight East-Central European countries which joined the EU in 2004) have been leaving the UK than have been arriving. The Institute for Public Policy Research estimated in 2008 that half of A8 migrants who arrived after 2004 had already left,[10] and the IPS suggests that the number of returnees (intending to be at their place of return for at least one year) was 66,000 in 2008.[11]

It seems that, at least in the Polish case, many of these returns were planned. A 2009 survey of returnees found that 76% had come back to Poland because they had planned to do so.[12] There is a difference between temporary migrants returning individually when planned, and a sudden wave of returns by people who are cutting short their stay abroad or abandoning intentions to settle because of the economic downturn in 2008-09. Some Polish and many British newspapers have carried headlines suggesting that the latter phenomenon had occurred and that such a mass return was well underway. For example:

'Tide turns as Poles end great migration' (*The Times*, 16 February 2008)[13]

'UK Poles return home' (*Daily Telegraph*, 21 February 2009)[14]

'Great return from the Isles' (*Gazeta Wyborcza*, 14 April 2008)[15]

'Poles return en masse with all their earnings' (*Gazeta Opolska*, 19 August 2008)[16]

'Polonia is bankrupt and fleeing Chicago' (*Dziennik*, 5 March 2009)[17]

In view of Poland's strong economic growth in the years after EU accession, and particularly the good performance of the Polish economy after the onset of the global recession in 2008, journalists – apparently assuming that economic cost-benefit calculations entirely determine migrants' behaviour – asserted that there was no reason for Poles to stay abroad:

As the country slides deeper into recession, the building trade contracts and the pound plummets against the zloty, there is little reason for many of the estimated 700,000 Poles who flocked to Britain after their country joined the EU in 2004 to remain.[18]

However, there seems to be little real evidence that the recession produced this effect. A 2009 survey, under the direction of Krystyna Iglicka, indicated that 'the economic crisis has not, so far, led to mass returns'.[19] A number of Polish media reports in 2008-09 also cast doubts on the reality of the return wave, for example quoting the Polish parliamentary speaker[20] and an official of the Polish Embassy in London to the effect that 'returns are not on a mass scale'.[21] Research in the Republic of Ireland came to the same conclusion.[22]

Assertions about mass returns are sometimes based on opinion polls showing that Poles in the UK hope or intend to return, but such findings are unsurprising. Polish migrants to the UK are hardly unique, since migrants everywhere tend to hope to return, a hope that often leads them to believe that they will. Scholars use the term 'myth of return' to refer to this belief that some day they will return to their home.

The myth of return is conceptualised as the completion of migration. Return is therefore the opposite of emigration. It will be a rest from migration, an opportunity to spend money earned abroad. Media articles and broadcasts, too, tend to present return as final. This chapter argues that return, for Poles in the UK, is not the antithesis of migration, but in many respects just migration in the opposite direction. Therefore, formulating a return migration strategy is little different to forming the original migration strategy. The following list of patterns in return migration, which approximately follows the structure of the chapter, should remind the reader of points already made in the first part of the book, about how and why migrants migrate from Poland to the West.

Patterns in return migration

1) It is unclear how long returnees will stay in Poland (despite the common media assumption that return is final).
   a) Often return is speculative: migrants feel to a greater or lesser degree that they would like to stay in Poland, but at the back or front of their minds is the idea that if they cannot shape a livelihood in Poland it may be possible to return to Western Europe.
   b) 'Double return migration' is common: people are returning to Western Europe from Poland.
   c) For families who had reunified abroad, return can be 'incomplete' in the sense that the family splits up again. Some members go back to Poland, but some remain abroad.
   d) Return may also be 'incomplete' in the sense that an individual spends part of the year in Poland and part in the West.
2) Decisions about return are made on the basis of *comparisons* between life in the UK and imagined future life in Poland.

a) However, this is not simply a question of weighing up economic costs and benefits in each location: emotional costs and benefits are also very important.

b) Decisions have to be negotiated between household members who may have different opinions about return. Chapter Eight argued that individual family members can become caught up in vicious or virtuous integration circles and these help contribute to differences of opinion. If a stalemate is reached, it is likely that the family will remain in the UK.

3) Migrants prefer to migrate to places where they have something already fixed up, which often means returning to their home locality.

a) The economy of that specific location is very important, given that some parts of Poland are flourishing more than others.

b) Employment and housing are important but so are emotional factors.

c) However, information about all of these factors may be of different qualities and images and preconceptions are important; for some migrants, there is a fear of return.

d) Decisions may be made in response to persuasion from friends and family back in Poland.

4) Inspection visits can be part of the return migration process.

a) Holidays (probably often subconsciously) function as inspection visits.

b) The quality of the holiday is important: if it is stressful and shows up negative aspects of life in Poland, the migrant is less likely to want to return to Poland for good.

As already suggested, emotional factors are usually considered to be paramount in return migration.[23] Frelak and Roguska's spring 2008 survey of returnees showed that only 3% had been motivated to return by 'improvements in the Polish economy'. The most common reasons for return to Poland were 'homesickness' (36%) and 'family and friends in Poland' (29%).[24] However, Iglicka's February–March 2009 survey, after the onset of recession, found that losing one's job was the reason most commonly cited by respondents (60%; additionally, 40% named 'family reasons', 15% 'inability to find work abroad', 4% 'prospect of better work in Poland', 2% 'had been accompanying spouse abroad' and 9% 'other').[25]

When discussing hierarchies of factors promoting return, it is obviously important to consider characteristics of specific migrants. As Orellana et al observe, migrants' children are more than mere appendages of their parents: 'the presence of the children is central to the families' decision-making processes'.[26] Certain factors are particularly important to families and it is these which will be highlighted in the following discussion. Couples and families are tied in more ways to the receiving community – and often more tightly, if for example, children go to school. Hence it takes more to uproot them: factors encouraging return have to be strong and also multiple. A simple turn in economic fortunes on a national level is unlikely to be enough to dislodge them. Even if one spouse loses his or her job it is not easy for the family to go. As Renata in Bath remarked, a single person can often up and go, saying "Goodbye, England!", but a family does not always have this luxury. Somerville and Sumption, in their 2009 analysis of whether migrants were likely to leave the UK because of recession, also concluded that families were likely to stay.[27] However, perhaps it is not quite fair to see children as a 'burden' in this situation. Orellana et al argue that children's *opportunities* for development are often central to parents' migration livelihood strategies.[28] If return will disrupt such development it is unlikely to be undertaken.

Another recurring theme is that people go back to Poland only to return to the West shortly afterwards. This can be part of a strategy of circular migration, or it can be a double return migration,[29] an unexpected decision to return abroad because of disillusionment arising from the experience of living in Poland again:

> I'm returning to Poland after five years. I'm giving myself one last chance.... But I don't have great expectations. I can always go off again, to Australia, New Zealand or Canada, where I've been offered jobs and visas. So it might be that this is a farewell visit to Poland. (Internet forum participant)[30]

Frelak and Roguska's 2008 study found returnees almost evenly divided between those who planned to stay in Poland, those who planned to go back abroad and those who did not know. Iglicka's 2009 percentages were: Poland 47%, abroad 23%, don't know 30%.[31] In her survey, 37.8% of planned returns were to the UK, 13.3% to Greece and 11.1% to Germany.[32] In some cases, double return migrants go back to the same country where they had been working abroad: 62% of planned returns in Iglicka's survey fell into this category.[33] Other double return migrants try out somewhere new. Given that Germany neighbours Poland and that, until overtaken by the UK very recently, it was the most popular destination for work abroad, it would seem to be an obvious alternative choice. In 2004 the old EU member states were given the option of introducing a seven-year transition period before they had to completely open their labour markets to the new member states: Germany's transition period will therefore expire in 2011, giving Poles open access to work in Germany. Iglicka's study asked whether those returnees who planned to go back abroad, or were not yet sure, would go to work in Germany, if it opened its labour market – 41% said they would, 31% were not sure and 28% said not.[34]

Return: the perspective from Poland

> On the television you hear that lots of people are coming back to Poland. On a mass scale.... But I don't think there are! You can't see it. And there are still people who are going off for the first time. In our region it's not the case that masses of people are coming back. Of course there are situations like everywhere where things didn't work

out for someone and they came home. But not on such a mass scale. I don't think so. (Magda, Sanok, September 2008)

The overwhelming impression from the interviews in Poland was that interviewees did not observe a great wave of return, still less, permanent return. It is true that in Sanok in spring 2008 the job centre had noticed an increase in applications from people who had returned from the UK, Italy and other places in Western Europe in response to newspaper reports that the Polish job market had improved significantly. However, when they realised that the job centre had little to offer, many went back abroad.[35] The only small wave mentioned in Grajewo, in 2009, was of returnees from Iceland, which had been particularly badly affected by the economic downturn. One interviewee guessed that half the people who had worked in Iceland had returned to Grajewo, although other interviewees did not seem to share this opinion and told tales of Grajewans who were staying on. In 2009, some interviewees in Grajewo had friends and family who were still planning to go abroad in the near future – for example, because they had contacts who could find, or had already found them work abroad.

Of course, interviewees' impressions were highly subjective, and their use of language varied: to one person five is 'many', to another 'hardly any'. Several interviewees asserted that people were returning but could not name any of their actual acquaintances who had done so, and it seemed that their impressions were perhaps just from media reports. Although interviewees rarely moralised about migration, there did seem to be some connection between interviewees' overall views on the advisability of migration and their impressions about stay and return. Alicja and Paulina, who were of all the interviewees perhaps the most hostile towards migration, also asserted, in September 2008, that quite a lot of people were returning to Sanok, including families. At the opposite extreme, Celina (Grajewo) who was exceptionally enthusiastic about migration, said (in March 2009) "People don't return from abroad and from what you hear more and more want to go there."

There was also a difference between Sanok and Grajewo: it seemed that there might be more people returning to Sanok, which would be understandable given that interviewees were also slightly more upbeat about the local economy and the fact that the town has better economic indicators (see Chapter Three). In Grajewo some interviewees mentioned individuals – not generally families – who had returned from the USA, usually because of the falling value of the dollar. However, several interviewees also suggested that people returned from the USA only to migrate again, either to the USA or to places in Europe. There was also evidence of European double return migration in both Sanok and Grajewo. For example, Joanna's husband had come back from London to Grajewo in 2008 after working as a builder for seven years because he was finding it hard to get jobs. In March 2009 he was working in Germany, but was not very happy there; hence he was looking for another job in the UK. Although he appreciated the fact that Germany was geographically closer to Grajewo, he said, finishing his sentence in English:

> It's good in England. It's a different way of life. In Germany it's different. Everything's shut. On Sunday everything's shut, all the shops, everything. There's nothing! After work you go home. In England, *finish, go to pub, drink!*

Also in 2009, Edyta told the story of a former colleague who had returned from the USA to Grajewo for emotional reasons but returned to the USA for economic reasons:

> There was a woman who used to work with me, Pani Iwona.... Then she went off to the States. But she said her children couldn't adapt to life in the States. They couldn't get used to the school. And she couldn't cope either.... So, she returned to Poland. But [after a while], when she came to visit us she said 'Girls, this is no life, here in Poland. In the USA.... I could even save money from my wages.... On Sundays I could take the children swimming, I could afford it. But here in Grajewo, if I didn't have those dollars I'd saved, I wouldn't be able to manage.' She lasted out in Poland for three months, then packed her bags and went back to the USA with her children.... Her brother sent her money for the tickets, and off they went.

As Massey et al observe, 'although migrants may begin as target earners seeking to make one trip and earn money for a narrow purpose, after migrating they acquire a concept of social mobility and a taste for consumer goods and styles of life that are difficult to attain through local labour. Once someone has migrated, therefore, he or she is very likely to migrate again.'[36] Interviewees in Poland expressed complete sympathy with migrants who adopted this attitude. For instance, in Grajewo Ewa observed: "If a Pole goes abroad, he gets a taste for it. He earns that money, counts his wages, and compares what he earned in a month abroad, and how much he would have done in Poland."

Perhaps the ideal solution, for some households, is incomplete migration where the migrant is gainfully employed in both Poland and abroad (not, as often happens, unemployed in Poland in between spells of work in the West). For example, Teresa, interviewed in 2007 in Wielkopolska, said her husband was "fed up" with working in Norway while his family remained in Poland and he travelled back and forward every month. He planned to work in Norway for a full three years, then return to live in Poland and after that just work two to three months a year in Norway. Teresa said that since he was a very good housepainter, who was much in demand locally, there would be no problem in finding work back in Poland.

Return: the perspective from the West of England

> A few people are leaving, but there are also a lot who are coming. There
> are more families now. Not men on their own. (Sylwia, February 2009)

Interviewees in England, like their counterparts in Poland, tended to feel that
media reports exaggerated the scale of returns and some pointed out that new
people were still arriving. In general, UK interviewees in 2009 had the impression
that isolated individuals were returning to Poland rather than a whole wave of
people; that families seldom or never returned; and that people who did return
to Poland were quite likely to come back to the West. In Bristol, Dorota, for
example, exploded with indignation:

> Last year there was lots of information on the [Polish] TV and in
> newspapers that masses of Poles were returning from England. It's not
> true. It's not true. Young people return. If they are about 20, those single
> people. They've gone back. But among my friends, people I know, and
> my friends' friends, I'm talking about families, no one has returned. No
> one, absolutely no one. Single people yes, plenty of them have gone.
> But not families.... I've even read articles on the internet and I swear
> they are so misleading, how could they think that so many Poles go
> back! What they write has no connection to reality. Because it's quite
> the opposite. Families stay.

Referring to Bath, Katarzyna said:

> It's a vicious circle, because some people come, others go, they go back
> to Poland thinking they'll stay, and some manage to, but others don't,
> so back they go abroad. That's how it keeps on and on ... I think it's
> just propaganda [*nagonka*] to say people are returning, it's not true.
> People do return to Poland, but they see what it's like, and they come
> back here.... Most people with families stay here in England. Their
> children have started school and somehow they make ends meet....
> If you have the responsibility of supporting a family you can't afford
> to return, just in case [it's impossible to find a decent job in Poland].

Katarzyna's sentiment, that it was risky for a family to attempt return to Poland,
was echoed by other UK interviewees:

> In Poland they lay off workers, too, whole factories are laying off
> people.... If the entire family is in England and the child goes to
> school and [at least] one parent has work on a contract, then they
> stay put. (Jagoda)

> Some people do go back. From Piotr's workplace someone last year, and a couple of people more recently, and in our group of friends we also hear about people going back. My friend, whose children are five and seven, has decided to go back with her daughters. They've bought a ticket for the end of August. And only her husband will stay. But I'm a bit surprised because … they don't have a flat in Poland and they won't live with their parents and they say they are going to rent a flat. It's a hard way to return. They don't have any security. People are different. I personally like to get things arranged, not to go somewhere with nothing fixed up [*w ciemno*]. (Monika)

As Monika's account indicates, sometimes families split up, returning to the model of just the breadwinner earning money abroad, rather than taking the risk of both spouses trying to shape new livelihoods in Poland. In other cases, planned reunifications in the UK are postponed or cancelled:

> Some people are going back to Poland, and some people are coming to England. I don't know. All I can say is that I have one friend who went back because he lost his job in England and was able to fix up work in Poland. His family is in Poland and if he hadn't lost his job they would have joined him in the UK. Among my friends he's the only case. Because the rest of my friends say they'll stay, at least for the time being they mean to stay. Of course, all sorts of things can happen in life. (Wanda)

My impression from conversations I heard among local Poles in 2008–09 was that return was 'in the air', a topic of conversation and general interest, and that because of this people speculated about their own potential for return, often in a joking way. Only two or three interviewees or their family members appeared to have seriously contemplated return because of the crisis, but afterwards even they had second thoughts. Bernadeta's boyfriend was one of those who had contemplated return, then changed his mind:

> My brother did want to come to England recently, but we told him it's too hard to get work, it's not worth helping him to come….The worst thing is the job situation [in Bristol].We personally haven't felt it because my boyfriend and I both work, but in general you can see it's hard….Though it seems to me that people [who are already here] are just sticking out the difficult time….They used to earn more, you could do more overtime, now it's hard, but they stay put…. Last year [my boyfriend] was thinking of returning, but he changed his mind … because of the recession, he thought it would be bad in Poland too. The job situation got a bit better in Poland last year but then it got worse again. It's hard, there's no sense going back. (Bernadeta)

Maria also hinted that they might have gone home, since earlier in the year her husband's employer had seemed on the brink of collapse and she had only very part-time work:

> People waited it out. If they had savings, they waited. But it would have been hard for us to wait if Rafał had completely lost his job! It's easier if you don't have children, those couples or single people, they earn £800–£1,000 and just have to pay rent on their room. And the rest they can spend. So it's easier for them to save.

It was her impression, by June 2009, that the worst of the crisis was over: there was more work coming into the agencies. Hence people had 'waited it out' successfully. The UK interviewees could also tell cautionary tales about how poorly returnees were faring in Poland. The verb they used to describe returnees 'living' in Poland was *siedzi*, 'sitting', which implies staying, rather than living. You 'sit' in prison, or abroad. For example, 'He's sitting in the USA' (*on siedzi w Ameryce*) is a phrase commonly heard in Grajewo. It implies that he may have been there a long time, but is not going to live in the USA for ever. The fact that UK-based interviewees made comments like "he's sitting in Warsaw" spoke volumes about their expectations that this was only a temporary return.

Malwina described why, in the only case she knew of a family who had gone back, the return might not be permanent. They had returned because the wife was unemployed, they had two tiny children and the husband had only agency work in Bristol:

> But I think they're finding it hard. He phoned me and said [he had a job] for 1,500 zl … and they live in Warsaw, it's expensive there, and he said they would probably come back here. I don't know. Because he adored it here, he really liked it, so it was hard for him to go back to Poland. You get used to it. He liked going sightseeing, travelling round everywhere. He adored it. He misses it, [now] that he had to go back to Poland.

In keeping with Iglicka's suggestion that often returnees go home because they had poor English and never integrated, Dominika said that Poles who returned to Poland were those who had just come to earn something and did not bother to learn English, hence did not feel at home in England. They might go back to Poland, but then they tended to re-emigrate after six months or so. Her impression was that the second time, they were more serious about learning the language and they began to think about staying for a long time. Double return migrants, in her opinion, realised the need to 'break through the linguistic, religious and cultural barriers' which had prevented their integration on their first visit. Predictably, an extra twist, mentioned by some interviewees, was that households could argue about the wisdom of double return migration. Husbands and wives could have quite opposite views.

UK interviewees' thoughts about their own return

Although none of the UK interviewees had changed their plans and decided to return to Poland, many of them had changed them in the opposite direction, staying on in England longer than they had originally expected to do. Sometimes they gave the impression of being at the mercy of fate:

> When we came here, it was for two years and then to go back. Those two years have stretched out [into five].... It'll be 20 years before we return! (Agnieszka)

> The time has flown by somehow. Who knows where and how? It's almost three years! (Sylwia)

Eade et al distinguish between 'hamsters' (who save up as much as they can as fast as they can, spend as little as possible and go home) and 'stayers'.[37] The interviewees tended to divide into these categories, either saying that they wanted to save for a house and go home quickly, or that they were probably staying for a long time. However, the 'hamsters' frequently also stated reasons why they might actually stay longer than originally anticipated. For example, in 2006 Kinga specified "five years maximum" very emphatically, but later in the interview said it would depend on the economic situation in Poland: she certainly would not go back if it was the same as now. Sylwia, interviewed in 2007, said that at first they thought they might go back in five or six years and there was a time quite recently when she had felt determined to return. They had changed their minds because they were so depressed by the politics and economics of Poland. "Poland would have to change" for the family to go back. Overall, there seemed to be a trend for hamsters to turn into stayers: not stayers 'for ever', but for an undetermined period. The provisional quality of these 'decisions' is encapsulated in Anna's comment, quoted at the head of Chapter One: "For the time being we've chosen England".

Changing plans implies missing deadlines set for return:

> We have some friends in Bristol with their own house in Poland. And they live in Bristol. They're always just about to return, just about to return, just one more year, just one more, just one more. And so they keep on putting it off. My impression is, if someone has a steady job in England ... [particularly] if both parents work, it's hard to leave. (Malwina)

Sometimes, like Agnieszka, the interviewees themselves had set down specific time limits ("two years and then go back"). In other cases, family members did the same. For example, Aneta was asked by her small son to name a time limit for their stay in Bristol. She said two years, after which he said he felt better about staying, although when I interviewed Aneta they had actually been in England for longer.

Plans can change for financial reasons, typically because it takes longer than expected to earn the necessary money to pay off Polish debts or to save for a house. Aneta, for example, was saving for a house. However, Agnieszka and her family stayed on in Bath even after they had purchased a flat in Poland. This was not because they had definitely decided to stay. She asserted "We are torn in two. That's the worst thing. . . . We don't know whether to go back or to stay." At one point in the interview she made the following statements, all in one go:

> It's easier to live in England. Well, why should we go back to Poland, to a worse life? Of course not. Although you do miss Poland the whole time. As I said, I'd like to pack up and go home. Although after five years I also miss England [when I'm in Poland]. We've got used to it a bit, here in England.

Agnieszka also pointed out that badly wanting to go home was a feeling that flared up from time to time, prompted by some news from home, such as a wedding that they would not be able to attend, or by a feeling of depression. "My husband sometimes says 'How I wish I was in Poland' but then after a few days we just go back to our normal way of life here and we don't feel like going back." Bożena (with three children and two jobs) told a similar story. She mentioned various reasons why the family should stay in Bath, but also confessed that sometimes she felt like changing her mind: "There are days when you are completely fed up with everything."

Times of economic crisis also promote mood swings, including upswings:

> The fact that the pound is weak does make people hesitate [about staying] because there's that separation from your relatives in Poland and the money doesn't go so far. But as soon as the pound goes up morale rises at once! (Edyta)

As indicated earlier in this book, decisions to migrate are always made on the basis of comparisons between the two locations concerned. To pessimists, such comparisons can be between two evils; for optimists, the reverse is true. Some UK interviewees seemed to be staying in England largely because of a perception that there was 'nothing to go back to' in their home town or village; their livelihoods in England might not be very successful, but at least they could make a living in the UK, which they did not think was possible in Poland. Other interviewees emphasised the positive aspects of their jobs and lives in England, but also spoke affectionately about Poland: being in England suited them better, for the time being, but this did not mean that they spoke negatively about Poland. Their identities as optimists or pessimists were quite important factors in shaping their plans, since they had to try to imagine the situation in the future. In most people's perceptions, the situation could change in either country. Katarzyna, when asked how long she might stay in Bath, replied: "I don't know how things will turn out, do I? In Poland, and here."

However, as already suggested, the calculation is not simply about the economic costs and benefits in each location, but also about emotional factors. For some, the ties are in England. Bernadeta, for instance, stated that: "Of my friends with whom I'm still in contact, no one is in Elbląg, they're all in England, though not in Bristol." For others, the main ties are in Poland. Ilona, for example, had described her husband's difficulty in learning English and his awkwardness about the fact that, as a consequence, she was the person who organised the family's affairs in Bath, not him. He obviously felt 'segregated' in England (see Chapter Eight). However, it also transpired that his poor integration was connected to wanting to be back with his extended family in Poland:

> He comes from a big family, he has lots and lots of brothers and sisters and he really misses them. He feels really bad in England because he wants to be spending time with them. He's really sad he's in England on his own, I mean, he does have us, but still he feels bad, because he'd like to be with family. He misses his family, that's why he wants to be in Poland.

Decisions have to be negotiated between household members who may have different opinions about return. Chapter Eight argued that individual family members can become caught up in vicious or virtuous integration circles and these help contribute to differences of opinion. The context of Ilona's explanation about her husband's ties was the following dialogue, sections of which have already been quoted:

> Ilona: We decided to take the children and spend three years in England saving for that house in Poland. Well, a flat.... It will be better living in Poland, our family will be there, and at Christmas and Easter, well, in general it will be better than being alone in England. That's why we want to return. We really wouldn't like to stay in England for ever.
>
> Anne: But why not?
>
> Ilona: Well, actually, if it was just for me, well I would like to stay here in England. We have work, I could go to college and learn perfect English. But my husband doesn't want to stay. He comes from a big family [etc, see above...] that's why he wants to be in Poland. I keep saying, I try to explain that perhaps we'd go to Poland and wouldn't be able to get work. It's hard to return. Perhaps I'd get a job, and him

not. But he doesn't want to be in England, he doesn't want to live here. And we don't want for me to be here and him in Poland. We have to stick together as a family.

Since Ilona's children were very small, the decision – to stay or to go – could be negotiated between her and her husband. In families with older children their views also have to be taken into account. In Grajewo, Jolanta was hoping that her mother would come back to Poland (where Jolanta was living in the family flat with her husband and a baby the grandmother had never seen), but Jolanta's 12-year-old sister was an important player:

> Mum isn't happy in the USA and she wants to come back to Poland. Only Dad doesn't want to come. Well, now they're in a dilemma, either they come back together, or they separate. It's true, because if you are a married couple you have to somehow agree about things, especially because my youngest sister [happily settled in the USA] is 12, she's still a child. So if Mum came back alone, she'd leave her daughter and her husband. That's why I think probably she will have to give in, because Dad is totally against returning. He's been there a long time, nearly eight years, and he's got used to it there.

Here, the 12-year-old sided with her father against her mother, but sometimes the children's wishes conflict with both the parents wishes'. Sylwia's 11-year-old son was a bright boy who soon felt comfortable at school in Trowbridge. Two-and-a-half years after arrival, his best friend was an English girl, he preferred the company of English friends and he told his parents he was not going back to Poland, even though they were discussing it as a serious option. "When we talk about going back, he says 'No'. He wants to do all his schooling in England." In 2007, Hanna and her husband were toying with the idea of returning, and seemed prepared to over-rule their children's wishes. She said "We [the parents] would prefer to buy a house in Poland, despite the fact that our sons don't want to go back." Uniquely among the UK interviewees, Iwona reported that her husband had been considering moving to a third country, but their teenage daughters vetoed the idea:

> We're not saying any longer that we're staying in England for good. We've come to the conclusion that time will tell. There was a point when my husband contacted his friend in Australia. When the girls heard about the insects there was an outcry. And they said they liked it in the UK. And they're not intending to go anywhere. So that was the end of that idea.

The interviewees' discussions of when and why they would or would not leave the UK constantly referred back to their children's integration, and particularly, their schooling in England. The parents might be homesick, but their perception was that, in the end, the children's well-being was paramount. Parents of younger children understand that children can quickly become embedded in their English environment once they start school. According to interviewees in both Poland and England, many couples' original intentions are to return to Poland before their children reach school age. In other words, to have a child starting school can be perceived as a point of no return, the end of temporariness and flexibility for young parents. I was told that in Sanok kindergartens one could find children with birth certificates reading 'London'. One Polish interviewee, Iwona, had indeed returned to Sanok from London partly for this reason, although before 2004. The family was in England illegally and they did not know how to arrange school for their son in England. She commented that had her son gone to school in London, they would probably still be there.

Two of the UK interviewees were still hoping to return to Poland in time for their children to start school there at age six or seven. Ilona and her husband were with a daughter aged four (who they had not registered to start at a UK school that autumn) and a son aged three. As already mentioned, the couple had hoped to stay in England for just three years to save for a flat and those three years had nearly expired, with too little money saved. The family's dilemma was not just whether to return, but also when. Should they return to Poland immediately, even though they had not saved enough and would need a sizeable mortgage, or should they risk putting their child(ren) into an English school? Patrycja and her husband had similar plans:

> We hope that we are in England just for a short while, I don't think we are going to stay. We are thinking of returning, so that perhaps, we'll be here perhaps another two years and then return to Poland. So that our son [aged five] will learn a little English, study a bit at English school, but not be behind at school in Poland. (Patrycja)

Other parents had delayed their return so that their children, now aged seven or eight, were well ensconced in English schools. Bernadeta, for example, explained that she felt she had already taken the fatal decision:

> We were thinking, earlier, that we'd return to Poland, because Wika would be starting school there, if we went to Poland. But we decided to stay here, for the time being. I did say, 'If we stay, we won't be able to go back, because Wika won't cope in a Polish school.' So we'll have to stay. That's how it seems to me.

The parents of older children, who were already at junior or secondary school, tended to be very sure that they were not going back while their children were still at school in England.[38] The following are just two of a number of similar comments:

Families stay put. Children go to school, and it's very hard to uproot them. I couldn't stop my daughter's schooling here and go to Poland for her to go to school there, well, it would be pointless! (Dorota)

We want to stay. If the children have started school here, they must finish those schools. I can't imagine taking them out of school half way through primary or secondary and putting them into a Polish school, the system in Poland is different. (Maria)

As these quotations also suggest, parents were also partly concerned about their children's ability to cope in a Polish school, given the perception that the 'standard was higher' in Poland. Overall, the parents had the impression that their children preferred being at school in the UK and part of the reason (in addition to those described in Chapter Eight) was the comparisons with how they imagined schooling in Poland. Agnieszka, for example, asserted "Everyone who comes here with children finds that children don't want to go back precisely because of school."

Children at secondary school, particularly after Year 9, can get trapped into the examination system and it becomes hard to leave in the middle of studying for GCSEs or A levels. At the same time, it would be even more difficult for secondary age than for primary school children to transfer back into the Polish system, so parents really have little choice but to keep their children in the UK after they reach the age of 14:

My [woman] friend, a close friend, went to England with her son. He'd just begun the *gimnazjum* [middle school] when they were in Poland. And now she's waiting for him to finish his school education in England because he wouldn't be able to cope in Poland.... He's 17 now and they simply can't come back to Sanok, although that's what she'd like to do – not until he leaves school in England. That's the only time she can come back, with her son. She can't see another way out, if he came back here, he wouldn't cope in any school. (Jadwiga)

Children do in fact return from abroad and re-enter schools in Poland, but in both such stories I heard from interviewees in Poland return happened soon after the child had migrated. The children did not adapt quickly to life and school abroad, so were brought back to Poland by their mothers. In one case the whole family abandoned their migration project. In the other, the son was left with an elder brother in Grajewo while his parents and younger sibling remained in the USA.

Parents who think further ahead realise that even children leaving school is not an opportunity to go back to Poland, since by then the children may have strong emotional reasons to stay in England and the parents will not want to part from them:

Anne: So do you think you might stay here? I know it's a hard question to answer. [laughter all round]

Monika: I don't know, I really don't know. For the moment.

Piotr: We intend to go back sometime.

Monika: It also depends on what the children decide to do. If they decide to stay, our family will be here. With the children. Obviously in Poland you have a brother or sister or something, mum and dad are there at the moment, but I think it depends on the children, what they decide to later.

Piotr: We intend to be here 15 years [until their youngest child finished school].

Monika: We 'intend', but! 'But', there's always a 'but'. And another thing is that we couldn't uproot the children and put them back into Polish schools. We don't know if they'd get back into the right class for them.

Piotr: In England schools aren't so good.

Monika: We have to look at things from the point of view of the children's interests. So as not to harm them too much again.

The dialogue also illustrates once more the potential for different viewpoints between spouses. Of the two, Monika seemed better integrated and therefore more open to the idea of remaining in England than Piotr, who after four years in England believed that he would never be able to learn English and obviously found it hard to imagine staying for ever.[39]

Perceptions of Poland

For those coming originally from a depressed part of Poland, it might seem to make most sense to 'return' to a Polish city where there is plenty of employment. During 2009, different Polish cities took it in turns to advertise themselves to Poles in the UK, holding meetings in London to inform migrants about employment opportunities.[40] However, just as would-be migrants in Poland often spurn the idea of internal migration (see Chapter Three), so, too, there are many potential return migrants who do not want to change their place of residence in Poland. Among the UK interviewees, there was only one couple, Ilona and her husband, who were thinking of moving to a city:

> We keep an eye on house prices. In Kraków, flats aren't so expensive. They're much dearer in Warsaw. We are interested in a three-room flat. Of course we would like five or six, but three is affordable.... My husband dreams of more!... At the moment we don't know. When the children go to bed, if we have a spare moment we go on the internet and look.

Ilona thought that the employment situation was improving slightly in her home town, but not to the extent that there would be a real choice of jobs. Moreover, she wanted to give her children more leisure opportunities.

Other interviewees assumed that they would be going back to their extended family, which was hardly surprising, considering that missing their parents and siblings was one of their chief reasons for wanting to return. They kept a close eye on the employment situation in their specific home town and this influenced their decisions. For instance, Dominika, interviewed in early 2009, mentioned that her brother (who had been in Bath working for three years) was going back to Poland that summer to get married and had originally planned to stay in Poland. However, because of the economic crisis in Poland, and high unemployment in the particular small town where he had lived, he and his wife had changed their minds and would return to England where he had a steady job.

Interviewees acquired information about the situation in Poland from various sources. They were sceptical about media accounts of Poland-wide economic growth. Agnieszka, for example, complained that, "People who have gone back say that it's nothing like how it's described on television, or by the government." Ilona, as already mentioned, used the internet to check property prices. Presumably many people rely on relatives, although they may not necessarily be persuaded by their accounts. Marianna, interviewed in summer 2008, had just hosted her boyfriend's father in Bath:

> At the moment, I could say that I'd like to remain here, but we'll see how I get on. And we'll see if there's any reason to go back to Poland because if things just get worse I don't see any point in going back [My boyfriend's father says that where they live in Poland] ... things are beginning to happen, there's some improvement. Perhaps something actually is beginning to improve in Poland but I don't believe it's really good enough to go back. At the moment I don't see it like that.

Just as potential migrants in Poland may fear migrating and be reluctant to adopt it as a livelihood strategy for this reason, so too migrants abroad may be afraid to return even if they are not doing well abroad. Alicja's sister-in-law and her family, for example, had lived in London for 10 years and, according to Alicja, "they are more or less settled, even though they are not doing particularly well". They knew that there were some job openings in Sanok and Alicja implied that she had been trying to persuade them to come home, but she sensed that they were afraid to come back and look for work. According to her, "They're simply scared. They're scared to start.... They're afraid and they keep putting off their return." To help overcome such anxieties, the Polish government has set up an advice service for returning Poles, which has been well-subscribed.[41]

Having a house in Poland was an obvious reason for returning to a particular place, rather than going to a more flourishing location where it would be expensive to rent. Moreover, it could provide a secure base from which to rebuild a Polish livelihood, avoiding the need to go into the unknown and allaying fears about return. Polish statistics about the number of people officially deregistering from their Polish address to go abroad show how comparatively rarely this happens. In 2006, only 7,861 Poles aged under 20 were registered with the authorities as having abandoned residence in Poland,[42] clearly a much smaller figure than the number of Polish children moving abroad. Over a third of the UK interviewees had housing in Poland and only two had sold property (one several years after moving to the UK, and then only in order to purchase a house in Bath). Once again, this testifies to Polish migrants' propensity to keep their options open as long as possible.

> Jolanta: When we're on holiday we live in our own home.
>
> Anne: Does that mean you want to go back?
>
> Jolanta: For the moment we're not planning to go back. The flat may as well stay [*niech stoi te mieszkanie*].

Interviewees in Poland also asserted that you must keep your flat in Poland, recalling examples of wise neighbours who came back for holidays, and (more rarely) foolish neighbours who had cut their moorings and then been stuck abroad:

> You shouldn't sell your flat here and go abroad, because you don't know what to expect. That's the other side of it. You don't know how things will work out. And if they don't, then you always have something to come back to. Because you have a flat, a roof over your head. Otherwise you may end up like some people do. I know it for a fact because my ex-neighbours ... went off, sold their flat, everything, and there they are stuck in the USA. And they are so sorry they sold their flat, they say if they had a flat they would come back to Poland like a shot. (Eliza, Grajewo, 2008)

Four interviewees had come back to Poland because of perceptions about the health service. They had become pregnant abroad and they (and/or their husbands) wanted the baby to be born in Poland. Other interviewees had daughters-in-law and other relatives who had come back for the same reason. Interviewees suggested an assortment of reasons why it was better for pregnant women to go back to Poland, including the language barrier in the UK and a perception, widely shared among Poles in the UK, that Polish healthcare is better than the NHS.[43] Angelika gave a detailed explanation of why she returned from Sanok to London and her account is interesting because it shows how family ties to Poland, and the wish to be 'at home' can be the most important pull factors. Angelika had been invited to London by a cousin before 2004 and worked for three years as a bar attendant and cleaner. However, when she became pregnant, she decided to come home. She said this was because she felt the medical care for pregnant women was better in Poland. Her husband stayed in London, since he was a roofer by profession and had lots of work in the UK. Angelika claimed that if she had not become pregnant she would still be living in London. It seems the pregnancy was partly an excuse to come back to Sanok. Despite missing her husband – whom she was currently trying to persuade to return to Poland – she was happy to be with her mother and brother. An important factor, too, was the spacious house that she and her husband had built in Sanok with their foreign earnings. Angelika had not liked living in central London, where not only had she and her husband been living in cramped accommodation, but also her cousin's family was sharing four to a small room. She could not imagine living with a child in such squalid conditions.

Holidays in Poland and their impact on decisions about 'permanent' return

Chapters Five and Nine described how family members frequently went on holiday to visit one another in the UK. It is also common for Poles in the UK to go home for visits and interviewees in Poland noticed an "avalanche of English people"[44] at Christmas, Easter and in the summer holidays. The cars parked outside church had British licence plates and the hairdressers were overworked.

Many interviewees went back to Poland at least once a year, and some went back as often as four times a year. Factors facilitating frequent travel included the wife not having a paid job in England, having a small number of children and living in the west of Poland, which was more accessible by car. This last was an important consideration, because air tickets were often considered to be expensive – especially in holiday seasons – and because people liked to be mobile in Poland and also to bring things back to England. Distance and poor roads in Poland deterred people from taking their cars to eastern corners of Poland.

However, as already suggested, it should not be assumed that all migrants are equally free to engage in transnational activities. Poorer families, those with three to five children, where parents had extensive work commitments, and so forth, were naturally less free to come and go, although sometimes older children travelled back on their own. Schools could also cause problems for families wishing to visit Poland. Sylwia, re-interviewed in 2009, reported that in Trowbridge, whereas previously large numbers of Polish parents had taken their children back to Poland whenever was convenient for them, now they were being threatened with fines of £50 if they removed their child from school during term-time.

How often interviewees went back was also connected to how settled they felt in the UK. Several said that they preferred to receive guests in their own homes in England than to go to Poland. As described in Chapter Nine, some had begun to enjoy more comfortable, and in some cases, more spacious housing. Interviewees who were pregnant or had babies could also have limited ability to travel, or simply feel more like being at home and waiting to be visited.

A handful of interviewees had never been back to Poland, for various reasons. It was clear from how they acknowledged this fact that they felt it to be very unusual. Dorota said that more recently, the reason for staying in Bristol was that she enjoyed having guests in their new council house. At the start, however, she was afraid that she would be too homesick if she returned:

> At first I was afraid to go back because I was afraid I might not come back to England. Because it was really hard at the beginning. I missed my friends, everything. Absolutely everything that I'd left behind in Poland. So sometimes I had little spells of depression. And I pushed it to the back of my mind, I just didn't want to think about it. I was just afraid that if I went I wouldn't come back.

Travelling back to Poland for holidays can produce varied effects, however. One is to make migrants feel more confused. Agnieszka, for example, complained: "When I go back to Poland for holidays, well, that's where my home is too. Because everything's there. But … who knows where my home actually is? It's hard, sometimes you think about it and you don't know where on earth your home actually is."

Travel for short visits to Poland, like other transnational activities, can facilitate stay in the UK because it is a kind of relief for homesickness. 'Visits home represent an important aspect of migrants' care for themselves – the best cure for homesickness being an opportunity to return to one's roots and breathe the "native air" for a few weeks.'[45] For example, Patrycja described how her husband, working alone in the UK for two-and-a-half years, often felt like giving up, but hung on partly because he was able to come home every three months for a short visit. Overall, however, visits to Poland create both pulls and pushes. Some aspects of Poland make (some) migrants more determined to return for good, others estrange them further.

Homesick migrants could find their preference for being in Poland much intensified by the experience of going on holiday. As Agnieszka said, "You feel so homesick when you go back to visit." Some migrants can never really integrate in the UK because they maintain such a strong emotional attachment to Poland, as a result of frequent visits. Alicja criticised her sister-in-law for visits to Sanok that meant that she and her children could not let go of ties in Poland:

If my husband's sister didn't come to Poland so often she would definitely be more accepting of life in England. But she has that constant contact with her mother and siblings. They come to Poland at least every six months and in the summer they come for a long time. They have time to get used to everything here. And then they have to go back and get used to England again.

Some interviewees had kept very good houses in Poland and to return to these was most definitely to return 'home'. Marzena's family, for example, had, before going to England, recently moved from a cramped urban flat into a house on the edge of a village. She said: "We always dreamed of having our own little house. It's lovely, a quiet place, near the forest." Sylwia and her husband were in a dilemma because they had inherited a dream house in Poland. The house was in a remote village, where they did not think they would find any work, and there was no other practical reason to go back, yet owning the house created a powerful emotional pull. "We have almost a hectare of land. We have a lot of land. We have fruit trees, a big orchard, we have lots of land. Well, and our own house … to which we can always return."

Interviewees also felt home was in Poland because that was where they went to the doctor, the dentist and the hairdresser. It seems to be commonplace, irrespective of age or social class, for Poles to make such appointments in Poland, even if they only go back for a short stay; the same is also true for EU citizens of other countries.[46] A 2008 report on Poles in Hammersmith and Fulham quotes a presumably young and childless migrant: "It works pretty well: you go to Poland for a week, have fun with your friends, party and go to the doctor to have a check-up."[47] To the parents in the research project, however, such visits within visits were a mixed blessing. On the one hand, it was nice to have your hair done and see your friends. On the other hand, you could feel so stressed you ended up wishing you were in England.[48]

You just run around.... Those three weeks are all taken up with organising things and looking after your health, 'mending' everything, making appointments for six months later.... You want to go to Poland, but when you're there it's not relaxing. It would be nice to go just for five days and do nothing but rest.... People go to the doctor in particular. Our health system is completely different.... It's better for me in Poland. In England the doctor just prescribes paracetamol.... People always go to the dentist in Poland.... It's good quality, cheaper and they know you because they have always looked after your teeth....You've probably noticed that I haven't been to the hairdresser in England! I'm waiting for Poland. It's true most Poles go to the hairdresser in Poland. It's cheaper and I think if you have a favourite hairdresser in Poland that's where you want to go. I've never been to the hairdresser in England. I have a hairdresser in Poland, a hairdresser is someone you can go to and she knows how to cut your particular hair. (Agnieszka)

There are masses of things you have to do. Everyone wants you to go and visit them. Everyone wants to visit you. It's so tiring, and you have to do shopping as well, I always buy myself books and we want to buy some books for our daughter in Poland....We go to the dentist and my husband gets the car repaired. And we took our daughter to a speech therapist.... It would be nicer to sit in your garden and relax. (Katarzyna)

Five of the UK interviewees had recently been on holidays to France or to southern Europe and enjoyed them; part of the enjoyment came from not having to clean or cook, deal with officials or go to the dentist. It was easy to see how non-Polish holidays could eventually become a habit and that less frequent visits to Poland would result in the loosening of ties.

The rushed nature of migrants' short holidays in Poland can also cause offence to their friends and family. If holiday-makers cannot make time to see them properly, this in turn must lead to a weakening of relationships and therefore a weakening of migrants ties to Poland:

My sister was in Poland for Easter, she came to see us, stayed in Grajewo for three days ... but she spent the whole time running about ... and my mother complained they didn't even have time to sit down and chat. (Eliza, Grajewo)

They say 'I would stop to chat, but I'm going to the dentist.' They have those two weeks and spend most of the time at the dentist. (Elwira, Sanok)

When people who moved to England sold their Polish house, or rented it to strangers, they have to stay with their parents, which partly solves the problem of not seeing each other during the holiday, but can also be uncomfortable, leading to the realisation that 'home' is in England:

It already does [seem like home]. When we come back from Poland, we feel we are coming home. When we go to Poland we stay with my parents or his and it's cramped so when we leave we say 'We're going home!'

However, the most common complaint about Poland was the cost of living. Edyta's comment was typical:

> We also have to save up to go to Poland because even if we live with
> my parents the money goes so fast. Recently I was in the shop with
> my sister buying basic things for the children and when she got home
> she thought she must have been cheated: she spent 800 zl on one
> shopping bag's worth of stuff.

Not only did other UK interviewees express the same feeling of shock, they
also mentioned that they had gone on shopping trips with their sisters and told
them how horrified they had been by Polish prices. Interviewees in Poland told
exactly the same stories about their sisters coming home for visits, going shopping
and being appalled by the prices. It is easy to see how siblings in Poland become
convinced that it would be easier for their families to live in the UK.

Conclusion

Many Polish migrants to the UK plan to be abroad only temporarily or have quite
open-ended plans and are ready to return home if, for example, they get a job
offer in Poland or things do not work out for them in the UK. Hence there is a
constant flow of people returning to Poland. Nonetheless, there is also a substantial
proportion of Polish migrants in the UK who are planning to remain in the UK
for the foreseeable future. Often the interviewees asserted that 'all Polish families'
were in this situation, and while this is obviously an exaggeration, it is clear that
there are many reasons for families to stay.

Newspaper reports which assume that economic recession in the UK will
automatically cause a 'wave' of return are making a false assumption, since the
overall economic situation in the receiving country is far from being the main
factor influencing migrants' decision making about how long to stay. First,
migrants make decisions on the basis of their individual livelihoods, not the
national economy. If they have jobs in the UK they are unlikely to abandon these
voluntarily. Second, decisions are always made on a comparative basis. Almost all
the interviewees could only envisage return as return to their home locality in
Poland, because that was where they had left their friends and family. Thinking
about livelihoods in those specific home towns, they often came to the conclusion
that it would be better to remain abroad.

Third, and even more importantly, economic factors are not the only ones
shaping thoughts about stay or return. The more integrated interviewees felt in
the UK, in all the dimensions discussed in Chapters Eight and Nine, the less they
felt like returning to Poland. Visits home were often stressful occasions which only
confirmed their feeling that they were better off in England and that their homes,
together with their own and their children's friendships in the UK, constituted
important ties to the UK. Conversely, interviewees who were more segregated
in England were more likely to see the positive sides of Poland when they went
home for short visits and to feel even more strongly that their emotional ties
were to Poland. Of course, there is also a third and very uncomfortable outcome,

vividly described by Agnieszka, of being "torn in two" – unable to decide where home should be and unhappy about living in a state of uncertainty.

The likelihood for prolonged indecision is only exacerbated when, as often seems to happen, different members of the family become integrated to different extents and this can lead to difficult discussions and negotiations. In the end, however, the decision about whether to return or to stay is likely to be made on the basis of what is assessed to be in the best interests of the children. In families where children were already at school and well settled, there was universal agreement that the family should not disrupt their schooling by further migration.

Notes

[1] Faist (2000, p 19).

[2] Cerase (1974) was influential in framing analysis of return in terms of success or failure.

[3] Glick Schiller et al (1992, p ix).

[4] Cassarino (2004, p 268).

[5] Morawska (2001).

[6] King (2000, p 15).

[7] King (2000, p 20).

[8] Galasińska (2010, pp 314, 311).

[9] IPS interviewers question about one in 500 people leaving and entering the UK by the major entry/exit points.

[10] Pollard et al (2008, pp 19-20).

[11] ONS (2009a, pp 3, 6).

[12] Iglicka (2009, p 12).

[13] Mostrous and Seib (2008).

[14] Harrison (2009).

[15] Pawłowska-Salińska (2008).

[16] Jasińska (2008).

[17] Czubkowska (2009).

[18] Harrison (2009).

[19] Iglicka (2009, p 5).

[20] Anon (2008a).

[21] Cieślak-Wróblewska (2009).

[22] Krings et al (2009) argue that 'there is only limited evidence to suggest that the current downturn will trigger large-scale outward migration from Ireland. This is for at least three reasons. A clear majority of NMS (new member state) migrants remain in employment.... Furthermore, even if migrants should lose their jobs, welfare state arrangements in Ireland

offer some protection against destitution. Moreover, the decision to migrate is not just reached on the basis of economic considerations alone. Social networks are particularly important in sustaining the migration process.'

[23] King (2000, pp 14-15). He also states (p 16) that 'while at an aggregate level it can be demonstrated that a link exists between economic crisis in the host country and return migration, most studies which look at individual-scale aspects of the return decision find that economic arguments are contextual rather than paramount'.

[24] Frelak and Roguska (2008, p 14).

[25] Iglicka (2009, p 13).

[26] Orellana et al (2001, p 587).

[27] Somerville and Sumption (2009, p 6). Of course, some families do go home: of the 47 respondents in Iglicka's 2009 study who had left Western Europe prematurely, 13 had dependent children (Iglicka, 2009, p 14).

[28] Orellana et al (2001, p 587).

[29] Scholars tend to label this phenomenon 're-(e)migration', but this is confusing, because the same label is often given to simple return migration (that is, the second journey, not the third). The word 'return' in the phrase 'double return' is particularly apposite if the migrant feels they have already made a home in the foreign country and are 'returning' to a preferred location of residence, or feel that the West in general is such a preferred location.

[30] *Gazeta Wyborcza*, 5 March 2010 (http://forum.gazeta.pl/forum/w,30,108259918,,Anglia_nawet_w_kryzysie_lepsza_od_Polski.html?s=1&v=2Top of Form).

[31] Frelak and Roguska (2008, p 15); Iglicka (2009, p 18). A survey for Money.pl in autumn 2008 found that nearly half of respondents were not sure whether their return would be final and nearly 12% knew for sure that they would migrate again (Dwornik, 2008, last paragraph).

[32] Iglicka (2009, p 20).

[33] Iglicka (2009, p 19).

[34] Iglicka (2009, p 25).

[35] Interview with EURES officer at Sanok Job Centre (PUP), 18 September 2008.

[36] Massey et al (1998, p 47).

[37] Eade et al (2006, pp 10-11).

[38] For a similar finding (in London) see Sales et al (2008, p 15) or Ryan et al (2009, p 71).

[39] Chapter Nine also contains their dialogue about Polish food, in which Piotr emphasises that Polish food is nicer and that they buy Polish food, whereas Monika talks about trying out new dishes. See Temple (2001) for analysis of an interview with another Polish couple with varying attitudes towards Polishness.

[40] Poland Street (2009).

[41] The website is www.powroty.pl (*powroty* = returns). See also www.polacy.gov.pl. Information on take-up from Paweł Kaczmarczyk, Warsaw, 9 March 2009.

[42] GUS (2007b, p 449).

[43] Cook et al (2008); Garapich (2008a); Goodwin and Goodwin (2009).

[44] Elwira, Sanok.

[45] Vullnetari and King (2008, p 144).

[46] Cook et al (2008, p 36).

[47] Garapich (2008a, p 34).

[48] For a discussion of similar emotions among Irish returnees, see Ní Laoire (2007).

ELEVEN

Conclusions

There will be as many Poles in Britain as English people! [laughter] And here there won't be anyone, it will be deserted. (Edyta, Grajewo, 2009)

I think that everywhere life is the same, work, for example, is the same, it's just that wages are different. (Emilia, north-east Poland, 2007)

This book has discussed migration from Poland since EU accession in 2004, with a special focus on migration by working-class families to England. It has explored the causes of migration, looking at why some people migrate but others do not. It has also investigated more specifically why parents choose to migrate with their children. The second part of the book has considered factors shaping migrants' decisions about how long to stay abroad, whether Polish families were likely to remain in the UK for an extended period and what they understood by 'return'. In addition, the book has contributed to discussions on various aspects of migration theory, particularly theories about why individuals and families migrate, networks, migration culture, integration and transnationalism. Along the way, the book has illustrated aspects of life in contemporary Poland, particularly life in small towns and villages. Society in Poland, as in other post-communist countries, is changing rapidly, partly in response to migration, and this book has attempted to chart some of those changes. This concluding chapter summarises the book's empirical findings before presenting its main theoretical contributions, using two case studies to illustrate why it is useful to apply a livelihood strategy approach to migration.

Research findings

The opening of the UK labour market to citizens of new EU member states was a necessary precondition for mass migration to the UK by Polish families, as by Poles in general. However, the new immigration regulations do not explain why some people chose to leave Poland while others remained behind. Nor do they explain why some locations in Poland have much higher rates of migration than others. The causes of mass migration lie largely in the economic situations of specific geographical areas and social groups. In early 2004, about one fifth of the Polish workforce was unemployed, with some locations having unemployment rates much higher than 20%. By 2007-08, unemployment was less significant for Poland as a whole, but still a common experience among some groups of people, particularly women over the age of 40, and in certain locations, such as Grajewo.

Moreover, in small towns and villages even employed people often found it hard to make a living because there were few opportunities to supplement basic wages with overtime, second jobs and other additional earnings. More universal economic push factors to migrate, in cities as well as small towns, were job insecurity and, above all, low wages.

People migrated largely to cover everyday expenses, securing what interviewees termed a "decent" or "normal" standard of living. Migrants wanted to be able to buy consumer goods such as cars and household equipment, not simply to scrape by from month to month. If they migrated in order to be able to invest, it was usually to invest in housing. Many parents also migrated to pay for their children's university studies. Business failure and debts were another reason to migrate. Much more rarely were migrants planning to invest in business ventures in Poland with money earned abroad. Interviewees tended to feel pessimistic about the prospects for making a living anywhere in Poland, and this helps explain their reluctance to migrate internally. Moreover, they believed that the cost of living, relative to wages, was lower in Western Europe than in Polish cities, and that they could easily earn enough to pay for their initial accommodation abroad, unlike in Poland. Hence it was easier to get a foothold in a foreign country and it was not seen as risky to experiment with migration to the West. Because of cheap international travel, Europe was on their doorstep. Again, this facilitated experimental migration, based on the attitude that if things did not work out, the migrant could easily come back. Western Europe was also often viewed as being culturally similar to Poland. Typically, migrants had open-ended plans and, at the outset, migration was seldom intended to be a permanent move to a foreign country. Employers in Poland often granted extended periods of unpaid leave and this also facilitated experimental migration.

In the 1990s it had become common in some Polish regions for parents to migrate to Western Europe. Usually it was the husband who migrated, although women also worked abroad, particularly in Italy and other countries where there was a demand for carers and domestic workers. The other spouse and the children remained in Poland. This practice partly occurred because migrants were working abroad illegally, but there were also other reasons why parents were and are still reluctant to uproot their families. Reluctance to loosen ties with the extended family is one of the most significant causes of households remaining in Poland, although sometimes the pioneer migrants decide it would be best for the whole nuclear family to live together abroad and they try to persuade their families to join them. They do not always succeed, and there are probably thousands of failed migration attempts, when spouses in Poland, and sometimes also children, refuse to go abroad. Overall, there remain many families divided by migration. Such families generally seem to consider that it is economically viable for one parent to live frugally abroad, while most of the family's spending takes place in Poland.

Motives for family reunification among the interviewees were usually non-economic. While it is true that some UK interviewees mentioned the expense of maintaining separate households in Poland and the UK, they were in the minority. Much more common were assertions that "a family should stick together", stories of how much family members had missed one another while the pioneer migrant was abroad alone and a belief that children would have a better start in life as a result of migration. There was often a conscious rejection of the 1990s model of migration by one parent. Although such migration is often conceptualised and justified as "self-sacrificing", such self-sacrifice is out of fashion. Interviewees were not embarrassed to talk about the importance of emotional fulfilment, particularly the need for fathers and children to be together. In Grajewo and Sanok, I encountered a similar preference for migration with children. Many interviewees had experienced the pain of the one-parent model at first hand: they had left their children to work abroad, or had been left by their own parents. It is evident that local migration norms in Poland are changing and that when families migrate with children this is not simply connected to new opportunities for family migration to the UK opened by EU accession. This was fully confirmed by the Podkarpacie opinion poll, which showed high levels of concern about the impact of single parent migration (broken marriages, unhappy children, over-burdened grandparents) and very considerable support for migration with children, especially among younger respondents.

In high-migration localities such as Grajewo or Sanok family migration also occurs as a result of chain migration, with, for example, migrant families already in the UK inviting over their sisters, brothers and friends. In Grajewo and Sanok there is an entrenched belief that you must migrate to be with someone you know, preferably another family member. This helps explain why there are so many families from Sanok specifically in London. People from places in Poland where there are fewer migrants do not have these helpful contacts, however, and they are braver about using formal institutions such as recruitment agencies. Many Bath interviewees, for example, were married to bus drivers who had responded to advertisements by recruitment agencies in Poland.

This book has also investigated how migrants decided the duration of their stay abroad. Research on return migration (both in general and, until recently, to Poland) shows that emotional reasons tend to preponderate over economic ones. In 2009, by contrast, some Poles were returning unexpectedly to Poland because they had lost jobs in the UK, although there was no evidence of mass return. Parents, in particular, seemed disposed to stay. Even if they had lost their jobs in the UK, or were afraid of doing so, parents preferred to stay in England rather than disrupt their children's lives by returning to Poland. This was particularly true in the case of school-age children. Usually, the children had already put down roots, learned English and acquired English friends. They were often doing very well at school. Parents had pangs of conscience about having uprooted their children once, when they moved from Poland to the UK, and they hesitated to disrupt their lives for a second time.

How parents make decisions about stay and return should be understood in the context of their overall integration into British society and their sense of being at home, or not being at home. The interviewees were often well-integrated in the sense that they were reasonably satisfied with their own work and with their children's schools. Housing was often more problematic, since people on six-month housing contracts were not able to feel settled in a particular neighbourhood. However, by far the main obstacle to integration was the interviewees' poor knowledge of English. As a result, most had no English friends and they encountered various practical problems as a result of communication difficulties. They were keen to improve their language skills but found it hard to access language classes. Maintaining Polish identity, on the other hand, became easier over the period covered by the research, 2006-09. By 2009, new arrivals were quickly able to feel at home because there was a sizeable number of Poles, even in places like Bath which previously did not have a Polish population. They were able to attend Polish masses, to buy Polish food, to have their hair cut by Polish hairdressers and to send their children to Polish Saturday schools. Most importantly, many quickly built up a circle of Polish friends.

As in other migrant communities, different family members experience integration very differently from one another. For example, there were cases where the wife was much happier in the UK than her husband, because she spoke better English and/or liked her job better. Almost always, children were more integrated than their parents. Parents and children are tied to different degrees to friends and family back in Poland, and will have different perceptions about whether or not they would like to live there again. Obviously these varying perspectives have a bearing on decisions about return, which need to be negotiated within the household.

With regard to methodology, the multi-sited character of the research on which the book is based facilitated understanding of some phenomena which might have seemed puzzling or insignificant had they been observed only in the sending or receiving society. For example, there was widespread conviction among the Polish interviewees that you would be exploited and your job would be insecure if you were employed in the private sector, particularly in small businesses. This expectation definitely helped shape the livelihood strategies of UK interviewees and explained why, when reflecting on the positive aspects of their UK jobs, working in the state sector often came high up the list. To take another example, UK-based interviewees almost all complained that they found it stressful to make visits back to Poland. I could see how this might put migrants off taking such 'holidays'. However, it was only when I began to talk to people in Poland about their perceptions of these visits that I began to appreciate the dynamics of the situation. One such dynamic is the widening rift between migrants and stayers. The interviewees in Poland were equally stressed by the fact that their friends and relatives did not spend much time with them when they returned on holiday, but (as they saw it) preferred to go to the hairdresser. Another dynamic is the reinforcement of the conviction of all parties that life is easier in the West: interviewees in both the UK and Poland related how they had gone shopping with their sisters, in Poland, and been horrified by the prices. One UK-based sister's outburst over the shopping would no doubt help encourage the Poland-based sister to consider migration as a livelihood strategy for herself. A more general reflection concerned the importance of the *quality* of relations within individual families. Interviewees in Poland told many stories of families where strained relations were exacerbated by migration. This threw into sharp relief the solidarity and teamwork which often seemed to characterise families who had migrated together.

The livelihood strategy approach

This book has also sought to contribute to several areas of migration theory. With reference to why people migrate, it has illustrated the helpfulness of applying a livelihood strategy approach. This approach is holistic, and perhaps this is the reason why it is not more popular, since it demands a wide-ranging exploration of the environments from which migrants originate. It is useful for many reasons. First, it is helpful because it sheds light on the choices available in particular geographical locations. People often migrate because they cannot find alternative livelihoods locally and this implies the need for migration scholars to look in depth at local perceptions about the economies of sending locations. This may reveal a very different picture from that presented by aggregate national statistics or even by local statistics, if local residents are stubbornly pessimistic and unwilling to believe any official assertions about economic growth.

Second, household strategies are important in decision making about migration, so there is merit in an approach that focuses on the household rather than the individual (except sometimes in the case of young, single people). Every household has its own combination of assets and liabilities and goes through its own process of discussing and formulating a migration strategy. Some of the most informative accounts of migrant decision making (for example, Grasmuck and Pessar, 1991 or Toro-Morn, 1995) are precisely those that explore the relationships within families which influence how migration strategies are shaped.

Third, since livelihoods are about all types of resource, not just financial ones, the livelihood approach focuses our attention on the personal and social capital of migrants: assets such as migration experience, language skills and useful contacts. As many migration analysts have observed, social networks can be a resource for would-be migrants, but it is also important to remember that networks are not just ladders from one country to another but also webs of emotional ties which often prevent people from migrating in the first place.

Understanding livelihoods means understanding cultural as well as economic contexts. Successful livelihoods must be appropriate within a specific culture – norms and conventions which help determine how individuals behave. This book has used the concept of 'migration culture' to understand migration behaviour. Migration cultures in Poland constitute quite a complex set of assumptions, and the book has attempted to identify the different kinds of assumption which shape migration decisions, as well as to understand their origins. Evidence of this culture was drawn from the opinion poll, conducted in Poland's highest sending region, as well as analysis of how the interviewees talked about migration. As mentioned earlier, beliefs that you should migrate to be with 'someone you know' and that 'families should stick together' were both components of this culture in 2008–09. Nonetheless, it is important to recognise how quickly cultures can evolve. Although cultures are often presented as being slow to change, the research suggests the opposite: in some situations cultures evolve very fast. Migrating to be with somebody you know is a convention which is, to some extent, being abandoned by younger Poles, while the conviction that 'families should stick together' is becoming stronger.

Migration networks, as argued in Chapter One, are a cause of migration, as well as a mechanism. This book has explored in some detail how migrants use migration networks, within the context of local migration cultures. It is important to remember that not everyone has access to transnational migration networks, and by studying how networks are used it is possible to appreciate why some migrants take advantage of them while others do not. The prevalence of transnational migration networks in parts of Poland induces a sense that it is only possible to migrate by using social connections; this is enabling for some, since existing migrants feel under some obligation to 'collect' their friends and family, but it is constraining for others.

The case of Danuta and Jerzy illustrates the usefulness of considering the different facets of livelihood strategies in order to understand why people migrate, or not. Although case studies have been avoided up to now, in order not to compromise anonymity, it seems helpful at this juncture to present a particular case in detail.[1] It is impossible to find 'typical' cases, and the two cases discussed in this chapter are not presented because they are to be considered typical. The intention is merely to show the range of factors that need to be taken into consideration in order to understand migration decisions.

Danuta was toying with the idea of migration when first interviewed in March 2008. By 2009, she was almost convinced she had to go. The family's main asset was Jerzy's well-paid job at a the chipboard factory in Grajewo. Danuta was unemployed, although she had an allotment which she liked to tend, so she felt she was contributing to the household resources in a small way. The couple had two children, who both started university in September 2008. Although Jerzy could support the family under normal circumstances, he had told Danuta and the children that they would have to find some way of contributing towards the costs of both children studying at the same time.

Taking into account local perceptions of the economy in Grajewo, it was not surprising why the couple felt that Danuta should migrate, not Jerzy. The chipboard factory, despite a somewhat chequered recent history, was central to Grajewo's economy, and still regarded by interviewees as one of the town's few solid employers: it was seen as foolish to give up that sort of job to go abroad. Since Jerzy had a brother in the USA, he could have gone to work there on a six-month tourist visa (like many Grajewans), but working at the chipboard factory was a good reason to reject that strategy. Danuta, by contrast, had a vocational qualification which she could not use in Grajewo and she had been working in a shop before she became redundant. She completely shared the typical local pessimism about job prospects for women over the age of 40. Her pessimism was also founded on personal experience, since she had spent the year between the interviews looking for a job and found nothing except a temporary summer job, as a shop assistant.

Discussions about migration as a household strategy appeared to have been amicable and this could perhaps have facilitated migration. However, the fact that the family was so happy was a huge barrier to migration by either party. Danuta described herself as a "family person" and Jerzy appeared to be the same. For example, explaining to his brother why he had only come on a short holiday and did not want to work in the USA, he said: "When I came to America, you were the only person who was happy, but when I go back to Grajewo, there will be lots of people glad to see me." In other words, although the family might seem to have strong ties abroad – and in other families a sibling abroad was sufficient to start a process of chain migration – in this case, 'family' was definitely perceived to be in Grajewo only.

In terms of personality, Danuta was also ill-suited to be a (female) migrant. She lacked confidence and experience and she disliked cleaning. Fear was a very important barrier to her migration. At one point she said, "It's really hard, you want to go, but you're scared.... I don't know if I would, I mean, I don't know if I would go abroad. I really don't know. I suppose you have to really screw up your courage." She had never worked abroad and she knew she did not want to clean. She was horrified at her daughter's summer job in the USA: "It would be different if you cleaned just for an hour or two. But 12 hours day! That's a lot, that's a really long time. Sometimes you spend two or three hours cleaning your own flat and you've had enough". With regard to the local migration culture in Morawska's sense of a 'toolkit',[2] Danuta's views were typical for a middle-aged Grajewan. It was impossible to imagine migrating except to be with someone you knew: "I wish I had some kind of contact, a friend, or family. I can hardly go off to England or Italy and then look for something at the station after I arrive." She clearly felt 'forced' to migrate ("I suppose you have to really screw up your courage"), but at the same time she needed an opportunity in the form of an invitation from a friend, illustrating the common local perception that opportunity was needed as well as compulsion. (It was noticeable that Danuta would only consider using European contacts, and also that she did actually mention having friends who were working in Western Europe. The implication was that these friends were not likely to make her an offer. She needed closer contacts: "If my sister or sister-in-law or some cousin was somewhere abroad [in Europe] I'd have gone long ago.")

The migration culture condones migration by women alone if they have grown-up children, so this was not an inhibiting factor. In fact, mothers in Danuta's situation were often expected to migrate to pay their children's university fees and this was seen as a normal act of self-sacrifice. Danuta, however, preferred the new model of family migration which was gaining ascendancy locally: "I think it's better if they're abroad as a whole family, husband, wife and child, not that one parent should be abroad and the other in Poland. Really." She told the cautionary tale of her friend whose marriage had fallen apart after she went to Belgium on her own.

Considering the children as potential earners, but only in the university vacations, since they were both serious students, opened new prospects for family migration strategies. The daughter – as often seems to happen – had become very keen on further migration after her first trip abroad, when she had earned some pocket money in the USA during the summer holidays. (It seems quite common for older school-age children to make such visits to relatives in the USA.) Danuta was toying with the idea that she would go with her two children to work abroad during the summer holidays: a livelihood strategy which would remove the fear and loneliness of migration and increase her confidence. In other words, by working through the pros and cons of all the other possible migration strategies, she had finally arrived at the optimum variant: family migration (unfortunately without her husband).

Danuta and Jerzy's case illustrates many of the dilemmas facing parents with older children. Much of this book, however, has been about migration in families with small children. Here, norms about gender roles are particularly important, given that the migration culture is part of the wider cultural background of the sending society. This book has contributed to the literature about the connections between gender roles and migration, and how gender roles evolve within individual households in parallel with migration strategies. The connections are not always obvious, and it is particularly important not to make assumptions about family reunification. The 1990s saw a trend towards more lone migration by women to join sisters and friends working as carers in Italy, Belgium and Greece, a type of migration which enhanced women's sense of independence from their husbands and their economic power within the household. In such families, the wife was the breadwinner/carer (in that order) and the husband also combined both roles. Despite such female migration, however, it was still more common, in the 1990s, for husbands to migrate alone, confirming their breadwinner status. Migration by wives to join their husbands after 2004 could also be seen as a conventional arrangement. However, on closer examination, it is apparent that family reunification is a step towards, and evidence of, more equal relationships between the spouses. Not all wives are happy to stay in Poland and wait for their husband to send them remittances. Moreover, this book has illustrated that wives, and sometimes also children, have a major role to play in shaping the family's migration strategy. A decisive event in many families, and one which deserves attention from scholars, is the 'inspection visit', when other family members visit the husband shortly after his departure abroad. In other words, it is important to look closely at what is entailed by 'family reunification' for 21st-century migrants, and to recognise that it does not necessarily imply the playing out of conventional gender roles.

The impact of migration on sending communities is usually identified with economic remittances, although Levitt's concept of 'social remittances' has also been influential.[3] Using the concept of social remittances, this book has tentatively suggested that changing views about gender roles might be a form of social remittance, but only in the sense that Western ideas may reinforce new ideas about gender roles already circulating among younger and better-educated sections of the Polish population. The impact of migration on sending communities is also emotional, and Chapter Seven looked at the emotional costs of separation from friends and relatives from places like Sanok and Grajewo. It emphasised that absences and gaps are just as important a part of the migration story as the transnational links and networks which commonly receive more attention.

The livelihood strategy approach can also be used to understand migrants' lives abroad, not just to find out about their past experiences in Poland but also to conceptualise and explore their experiences in the UK. Integration is not just about having a job but also about feeling at home in the receiving community. To feel at home, new migrants need to become familiar with how things are done – the conventions guiding behaviour in the receiving culture – and with the range of livelihoods on offer. They need to know people in the local community. Only then will they have the sense of being reasonably free agents, able to shape their own livelihood strategy in the same way as they would attempt at home. Language is a fundamental prerequisite for achieving all these goals. It is not just a tool for performing everyday transactions (as often assumed) but also opens access to the receiving culture and society.

Patrycja's case illustrates the different aspects of livelihoods that are important to migrants, and the significance of a whole range of non-economic factors. Patrycja had lived in England for 18 months and was hoping to go back after two more years. She was a part-time cleaner and her husband was a bus driver, quite a common combination in the sample. In purely financial terms, their British livelihood was better than their Polish one. Patrycja had been unemployed in their village; she had tried to find work but "In Poland the situation is, they don't want to give you a job if you're a mother." In Bath, by contrast, she did not encounter such discrimination and was able to find part-time work. Her husband had worked in the family business in Poland, which she said was quite a good job by local standards, but they wanted to build a house, so he came to England to earn more money. On the face of it, they were typical 'target earners' and likely to return to Poland as soon as they had saved up enough money.

However, closer examination of the household's livelihood trajectory, including the varying resources and emotions of different family members, illustrated the actual complexity of the situation. On the one hand, return was associated with much more than simply the fulfilment of an economic plan. There were pressures to go back early, and these were partly linked to homesickness: they spent as much time as possible telephoning and sending emails to people in Poland, partly to compensate for the fact that they were not able to go home for many visits. Wanting to go home was also connected to a feeling of being defeated by situations they encountered in the UK. Patrycja's husband's attitude was "The sooner the better. If he could, he'd pack his bags and go today." Despite the fact that his job was well paid, he did not really like bus driving: he found it tiring, and passengers could be unpleasant. Patrycja's five-year-old son was also unhappy, since he was not learning much English at school and had only one friend, who was also Polish. In lessons "he doesn't take part and he's afraid even to repeat any words in English". Patrycja took the view that this was his character; in other words, it was likely to go on being a problem. Patrycja also knew little English and she relied a great deal on her husband. Like many interviewees, she referred to 'The Language Barrier'. She was not able to go to college to learn English after work because of her childcare responsibilities: they could not afford to pay a nanny and in any case she, as a mother, felt she had a duty to help her son with his homework. They only went to Polish mass, not English mass (although other interviewees who were less inhibited tried the English services and found them the same as Polish services). Finally, there was a problem for the whole family: the neat matching of work shifts, where Patrycja worked in the morning and her husband worked in the afternoon and evening, which meant that they "met only in passing".

There were also reasons to stay, however. Comparing livelihoods in her home locations in the two countries, as migrants do, Patrycja pointed out that there was always work to be had in the UK: even during the recession, it was possible to find something. She felt that she and her husband both had job security in the UK, unlike in Poland. The lower cost of living in England was also a big advantage, as was the fact that they could rent a house. With reference to their particular situation, the change from living with parents in Poland to living independently was a good reason to prefer their English lifestyle. They had found that they could buy "very nice" food at German supermarkets in Bristol, so they enjoyed shopping. They also used their weekends to travel around the region, for example, taking their son to the Dorset seaside, enjoyable occasions which helped to make them feel more positive about being in England. However, for Patrycja (in contrast to her husband), her work as a hotel cleaner seemed to be the most important factor anchoring her in the UK. This was not so much because of the pay, although she described this as being good (perhaps testifying to her overall good feelings about being in work). It was the social aspects of the job that she really enjoyed, and she also socialised with her (Polish) colleagues after work.

Integration, transnationalism and return

In many respects, Patrycja seemed more 'segregated' than 'integrated', but perhaps this was a situation that would change over time. Chapter One introduced the concept of 'sufficient integration' and, taking into account her positive feelings about being in work and about her house, Patrycja could perhaps be described as 'sufficiently integrated' to have moments when she wanted to stay in England. However, she was as yet far from being 'sufficiently integrated' in the Home Office sense of being able to 'confidently engage' with British society.[4] She could only live and work in the UK within the context of her family, because she depended on her husband to do everything that required the use of the English language. Had Patrycja been able to access English language lessons, her integration could no doubt have become far more complete, and a 'virtuous circle' might have ensued, where a feeling of being at home in some respects would be helped along by increasing language confidence.

Integration, however, is not just being able to operate within British society. It also involves retaining aspects of original ethnic identity and, insofar as possible, experiencing migration as an enrichment of the original identity, rather than subtracting from it. By focusing on the details of how migrants maintain and construct their sense of Polish identity abroad, it is possible to appreciate both the opportunities and the constraints which migrants of all ethnic groups actually encounter. The constraints are as important as the opportunities, particularly, perhaps, for working-class migrants. Transnationalism is sometimes presented as a universally available fruit of globalisation, but this book has contributed to the literature emphasising the limitations of transnationalism: activities often require money and time which not all migrants possess. (An example would be Patrycja's inability to make frequent visits back to Poland.) The book has also attempted to shed some light on the relationship between transnationalism and integration, adding to the literature which considers the two to be compatible and even mutually beneficial. For example, supplementary language schools for ethnic minority children might be viewed as unfavourable for integration, but the examples of Polish Saturday schools and parent and toddler groups in Bath and Bristol show that they are quite the reverse, since they organise events for the whole local community and are used by local service providers such as the police and the NHS to channel information to local Polish residents.

Transnationalism is also a helpful term because it implies links across borders, including links which may serve to draw the migrant back home: for example, emotional ties with friends and relatives in Poland. Scholars of transnationalism tend to argue that 'return' is simply a stage in the migration process, often to be followed by further migration, rather than a definitive end to migration, as has conventionally been assumed. This book has elaborated on this idea by comparing emigration and return strategies side by side and illustrating how, in many respects, the patterns of return migration are a mirror image of patterns of emigration. In other words, the return migration culture and the migration culture are inseparable. This is hardly surprising, given that most Polish migrants have been in the UK for such a short time. Return migrants, for example, often return experimentally: they are not sure how long they will stay in Poland. Sometimes one family member tests the water, leaving the others in England. Return is not made 'into the unknown': a job is usually fixed up in advance and the return migrant feels sufficiently well-informed about where he or she is going. Decisions about return are made on the basis of comparisons of local livelihoods: London *versus* Sanok, not the UK *versus* Poland. Return, at least among the interviewees, was generally associated with being with family and friends, return to a home town, not return to a different location in Poland. The interviewees had not entertained the idea of internal migration within Poland before they came to the UK and they still ruled it out. In all these ways, 'return' was conceptualised in exactly the same fashion as 'migration' had been a few years before.

However, return can, of course, never be identical to emigration, not least because migrants return 'home' as different people, even if they have been abroad only briefly. Another important respect in which return is often said to differ from emigration is the weight attributed to emotional factors. The decision about whether to return is not merely the outcome of weighing up economic costs and benefits in each location: emotional costs and benefits are also very significant, and in this regard this book backs up the findings of many other scholars. It looked in detail at the nature of some of these emotional factors. Decisions to return are made in the context of persuasion by friends and relatives. They are also made on the basis of holidays to Poland which function as 'inspection visits'. Returnees are not just keeping an eye on local economic developments, but also, inevitably, reflecting on how much they still feel 'at home' in Poland.

Overall, perhaps the most important argument of this book is that non-economic motives underlie migration decisions, at every stage. All migrants, not just families, live within societies where decisions are made not only as a result of rational cost–benefit calculations, but also in accordance with local norms. Moreover, people have multiple motivations and being a labour migrant does not prevent a person from wanting to travel and to see the world. In addition, almost every individual has emotional ties to people in different locations and they are tugged in different directions simultaneously. Parents whose closest ties are to their children will base their migration decisions primarily on their perceptions of what they perceive to be in the best interests of their children. These interests include much more than access to material possessions.

Note

[1] I have deliberately chosen a very harmonious family to avoid potentially causing embarrassment.

[2] Morawska (2001).

[3] Levitt (1998).

[4] Ager and Strang (2004).

The interviewees

Not including key informants, there were 115 interviews and 102 interviewees in total. Seventy-two first interviews (2007-08) and 10 repeat interviews (2009) were conducted in Poland. Thirty first interviews (2006-09) and three repeat interviews (2007, 2009) were conducted in the UK. Interviews in Poland took place in 2007 in Biedruszko, Brodnica (Wielkopolska), Gniezno, Książ Wielkopolski, Tarnowo Podgórne and Witkowo (one interview in each location), as well as Suwałki (3), Ełk (6), Kłodawa (3); in 2008 in Grajewo (33) and Sanok (21); and in 2009 in Grajewo (10). Interviews in England took place in Bath (17 interviews, 2006-09), Bristol (12 interviews, 2006-09), Frome (one interview, 2009) and Trowbridge (three interviews, 2007-09).

UK interviewees were 31 years old on average, Polish interviewees about 37. Twenty-three interviewees were under the age of 30 and 10 were over the age of 45.

The 30 UK interviewees had previously lived in almost every region of Poland. In total, the last Polish places of residence of UK interviewees included seven cities with populations of approximately 100,000 or more, seven towns of 40,000–70,000, eight towns under 40,000 and eight villages.

Most of the interviewees (73) were found by 'gatekeepers' – my personal contacts, or contacts of contacts. These gatekeepers were mostly teachers and kindergarten heads, as well as a nurse (the mother of a UK contact). Most of the gatekeepers have been thanked in the 'Acknowledgements' at the start of this book, but I have not mentioned by name those interviewees who, without reference to a gatekeeper, helped me directly to find other interviewees (the so-called 'snowball' method). In fact only 11 interviewees were contacted by the snowball method. I approached 23 interviewees (five in Poland and 18 in the UK) directly, persuading them to talk to me at English lessons or lunchtime breaks for cleaners at the University of Bath; at Saturday schools/toddler groups in the UK; at hotels in Poland; and through the social networking internet site *Nasza Klasa*. (In addition, one *Nasza Klasa* contact in Sanok, 'Olga', aged 24, did not want to be interviewed, but replied to questions by email.) I also requested all 13 repeat interviewees by contacting the interviewees directly. I found no interviewees through paper advertisements (which I posted in Polish shops in the UK, displayed at an event at the Saturday School in Bath and distributed to parents at a school in Sanok). I paid for interviews, except for the first few in the pilot survey. (The fee was 50 zl in Poland and £15, rising in 2008 to £20, in England.)

There were 14 key informants in the UK. Most were teachers: English teachers, teaching assistants at schools, a schools liaison officer working with Polish families and a Saturday school headteacher. The other key informants were three cleaning managers, one recruitment agency manager, one community development worker and the Trowbridge representative of the Polish Honorary Consul in Bristol. I also had many informal conversations with teachers at the Saturday School in Bath. In Poland I interviewed/had conversations with local education officers, House of Culture employees and a newspaper editor in Suwałki; a local historian and a hospital administrator in Grajewo; nursery and kindergarten heads in Sanok; travel agency workers in Ełk, Grajewo and Sanok; and job centre heads/employees, librarians, teachers and school secretaries in all four towns.

Some interviewees did not completely match my criteria because of misunderstandings on the part of the gatekeepers. Unfortunately five women turned out to have higher education (Polish Master's) but in places where this seemed to differentiate them from other respondents (for example, because they had different aspirations, such as non-manual work or private education for their children) I have not used information from the interviews. The five women were: Eliza and Hanna in the UK, Karolina and Irena in north-east Poland and Rozalia in Sanok. In Poland, Marcelina and Julita were not yet mothers (although Julita was heavily pregnant). In the UK, Agnieszka had been childless when she first arrived in the UK, but had her first baby shortly afterwards. I tried to interview only mothers with children under the age of 20 (although some also had older children); Henryka turned out to have only older children, but since her son and his family were living in England this was an interesting interview nonetheless.

The opinion poll

The opinion poll was conducted by telephone among 1,101 residents of Podkarpacie (excluding the city of Rzeszów) in March 2008. Although I wrote the questions, the information was collected by sociologists from the University of Rzeszów working for an independent firm, BD Center Consulting, run by Dr Paweł Walawender.

Questions

1   Since 1 May 2004, have whole families begun to migrate from your locality to Western Europe?

2.1   'If one parent in the family works abroad temporarily, it's better for the children if the father migrates, not the mother, even when the children are teenagers.'

2.2   'Mothers of small children should not leave their children and husbands to work abroad.'

2.3.1   'In my locality you can notice certain problems connected with parental migration: there are more lone-parent and broken families.'

2.3.2   'In my locality you can notice certain problems connected with parental migration: the children left in Poland have psychological and behavioural problems.'

2.3.3   'In my locality you can notice certain problems connected with parental migration: grandparents looking after migrants' children have too many responsibilities.'

3.1   'It's better for children under 12 years old to go abroad with both parents, rather than staying in Poland without one parent.'

3.2   'It's better for teenage children to go abroad with both parents, rather than staying in Poland without one parent.'

3.3   'If one parent has a good job offer, or has already found a good job in Western Europe, it's worthwhile for the whole family to try emigrating (they can return if it doesn't work out).'

3.4   'For lone mothers, migration is often a sensible escape route from a difficult financial situation; afterwards, they can bring their children to be with them and start a new life abroad.'

3.5   'In my locality, you can notice a certain social pressure on family members left behind in Poland to go and join the husband or wife who is already working abroad.'

3.6   'It's frightening to move with children to another country and I find it hard to understand parents who decide to do this.'

4.1   Do you agree that it's easier for families to live in England than in Poland?

4.2   Do you agree that English towns are less safe than Polish ones?

4.3   Do you agree that young children quickly adapt to life in a new country?

4.4   Do you agree that teenagers would quickly adapt to life in England, because they learned English at school?

4.5   Do you agree that the school syllabus in England is similar to the Polish syllabus?

5.1   Are there any members of your immediate family in England or who have been there over the past year?

5.2   What is the sex of that person/those people?

Respondents were also asked about their own age, educational level, financial status, whether they had been in the UK or to other Western countries, whether they had children under the age of 20 and, if so, whether they had lived with those children abroad. A record was kept of where they lived and the places of residence were categorised into four bands by BD Center Consulting: villages, plus three sizes of town (under 9,000, 9,000–50,000 and over 50,000 population). During the analysis, I also identified three sub-regions: the south-east periphery (128 respondents), the west (133) and the north (129). All sub-regions were on the borders of Podkarpacie and not adjacent to one another.

2001 Census data for Bath, Bristol, Frome and Trowbridge urban areas

	Bath	Bristol	Frome	Trowbridge
Population	90,144	551,066	24,171	34,401
% white British	91.26	90.35	97.01	95.06
% retired	13.51	11.93	12.33	13.28
% students (aged 16-74)	4.27	3.44	2.45	2.22
% employed in hotel and catering industries	7.33	4.16	5.20	3.77
% employed in manufacturing	10.02	12.02	19.86	21.52
% employed as managers and senior officials	16.71	13.49	13.09	13.64
% employed in professional occupations	17.43	12.69	8.95	8.68

Source: ONS (2004, Tables KS01, KS06, KS09a, KS11a, KS12a, KS18)

Bibliography

Aboim, S. (2010) 'Gender cultures and the division of labour in contemporary Europe: a cross-national perspective', *The Sociological Review*, vol 58, no 2, pp 171-96.

Ackers, L. (1998) *Shifting spaces:Women, citizenship and migration within the European Union*, Bristol:The Policy Press.

Ackers, L. (2004) 'Citizenship, migration and the valuation of care in the European Union', *Journal of Ethnic and Migration Studies*, vol 30, no 2, pp 373-96.

admin, 'Sieroty emigracji' (http://isanok.pl/index.php?option=com_content&task=view&id=681&Itemid=99999999).

Ager, A. and Strang, A. (2004) *Indicators of integration: Final report*, London: Home Office.

AKJ, KAI (2007) 'Powołanie małżeńskie i rodzinne', *Nasz Dziennik*, 20 August.

Al-Ali, N. (2002) 'Loss of status or new opportunities? Gender relations and transnational ties among Bosnian refugees', in D. Bryceson and U.Vuorela (eds) *The transnational family: New European frontiers and global networks*, Oxford: Berg, pp 83-102.

Alexander, C., Edwards, R. and Temple, B. (2007) 'Contesting cultural communities: language, ethnicity and citizenship in Britain', *Journal of Ethnic and Migration Studies*, vol 33, no 5, pp 783-800.

Anderson, B., Clark, N. and Parutis,V. (2007) *New EU members? Migrant workers' challenges and opportunities to UK trades unions:A Polish and Lithuanian case study*, London:Trades Union Congress.

Anderson, B., Ruhs, M., Rogaly, B. and Spencer, S. (2006) *Fair enough? Central and East European migrants in low-wage employment in the UK*, York:Joseph Rowntree Foundation.

Anon (1998) *Czym dla Polaków jest dom?*, Warsaw:CBOS (Centrum Badań Opinii Społecznej) [Centre for Public Opinion Research].

Anon (2007a) 'Najmłodsze ofiary emigracji', *Gazeta Współczesna*, 30 November (www.wspolczesna.pl/apps/pbcs.dll/article?AID=/20071130/MAGAZYN/71129012).

Anon (2007b) 'Osierocone dzieci polskich emigrantów', *Super Nowości*, reproduced by PAP, 12 October (http://wiadomosci.wp pl/kat,18453,wid,9288298,wiadomosc.html?ticaid=14f81).

Anon (2008a) 'Boruszewicz: nie ma masowych powrotów emigrantów' ['Boruszewicz: no mass return of emigrants'] (http://wyborcza.pl/1,75248,6053435,Borusewicz__nie_ma_masowych_powrotow_emigrantow.html).

Anon (2008b) 'Eurosieroty: zestawienie bibliograficzne w wyborze za lata 1998-2008', Kraków, Pedagogiczna Biblioteka Wojewódzka im Hugona Kołłątaja, Wydział Informacyjno-Bibliograficzny (www.pbw.edu.pl/images/Zestawienia/eurosieroty.doc).

Anon (2008c) 'Rośnie pokolenie eurosierot', *Rzeczpospolita*, 23 January.

Anon (2008d) 'Za granicę przez agencje', *Biuletyn Migracyjny* 13, Warsaw: CMR (Centre of Migration Research, Warsaw University), p 4.

Anon (2009a) *Kobiety 2009: Raport z badań*, Warsaw: CBOS (Centrum Badań Opinii Społecznej) [Centre for Public Opinion Research].

Anon (2009b) 'Mleczarnie czeka konsolidacja?', www.egrajewo.pl/wiadomosc,Mleczarnie_czeka_konsolidacja,8697.html.

Anon (2009c) 'Od listopada zasiłki rodzinne wzrosną o 40%', *Gazeta Prawna*, 12 August.

asz, PAP (2007) 'Milion Polek opuściło kraj', reprinted from *Polska. gazeta.pl*, 20 December (http://wiadomosci.gazeta.pl/wiadomosci/1,74877,4772785.html).

Audit Commission (2007) *Polski Bristol – An example of a church and community-based voluntary support group for new migrants*, London: Audit Commission.

Badora, B. et al (2009) 'Młodzież 2008' ['Youth 2008'], *Opinie i Diagnozy* [*Reviews and Diagnoses*], no 13, Warsaw: CBOS (Centrum Badań Opinii Społecznej) [Centre for Public Opinion Research].

Bafekr, S. (1999) 'Schools and their undocumented Polish and "Romany Gypsy" pupils', *International Journal of Educational Research*, vol 31, no 4, pp 295-302.

Bailey, A. and Boyle, P. (2004) 'Untying and retying family migration in the new Europe', *Journal of Ethnic and Migration Studies*, vol 30, no 2, pp 229-41.

Baldassar, L. (2007) 'Transnational families and aged care: the mobility of care and the migrancy of ageing', *Journal of Ethnic and Migration Studies*, vol 33, no 2, pp 275-97.

Baldock, C.V. (2000) 'Migrants and their parents: caregiving from a distance', *Family Issues*, vol 21, no 2, pp 205-24.

Bańkosz, R. (2008) *Sanok: Przewodnik*, Rzeszów: PIKiM.

Bauer, T., Epstein, G. and Gang, I.N. (2002) *Herd effects or migration networks? The location choice of Mexican immigrants in the US*, Bonn: IZA.

Berry, J.W. and Sabatier, C. (2010) 'Acculturation, discrimination, and adaptation among second generation immigrant youth in Montreal and Paris', *International Journal of Intercultural Relations*, vol 34, no 3, pp 191-207.

Blazyca, G. (2009) 'Managing transition economies', in S. White, J. Batt and P.G. Lewis (eds) *Developments in Central and East European Politics*, Basingstoke: Palgrave, pp 213-33.

Blunt, A. and Dowling, R. (2006) *Home*, London: Routledge.

Bobek, A. (2009) 'Polish migrants in Ireland: community formation and internal divisions', Paper presented at AHRC/CRONEM (Centre for Research on Nationalism, Ethnicity and Multiculturalism) Conference, University of Surrey, Guildford.

Bojar, H. (2005) 'Family values from the parental perspective', *Polish Sociological Review*, vol 3, no 151, pp 281-90.

Boyd, M. (1989) 'Family and personal networks in international migration', *International Migration Review*, vol 23, no 3, pp 638-70.

Bryceson, D. and Vuorela, U. (2002) 'Transnational families in the twenty-first century', in D. Bryceson and U. Vuorela (eds) *The transnational family: New European frontiers and global networks*, Oxford: Berg, pp 3-30.

Bukowski, M. (1996) 'The shifting meanings of civil and civic society in Poland', in C. Hann and E. Dunn (eds) *Civil society: Challenging Western models*, London: Routledge.

Burrell, K. (2006) *Moving lives: Narratives of nation and migration among Europeans in post-war Britain*, Aldershot: Ashgate.

Burrell, K. (2008) 'Time matters: temporal contexts of Polish transnationalism', in M.P. Smith and J. Eade (eds) *Transnational ties: Cities, migrations, and identities*, New Brunswick, NJ: Transaction Publishers, pp 15-38.

Burrell, K. (ed) (2009a) *Polish migration to the UK in the 'new' European Union: After 2004*, Farnham: Ashgate.

Burrell, K. (2009b) 'Introduction: migration to the UK from Poland: continuity and change in East-West European mobility', in K. Burrell (ed) *Polish migration to the UK in the 'new' European Union: After 2004*, Farnham: Ashgate, pp 1-19.

Byron, M. (1994) *Post-war Caribbean migration to Britain: The unfinished cycle*, Aldershot: Avebury.

Cantle, T. (2001) *Community cohesion: A report of the Independent Review Team*, London: Home Office.

Cassarino, J.-P. (2004) 'Theorising return migration: the conceptual approach to return migrants revisited', *International Journal on Multicultural Societies*, vol 6, no 2, pp 253-79.

Castles, S. and Miller, J.M. (2009) *The age of migration: International population movements in the modern world* (4th edn), Basingstoke: Palgrave Macmillan.

Cerami, A. (2005) 'Social policy in Central and Eastern Europe: the emergence of a new European model of solidarity?', Doctoral dissertation, University of Erfurt.

Cerase, F.P. (1974) 'Expectations and reality: a case study of return migration from the United States to southern Italy', *International Migration Review*, vol 8, no 2, pp 245-62.

Cieślak-Wróblewska, A. (2009) 'Polska emigracja wraca do kraju, ale powoli', *Rzeczpospolita*, 22 May (www.rp.pl).

Cieślińska, B. (1997) *Małe miasto w procesie przemian w latach 1988-1994. Monografia socjologiczna Moniek*, Białystok: Białystok University.

Cieślińska, B. (2008) 'The experience of labour emigration in the life of women from Podlasie', Paper presented at workshop on 'Temporary migration and community cohesion: the nature and impact of migration from East-Central to Western Europe', University of Bath.

Cook, J., Dwyer, P. and Waite, L. (2008) *New migrant communities in Leeds: A research report commissioned by Leeds City Council*, Leeds: University of Leeds, Leeds City Council and Nottingham Trent University.

Corden, A. and Sainsbury, R. (2006) 'Exploring "quality": research participants' perspectives on verbatim quotations', *International Journal of Social Research Methodology*, vol 9, no 2, pp 97-110.

Coyle, A. (2007a) 'The changing status of Polish women's migration and work in the "new" Europe', *European Journal of Women's Studies*, vol 14, no 1, pp 37-50.

Coyle, A. (2007b) 'Has transition left women behind? Polish women's labour markets at "home" and "abroad"', *Gender in Transition*, vol 8 (www.developmentandtransition.net/index.cfm?module=ActiveWeb&page=WebPage&DocumentID=660#).

CRE (Commission for Racial Equality) (nd) 'Ethnicity profile: South-West England' (http://83.137.212.42/sitearchive/cre/diversity/map/southwest/bristol.html).

Cwerner, S.B. (2001) 'The times of migration', *Journal of Ethnic and Migration Studies*, vol 27, no 1, pp 7-36.

Czubkowska, S. (2009) 'Polonia bankrutuje i ucieka z Chicago' ['Polonia is bankrupt and fleeing Chicago'], *Dziennik*, 5 March (www.dziennik.pl/wydarzenia/article334382/Polonia_bankrutuje_i_ucieka_z_Chicago.html).

Dahinden, J. (2005) 'Contesting transnationalism? Lessons from the study of Albanian migration networks from former Yugoslavia', *Global Networks*, vol 5, no 2, pp 191-208.

Dallas, I. (2007) *Polish community in Bristol and South Gloucestershire: Research report (January-April 2007)*, Bristol: Bristol City Council, South Gloucestershire Council and the Anglo Polish Society (Bristol and the South West).

Datta, A. (2008) 'Building differences: material geographies of home(s) among Polish builders in London', *Transactions of the Institute of British Geographers*, vol 33, no 4, pp 518-31.

Derczyński, W. (2004) 'Postrzeganie swego miejsca w strukturze społecznej, awanse i degradacje', *Komunikat z badań*, Warsaw: CBOS (Centrum Badań Opinii Społecznej) [Centre for Public Opinion Research].

DfID (Department for International Development) (1999) *Sustainable livelihoods guidance sheets* (www.nssd.net/pdf/sectiono.pdf).

Długosz, P. (2008) *Trauma wielkiej zmiany na Podkarpaciu*, Kraków: Nomos.

Domanowska, A. (2008) 'Koniec dolarów w Mońkach', www.gazeta.pl, 16 July.

Duany, J. (2002) 'Mobile livelihoods: the sociocultural practices of circular migrants between Puerto Rico and the United States', *International Migration Review*, vol 36, no 2, pp 355-88.

Dwornik, B. (2008) 'Obalamy mit – nie będzie masowych powrotów z emigracji', *Raport Money pl*, Wrocław: Money. pl.

Eade, J., Drinkwater, S. and Garapich, M.P. (2006) *Class and ethnicity – Polish migrants in London*, Guildford: CRONEM (Centre for Research on Nationalism, Ethnicity and Multiculturalism), Universities of Surrey and Roehampton.

Ellis, F. (2000) *Rural livelihoods and diversity in developing countries*, Oxford: Oxford University Press.

Elrick, T. (2008) 'The influence of migration on origin communities: insights from Polish migrations to the West', *Europe-Asia Studies*, vol 60, no 9, pp 1503-17.

Eurostat (2009) *Eurostat regional yearbook 2008*, Luxembourg: Eurostat.

Evergeti, V. and Zontini, E. (2006) 'Introduction: some critical reflections on social capital, migration and transnational families', *Ethnic and Racial Studies*, vol 29, no 6, pp 1025-39.

Faist, T. (2000) *The volume and dynamics of international migration and transnational social spaces*, Oxford: Oxford University Press.

Feliksiak, M. (2009) *Nastroje społeczne w maju: Komunikat z badań*, Warsaw: CBOS (Centrum Badań Opinii Społecznej) [Centre for Public Opinion Research].

Fihel, A. and Kaczmarczyk, P. (2009) 'Migration: a threat or a chance? Recent migration of Poles and its impact on the Polish labour market', in K. Burrell (ed) *Polish migration to the UK in the 'new' European Union: After 2004*, Farnham: Ashgate, pp 23-48.

Fihel, A., Kaczmarczyk, P. and Okólski, M. (2006) *Labour mobility in the enlarged European Union: International migration from the EU8 countries*, Warsaw: CMR (Centre of Migration Research, Warsaw University).

Fomina, J. (2009) *Światy równoległe – wizerunek własny Polaków w Wielkiej Brytanii*, Warsaw: ISP (Instytut Spraw Publicznych) [Institute of Public Affairs] (www.isp.org.pl/files/19756075301447910012547 42838.pdf).

FPE (Fundacja Prawo Europejskie) (2008) *Eurosieroctwo 2008: Materiał signalny (zapowiedź raportu)*, Warsaw: FPE.

Frejka, T., Okólski, M. and Sword, K. (1998) *In-depth studies on migration in Central and Eastern Europe: The case of Poland*, New York, NY and Geneva: United Nations.

Frelak, J. and Roguska, B. (2008) *Powroty do Polski: Wyniki badań*, Warsaw: Warsaw: ISP (Instytut Spraw Publicznych) [Institute of Public Affairs] (www.isp org.pl/files/6427608760871582001209562869.pdf).

Fuszara, M. (2005) *Kobiety w polityce*, Warsaw: Trio.

Galasińska, A. (2010) 'Leavers and stayers discuss returning home: internet discourses on migration in the context of the post-communist transformation', *Social Identities*, vol 16, no 3, pp 309-24.

Galasińska, A. and Kozłowska, O. (2009) 'Discourses of a "normal" life among post-accession migrants from Poland to Britain', in K. Burrell (ed) *Polish migration to the UK in the 'new' European Union: After 2004*, Farnham: Ashgate, pp 87-105.

Garapich, M.P. (2006) *London's Polish borders: Class and ethnicity among global city migrants*, Guildford: CRONEM (Centre for Research on Nationalism, Ethnicity and Multiculturalism), Universities of Surrey and Roehampton.

Garapich, M.P. (2008a) *Between the local and transnational – EU accession states migrants in the London Borough of Hammersmith and Fulham*, Guildford: CRONEM (Centre for Research on Nationalism, Ethnicity and Multiculturalism), Universities of Surrey and Roehampton (www.surrey.ac.uk/Arts/CRONEM/documents/Report_HF_CRONEM.pdf).

Garapich, M.P. (2008b) 'The migration industry and civil society: Polish immigrants in the United Kingdom before and after EU enlargement', *Journal of Ethnic and Migration Studies*, vol 34, no 5, pp 735-52.

Garapich, M.P. (2008c) 'Odyssean refugees, migrants and power: construction of the "other" and civic participation within the Polish community in the United Kingdom', in D. Reed-Danahay and C.B. Brettell, *Citizenship, political engagement and belonging: Immigrants in Europe and the United States*, New Brunswick, NJ: Rutgers University Press, pp 124–43.

Garapich, M.P. (2009) 'Migracje, społeczeństwo obywatelskie i władza. Uwarunkowania stowarzyszeniowości etnicznej i rozwoju społeczeństwa obywatelskiego wśród polskich emigrantów w Wielkiej Brytanii', in M. Duszczyk and M. Lesińska (eds) *Współczesne migracje: Dylematy Europy i Polski. Publikacja z okazji 15-lecia Ośrodka Badań nad Migracjami UW*, Warsaw: Wydawnictwo Petit, pp 39-69.

Giza, A. and Tefelski, M. (1998) 'The migration networks', in T. Frejka, M. Okólski and K. Sword, *In-depth studies on migration in Central and Eastern Europe: The case of Poland*, New York, NY and Geneva: United Nations, pp 123-33.

Glick Schiller, N., Basch, L. and Blanc-Szanton, C. (1992) *Towards a transnational perspective on migration: Race, class, ethnicity and nationalism reconsidered*, New York, NY: New York Academy of Sciences.

Glińska, E. (2007) 'Grajewo w opinii swoich mieszkańców (raport z badań ankietowych)', Grajewo (http://grajewo2.website.pl/rozne/raport_dorosli).

Gmelch, G. (1980) 'Return migration', *Annual Review of Anthropology*, vol 9, pp 135-59.

Goodwin, R. and Goodwin, K. (2009) *The acculturation of Polish immigrants into British Society: A multi-method investigation*, Final project report for the British Academy, London: Brunel University.

Goulbourne, H. (2006) 'Families, communities and social capital', *Community, Work and Family*, vol 9, no 3, pp 235-50.

Grasmuck, S. and Pessar, P.R. (1991) *Between two islands: Dominican international migration*, Berkeley, CA: University of California Press.

Grzymała-Kazłowska, A. (2005) 'From ethnic cooperation to in-group competition: undocumented Polish workers in Brussels', *Journal of Ethnic and Migration Studies*, vol 31, no 4, pp 675-97.

GUS (Główny Urząd Statystyczny) [Central Statistical Office] (2007a) *Kobiety w Polsce*, Warsaw: GUS.

GUS (2007b) *Rocznik Demograficzny 2007*, Warsaw: GUS.

GUS (2007c) 'stopa_bezrobocia_02_07' (www.stat.gov.pl/dane_spol-gosp/praca_ludnosc/index.htm).

GUS (2008a) *Rocznik Demograficzny 2008*, Warsaw, GUS.

GUS (2008b) 'Stopa bezrobocia rejestrowanego (2008)' (www.stat.gov.pl/bdr_n/app/dane_podgrup nowe_okno?p_zest_id=955630&p_typ=HTML).

GUS (2009a) 'Przeciętne miesięczne wynagrodzenie w gospodarce narodowej w latach 1950-2008 (podstawa wymiaru emerytur i rent)' (www.stat.gov.pl/gus/5840_1630_PLK_HTML.htm).

GUS (2009b) *Rocznik Demograficzny 2009*, Warsaw: GUS.

GUS (2009c) 'Stopa bezrobocia w latach 1990-2009' ['Unemployment rate during 1990-2009'] (www.stat.gov.pl/gus/5840_677_PLK_HTML.htm).

Guzik, M. (2005) *Szare Madonny*, Krosno: Krośnieńska Oficyna Wydawnicza.

Gwiazda, M. and Roguska, B. (2008) *Jak się żyje w województwie Podlaskim?*, Warsaw: CBOS (Centrum Badań Opinii Społecznej) [Centre for Public Opinion Research].

Hardy, J., Kozek, W. and Stenning, A. (2008) 'In the front line: women, work and new spaces of labour politics in Poland', *Gender, Place and Culture*, vol 15, no 2, pp 99-116.

Harney, N.D. and Baldassar, L. (2007) 'Tracking transnationalism: migrancy and its futures', *Journal of Ethnic and Migration Studies*, vol 33, no 2, pp 189-98.

Harrison, D. (2009) 'UK Poles return home', *Daily Telegraph*, 21 February.

Home Office (2009) *Accession monitoring report, May 2004-March 2009:A8 migrants*, London: Home Office.

Horváth, I. (2008) 'The culture of migration of rural Romanian youth', *Journal of Ethnic and Migration Studies*, vol 34, no 5, pp 771-86.

Hossain, M.I., Khan, I.A. and Seeley, J. (2003) 'Surviving on their feet: charting the mobile livelihoods of the poor in rural Bangladesh', Paper presented at the 'Staying Poor: Chronic Poverty and Development Policy' Conference, University of Manchester, 7-9 April.

Hudson, M., Phillips, J., Ray, K. and Barnes, H. (2007) *Social cohesion in diverse communities*, York: Joseph Rowntree Foundation.

Hugo-Bader, J. (2007) 'Syndrom F92', *Gazeta Wyborcza*, 16 October.

Iglicka, K. (2001) *Poland's postwar dynamic of migration*, Aldershot: Ashgate.

Iglicka, K. (ed) (2002) *Migracje powrotne Polaków: Powroty sukcesu czy rozczarowania?*, Warsaw: ISP (Instytut Spraw Publicznych) [Institute of Public Affairs].

Iglicka, K. (2008) *Kontrasty migracyjne Polski: Wymiar transatlantycki*, Warsaw: WN Scholar.

Iglicka, K. (2009) *Powroty Polaków w okresie kryzysu gospodarczego. W pętli pułapki migracyjnej. Raport z badań*, Warsaw: Centrum Stosunków Międzynarodowych, Warsaw University.

Jacobsen, K. (2002) 'Livelihoods in conflict: the pursuit of livelihoods by refugees and the impact on the human security of host communities', *International Migration*, vol 40, no 5, pp 95-123.

Jakubowski, S. (2008) 'Zapomniane sieroty emigracji', *PolskaLokalna Podkarpackie*, 10 April (http://polskalokalna.pl/wiadomosci/podkarpackie/news/zapomniane-sieroty-emigracji,1094004).

Jasińska, A. (2008) 'Polacy masowo wracają z Anglii z całym dobytkiem', *Gazeta Opolska*, 19 August.

Jaźwińska, E. (2001) 'Migracje niepełne ludności Polski: zróżnicowanie międzyregionalne', in E. Jaźwińska and M. Okólski (eds) *Ludzie na hustawce: Migracje między periferiami Polski i zachodu*, Warsaw: Scholar, pp 101-24.

Jaźwińska, E. and Okólski, M. (eds) (2001) *Ludzie na hustawce: Migracje między periferiami Polski i zachodu*, Warsaw: Scholar.

Jolly, S. with Reeves, H. (2005) *BRIDGE gender and migration overview report*, Brighton: Institute of Development Studies, University of Sussex.

Jordan, B. and Düvell, F. (2003) *Migration: The boundaries of equality and justice*, Cambridge: Polity Press.

Kaczmarczyk, P. (2008a) 'Pawel Kaczmarczyk', in *From brain drain to brain gain? The impact in Central and Eastern Europe of the free movement of workers*, European Policy Centre Dialogue Report (www.epc.eu/events_rep_details.php?cat_id=6&pub_id=899&year=2008).

Kaczmarczyk, P. (2008b) Sections 1, 6, 8 and 9 in P. Kaczmarczyk (ed) *Współczesne migracje zagraniczne Polaków: Aspekty lokalne i regionalne*, Warsaw: CMR (Centre of Migration Research, Warsaw University).

Kanji, N. (2002) 'Trading and trade-offs: women's livelihoods in Gorno-Badakhshan, Tajikistan', *Development in Practice*, vol 12, no 2, pp 138-52.

Kicinger, A. and Weinar, A. (eds) (2007) *State of the art of the migration research in Poland*, Warsaw: CMR (Centre of Migration Research, Warsaw University).

King, R. (2000) 'Generalizations from the history of return migration', in B. Ghosh (ed) *Return migration: Journey of hope or despair?*, Geneva: International Organisation for Migration and the United Nations, pp 7-55.

Kivisto, P. (2001) 'Theorizing transnational immigration: a critical review of current efforts', *Ethnic and Racial Studies*, vol 24, no 4, pp 549-77.

Korneluk, E. (1988) 'Grajewo w okresie międzywojennym', in A. Dobronski, W. Jarulank and W. Monkiewicz (eds) *Z przesłości Grajewa i okolic*, Grajewo: Towarzystwo przyjaciół ziemi Grajewskiej, pp 71-120.

Kowalczuk, K. (2010) *Mobilność i preferencje migracyjne Polaków*, Warsaw: CBOS (Centrum Badań Opinii Społecznej) [Centre for Public Opinion Research].

Kowalik-Malcolm, M. (nd) *Initiatives: The Family Club for Eastern Europeans in Bristol* (www.polishculture.co.uk/index.php?option=com_content&task=view&id=369&Itemid=34).

Kozerawska, M. (2008a) 'Eurosieroty', 21 May (http://wyborcza.pl/1,76842,5233172,EUrosieroty.html).

Kozerawska, M. (2008b) 'Eurosieroty: co dziesiąty ojciec wyjechał', 17 June (http://wyborcza.pl/1,76842,5295557,Eurosieroty__co_dziesiaty_ojciec_wyjechal.html).

Krings, T., Bobek, A., Moriarty, E., Salamonska, J. and Wickham, J. (2009) 'Migration and recession: Polish migrants in post-Celtic Tiger Ireland', *Sociological Research Online*, vol 14, no 2/3 (www.socresonline.org.uk/14/2/9.html).

Levitt, P. (1998) 'Social remittances: migration driven local-level forms of cultural diffusion', *International Migration Review*, vol 32, no 4, pp 926-48.

Levitt, P. (2003) 'Keeping feet in both worlds: transnational practices and immigrant incorporation in the United States', in C. Joppke and E. Morawska, *Toward assimilation and citizenship: Immigrants in liberal nation-states*, Basingstoke: Palgrave Macmillan.

Lipiński, Ł. (2006) 'Za pracą wyemigrowały ostatnio setki tysięcy...', www.gazeta.pl, 3 September.

Long, N. (2000) 'Exploring local/global transformations: a view from anthropology', in A. Arce and N. Long (eds) *Anthropology, development and modernities: Exploring discourses, counter-tendencies and violence*, London: Routledge, pp 184–201.

Lovenduski, J. and Woodall, J. (1987) *Politics and society in Eastern Europe*, Basingstoke: Macmillan.

Lukowski, W. (1998) 'A pendular society: hypotheses based on interviews', in T. Frejka, M. Okólski and K. Sword, *In-depth studies on migration in Central and Eastern Europe: The case of Poland*, New York, NY and Geneva: United Nations, pp 145–54.

McIlwaine, C., Datta, K., Evans, Y., Herbert, J., May, J. and Wills, J. (2006) *Gender and ethnic identities among low-paid migrant workers in London*, London: Queen Mary, University of London (www.geog.qmul.ac.uk/globalcities/reports/docs/workingpaper4.pdf).

Malinowski, M. and Szczepańska, B. (2002) 'Emigracja zagraniczna mieszkańców Podkarpacia', in M. Malinowski (ed) *Społeczeństwo Podkarpacia na przełomie wieków*, Rzeszów: Towarzystwo Naukowe w Rzeszowie, pp 139–61.

Mandel, J. (2004) 'Mobility matters: women's livelihood strategies in Porto Novo, Benin', *Gender, Place and Culture*, vol 11, no 2, pp 257–87.

Markova, E. and Black, R. (2007) *East European immigration and community cohesion*, York and Brighton: Joseph Rowntree Foundation and Centre for Migration Research, University of Sussex.

Massey, D.S., Arango, J., Hugo, G., Kouaouci, A., Pellegrino, A. and Taylor, J.E. (1998) *Worlds in motion: Understanding international migration at the end of the millennium*, Oxford: Clarendon Press.

Mincer, J. (1978) 'Family migration decisions', *Journal of Political Economy*, vol 86, no 5, pp 749–73.

Modzelewska, M. (2004) 'Gospodarka', *Gazeta Grajewska*, 3 March (www.grajewo.pl/content/view/22/57).

Modzelewski, H. (2009) 'Kalendarium Grajewa', http://www.grajewo.pl/web/strona-20-Historia_Grajewa+Kalendarium_Grajewa.html

Morawska, E. (2001) 'Structuring migration: the case of Polish income-seeking travelers to the West', *Theory and Society*, vol 30, no 1, pp 47–80.

Morawska, E. (2003) 'Immigrant transnationalism and assimilation: a variety of combinations and the analytic strategy it suggests', in C. Joppke and E. Morawska, *Toward assimilation and citizenship: Immigrants in liberal nation-states*, Basingstoke: Palgrave Macmillan.

Morokvasic, M. (2004) '"Settled in mobility": engendering post-Wall migration in Europe', *Feminist Review*, no 77, pp 7–25.

Mostrous, A. and Seib, C. (2008) 'Tide turns as Poles end great migration', *The Times Online*, 16 February (www.timesonline.co.uk/tol/news/uk/article3378877.ece).

Moszczyński, W. (2009) 'UK Recession increases hate crimes' (www.polishexpress.co.uk/art,uk_recession_increases_hate_crimes,3499.html).

Neto, F., Barros, J. and Schmitz, P.G. (2005) 'Acculturation attitudes and adaptation among Portuguese immigrants in Germany: integration or separation', *Psychology and Developing Societies*, vol 17, no 1, pp 19-32.

Ní Laoire, C. (2007) 'The "green green grass of home"? Return migration to rural Ireland', *Journal of Rural Studies*, vol 23, no 3, pp 332-44.

Okólski, M. (2007) *Europe in movement: Migration from/to Central and Eastern Europe*, Warsaw: CMR (Centre of Migration Research, Warsaw University).

Olwig, K.F. and Sørensen, N.N. (2002) 'Mobile livelihoods: making a living in the world', in N.N. Sørensen and K.F. Olwig (eds) *Work and migration: Life and livelihoods in a globalizing world*, London: Routledge, pp 1-19.

ONS (Office for National Statistics) (2004) *Census 2001: Key statistics for urban areas in the South West and Wales* (www.statistics.gov.uk/downloads/census2001/ks_urban_sw&w_part_1.pdf).

ONS (2009a) *Migration statistics quarterly report no 2 (August)* (www.statistics.gov.uk/pdfdir/mig0809.pdf).

ONS (2009b) *Mothers' country of birth: Table 3h Live births (numbers): Birthplace of mother and area of usual residence, 2008* (www.statistics.gov.uk/downloads/theme_population/Mothers_country_of_birth_Further_tables_commentary.xls#'Table 3h - 2008'!A1).

Orellana, M.F., Thorne, B., Chee, A. and Lam, W.S.E. (2001) 'Transnational childhoods: the participation of children in processes of family migration', *Social Problems*, vol 48, no 4, pp 572-91.

Osipowicz, D. (2002) *Rola sieci i kapitału społecznego w migracjach zarobkowych: Przykład Moniek,* Warsaw: CMR (Centre of Migration Research, Warsaw University).

Osipowicz, D. (2010) 'Social citizenship of Polish migrants in London: engagement and non-engagement with the British welfare state', Doctoral thesis, London: UCL Eprints.

Palloni, A., Massey, D.S., Ceballos, M., Espinosa, K. and Spittel, M. (2001) 'Social capital and international migration: a test using information on family networks', *The American Journal of Sociology*, vol 106, no 5, pp 1262-98.

Panagakos, A.N. and Horst, H.A. (2006) 'Return to Cyberia: technology and the social worlds of transnational migrants', *Global Networks*, vol 6, no 2, pp 109-24.

Parreñas, R. (2005) 'Long distance intimacy: class, gender and intergenerational relations between mothers and children in Filipino transnational families', *Global Networks*, vol 5, no 4, pp 317-36.

Parutis, V. (2006) '"At home" in migration', *Oikos (Lithuanian Migration and Diaspora Studies)*, vol 2, pp 9-29.

Parutis, V. (2009) '"At home" in migration: the social practices of constructing "home" among Polish and Lithuanian migrants in London', doctoral thesis, London: University College London.

Parutis, V. (2010) 'Returning home? East European migrants' discourses of return', *International Migration*.

Passerini, L., Lyon, D., Capussotti, E. and Laliotou, I. (2007) *Women migrants from East to West: Gender, mobility and belonging in contemporary Europe*, New York, NY: Berghahn Books.

Pawłowska-Salińska, K. (2008) 'Wielki powrót z Wysp', *Gazeta Wyborcza*, 14 April.

Pawluczuk, A. (2007) 'Grajewo w opinii młodzieży (raport z badań ankietowych)', Grajewo (www.grajewo.pl/images/pdf/Raport_mlodziez.pdf).

Phillips, D. (2009) 'Minority ethnic segregation, integration and citizenship: a European perspective', *Journal of Ethnic and Migration Studies*, vol 36, no 2, pp 209-25.

Pickup, F. and White, A. (2003) 'Livelihoods in postcommunist Russia: urban/rural comparisons', *Work, Employment and Society*, vol 17, no 3, pp 419-34.

Piechota, G. (2009) 'Przystanek Europa' ['Stop Europe'], www.gazeta.pl, 7 May.

Pierik, R. (2004) 'Conceptualizing cultural groups and cultural difference: the social mechanism approach', *Ethnicities*, vol 4, no 4, pp 523-44.

Pine, F. and Bridger, S. (1998) 'Introduction', in F. Pine and S. Bridger (eds) *Surviving post-socialism: Local strategies and regional responses*, London: Routledge.

Pinnawala, M. (2008) 'Engaging in trans-local management of households: aspects of livelihood and gender transformations among Sri Lankan women migrant workers', *Gender, Technology and Development*, vol 12, no 3, pp 439-59.

Podgórecki, A. (1994) *Polish society*, Westport, CT: Praeger.

Poland Street (2009) 'Projekt 12 miast' (www.polandstreet.org.uk/index.php?page=sekcja_ogolna&dzial=7&kat=11).

Pollard, N., Latorre, M. and Sriskandarajah, D. (2008) *Floodgates or turnstiles? Post-EU enlargement migration flows to (and from) the UK*, London: Institute for Public Policy Research.

Portes, A. (2001) 'Introduction: the debates and significance of immigrant transnationalism', *Global Networks*, vol 1, no 3, pp 181-93.

Portes, A. and Sensenbrenner, J. (1993) 'Embeddedness and immigration: notes on the social determinants of economic action', *The American Journal of Sociology*, vol 98, no 6, pp 1320-50.

Powiatowy Urząd Pracy w Kamiennej Górze (2004) *Stopa bezrobocia[1]pdf* (December) (www.pupkamiennagora.pl/?a=117).

Pratt, G. (2009) 'Circulating sadness: witnessing Filipina mothers' stories of family separation', *Gender, Place and Culture*, vol 16, no 1, pp 3-22.

Przybyła, M. (2007), 'Mama za granicą, dziecko w bidulu', *Praca i nauka za granicą*, 23 March, p 12.

Rabikowska, M. and Burrell, K. (2009) 'The material worlds of recent Polish migrants: transnationalism, food, shops and home', in K. Burrell (ed) *Polish migration to the UK in the 'new' European Union: After 2004*, Farnham: Ashgate, pp 211-32.

Raciborski, J. and Kublik, A. (2009) 'Wybory pokazały stary podział na Polskę A i B', www.wyborcza.pl, 8 June.

Redakcja (2006) *Dlaczego chcesz zostać lub wyjechać z kraju?*, 1 September (http://forum.gazeta.pl/forum/72,2.html?f=23&w=47881760).

Roberts, B.R. (1995) 'Socially expected durations and the economic adjustment of immigrants', in A. Portes (ed) *The economic sociology of immigration: Essays on networks, ethnicity and entrepreneurship*, New York, NY: Russell Sage Foundation, pp 42-86.

Robinson, D. (2007) 'European Union accession state migrants in social housing in England', *People, Place & Policy Online*, vol 1, no 3, pp 98-111.

Rudmin, F.W. (2003) 'Critical history of the acculturation psychology of assimilation, separation, integration and marginalization', *Review of General Psychology*, vol 7, no 1, pp 3-37.

Rudnik, J. (2005) *Jak znaleźć pracę w Wielkiej Brytanii*, Poznań: Sorus.

Ryan, L., Sales, R., Tilki, M. and Siara, B. (2007) *Recent Polish migrants in London: Social networks, transience and settlement*, Research report for RES-000-22-1552 ESRC study, London: Middlesex University.

Ryan, L., Sales, R., Tilki, M. and Siara, B. (2008) 'Social networks, social support and social capital: the experiences of recent Polish migrants in London', *Sociology*, vol 42, no 4, pp 672-90.

Ryan, L., Sales, R., Tilki, M. and Siara, B. (2009) 'Family strategies and transnational migration: recent Polish migrants in London', *Journal of Ethnic and Migration Studies*, vol 35, no 1, pp 61-77.

Rychard, A., Domański, H. and Śpiewak, P. (2006) *Polska: Jedna czy wiele?*, Warsaw: Trio.

Sądej, J. (2007a) 'Koszty ponoszą dzieci', *Nasz Dziennik*, 9 August.

Sądej, J. (2007b) 'Skutki rozstań ponosimy wszyscy', *Nasz Dziennik*, 25-26 August.

Sales, R., Ryan, L., Lopez Rodriguez, M. and D'Angelo, A. (2008) *Polish pupils in London schools: Opportunities and challenges*, London: University of Middlesex and Multiverse (www.multiverse.ac.uk/ViewArticle2.aspx?ContentId=15120).

Sassen, S. (1999) *Guests and aliens*, New York, NY: The New Press.

Schutta, P. (2007) 'Emigracja do domu dziecka', *Nowości*, 19 October (www.nowosci.com.pl/look/nowosci/article.tpl?IdLanguage=17&IdPublication=6&NrIssue=634&NrSection=80&NrArticle=80828&IdTag=34).

Shevchenko, O. (2009) *Crisis and the everyday in postsocialist Moscow*, Bloomington, IN: Indiana University Press.

Siara, B. (2009) 'UK Poles and the negotiation of gender and ethnicity in cyberspace', in K. Burrell (ed) *Polish migration to the UK in the 'new' European Union: After 2004*, Farnham: Ashgate, pp 167-87.

Slany, K. (ed) (2008) *Migracje kobiet: Perspektywa wielowymiarowa*, Kraków: Uniwersytet Jagielloński.

Slany, K. and Malek, A. (2005) 'Female emigration from Poland during the period of the systemic transformation (on the basis of the emigration from Poland to the USA and Italy', in K. Slany (ed) *International migration: A multidimensional analysis*, Kraków: AGH University of Science and Technology Press, pp 115-54.

Smith, J. and Jehlička, P. (2007) 'Stories around food, politics and change in Poland and the Czech Republic', *Transactions of the Institute of British Geographers*, vol 32, no 3, pp 395-410.

Snel, E., Engbersen, G. and Leerkes, A. (2006) 'Transnational involvement and social integration', *Global Networks*, vol 6, no 3, pp 285-308.

Somerville, W. and Sumption, M. (2009) *Immigration in the UK: The recession and beyond*, Washington, DC: Migration Policy Institute.

Spencer, S., Ruhs, M., Anderson, B. and Rogaly, B. (2007) *Migrants' lives beyond the workplace: The experiences of Central and East Europeans in the UK*, York: Joseph Rowntree Foundation.

Stańkowski, B. (2006) 'Współczesna rodzina podhalanska: wpływ emigracji zarobkowej na wychowanie dzieci i młodzieży – wyniki badań empirycznych', *Seminare*, vol 23, pp 239-59.

Stenning, A. (2004) 'Post-socialism and the changing geographies of the everyday in Poland', *Transactions of the Institute of British Geographers*, vol 29, no 1, pp 113-27.

Stenning, A., Champion, T., Conway, C., Coombes, M., Dawley, S., Dixon, L., Raybould, S. and Richardson, R. (2006) *Assessing the local and regional impacts of international migration: Final report of a research project for the Department of Communities and Local Government*, Newcastle: Centre for Urban and Regional Development Studies, Newcastle University.

Strzeszewski, M. (2006) *Znajomość języków obcych i wyjazdy zagraniczne: Komunikat z badań*, Warsaw: CBOS (Centrum Badań Opinii Społecznej) [Centre for Public Opinion Research].

Strzeszewski, M. (2008) *Jak się żyje w województwie Podkarpackim?*, Warsaw: CBOS (Centrum Badań Opinii Społecznej) [Centre for Public Opinion Research].

Sword, K. (1996) *Identity in flux. The Polish community in Britain*, London: School of Slavonic and East European Studies, University College London.

Szczepańska, J. (2006) *Kobiety i mężczyźni o podziale obowiązków domowych: Komunikat z badań*, Warsaw: CBOS (Centrum Badań Opinii Społecznej) [Centre for Public Opinion Research].

Szczepańska, J. (2008) *Więzi rodzinne*, Warsaw: CBOS (Centrum Badań Opinii Społecznej) [Centre for Public Opinion Research].

Szlachetka, M. (2008) 'Emigracja zarobkowa odbija się na szkole', 1 July, *Gazeta Lublin* (http://praca.gazeta.pl/gazetapraca/1,67738,4817235.html).

Sztompka, P. (1999) *Trust: A sociological theory*, Cambridge: Cambridge University Press.

Temple, B. (2001) 'Polish families: a narrative approach', *Journal of Family Issues*, vol 22, no 3, pp 386-99.

Temple, B. (2010) 'Feeling special: language in the lives of Polish people', *The Sociological Review*, vol 58, no 2, pp 286-304.

Thomas, W.I. and Znaniecki, F. (1984) *The Polish peasant in Europe and America* (edited and abridged by E. Zaretsky), Urbana and Chicago, IL: University of Illinois.

Tolia-Kelly, D. (2004) 'Locating processes of identification: studying the precipitates of re-memory through artefacts in the British Asian home', *Transactions of the Institute of British Geographers*, vol 29, no 3, pp 314-29.

Toro-Morn, M.I. (1995) 'Gender, class, family, and migration: Puerto Rican women in Chicago', *Gender and Society*, vol 9, no 6, pp 712-26.

Toruńczyk-Ruiz, S. (2008) *Being together or apart? Social networks and notions of belonging among recent Polish migrants in the Netherlands*, Warsaw: CMR (Centre of Migration Research, Warsaw University).

Trevena, P. (2005) *The Polish 'intelligentsia' in London: A case study of young graduates working in the secondary sector* (www.surrey.ac.uk/Arts/CRONEM/PolishIntelligentsia_1.ppt#257,1).

Triandafyllidou, A. (2006) 'Polish female migration in Europe: a gender approach', in A.Triandafyllidou (ed) *Contemporary Polish migration in Europe: Complex patterns of movement and settlement*, Lewiston, NY: Edwin Mellen, pp 225-42.

UN (United Nations) (2005) *2004 World survey on the role of women in development: Women and migration*, Geneva: UN.

UN (2008) *Human development report 2007-8* (http://hdrstats.undp org/indicators/147.html).

Urbańska, S. (2009) 'Transnarodowość jako perspektywa ujęcia macierzyństwa w warunkach migracji', in K. Slany (ed) *Migracje kobiet: Perspektywa wielowymiarowa*, Kraków: Uniwersytet Jagielloński, pp 75-85.

Urry, J. (2003) 'Social networks, travel and talk', *British Journal of Sociology*, vol 54, no 2, pp 155-75.

Urząd Pracy Podlasia (Labour Office, Podlasie) (2009) *Stopa bezrobocia, styczeń 2009* (www.up podlasie.pl/default.aspx?docId=15947).

Vertovec, S. (2001) 'Transnationalism and identity', *Journal of Ethnic and Migration Studies*, vol 27, no 4, pp 573-82.

Vullnetari, J. and King, R. (2008) '"Does your granny eat grass?" On mass migration, care drain and the fate of older people in rural Albania', *Global Networks*, vol 8, no 2, pp 139-71.

Wachowiak, A. (ed) (2002) *Przemiany orientacji życiowych kobiet zamężnych*, Poznań: Wydawnictwo Fundacji Humaniora (Humaniora Foundation).

Walczak, B. (2008) 'Szkoła i uczeń wobec migracji poaksecyjnej', *Biuletyn Migracyjny [Migration Bulletin]*, no 17 (supplement), Warsaw: CMR (Centre of Migration Research, Warsaw University).

Walczak, B. (2009) 'Dziecko w sytuacji rozłąki migracyjnej', in M. Duszczyk and M. Lesińska (eds) *Współczesne migracje: dylematy Europy i Polski: Publikacja z okazji 15-lecia Ośrodka Badań nad Migracjami UW*, Warsaw: Wydawnictwo Petit, pp 149-73.

Wallace, C. (2002a) 'Household strategies: their conceptual relevance and analytical scope in social research', *Sociology*, vol 36, no 2, pp 275-92.

Wallace, C. (2002b) 'Opening and closing borders: migration and mobility in East-Central Europe', *Journal of Ethnic and Migration Studies*, vol 28, no 4, pp 603-25.

Ward, C. (2008) 'Thinking outside the Berry boxes: new perspectives on identity, acculturation and intercultural relations', *International Journal of Intercultural Relations*, vol 32, no 2, pp 105-14.

Warzywoda-Kruszyńska, W. and Grotowska-Leder, J. (2006) 'Informal support networks of the population living in poverty (in villages and small towns)', *Polityka Społeczna*, vol 11-12.

Wasek, A. (2007) 'Siemiatyckie Eldorado?', *Nasz Dziennik*, 9 February.

Wciórka, B. (2008) *Zaufanie społeczne w latach 2002-8*, Warsaw: CBOS (Centrum Badań Opinii Społecznej) [Centre for Public Opinion Research].

Wciórka, B. (2009) *Opinie o sytuacji na rynku pracy i zagrożenie bezrobociem*, Warsaw: CBOS (Centrum Badań Opinii Społecznej) [Centre for Public Opinion Research].

Webster, W. (1998) *Imagining home: gender, race and national identity, 1945-64*, London: Routledge.

Wedel, J. (1986) *The private Poland*, New York, NY: Facts on File.

White, A. (2004) *Small-town Russia: Postcommunist livelihoods and identities. A portrait of the intelligentsia in Achit, Bednodemyanovsk and Zubtsov, 1999-2000*, London: RoutledgeCurzon.

White, A. (2007) 'Internal migration trends in Soviet and post-Soviet European Russia', *Europe-Asia Studies*, vol 59, no 6, pp 887-911.

White, A. (2009a) 'Family migration from small-town Poland: a livelihood strategy approach', in K. Burrell (ed) *Polish migration to the UK in the 'new' European Union: After 2004*, Farnham: Ashgate, pp 67-85.

White, A. (2009b) 'Internal migration, identity and livelihood strategies in contemporary Russia', *Journal of Ethnic and Migration Studies*, vol 35, no 4, pp 555-73.

White, A. and Ryan, L. (2008) 'Polish "temporary" migration: the formation and significance of social networks', *Europe-Asia Studies*, vol 60, no 9, pp 1467-502.

Wiles, J. (2008) 'Sense of home in a transnational social space: New Zealanders in London', *Global Networks*, vol 8, no 1, pp 116-37.

Winnicka, E. (2007) 'Eurosieroty', *Polityka w interia.pl*, 14 November (http://fakty.interia.pl/prasa/polityka/news/eurosieroty,%201010372).

Wodecka, D., Kulczycka, A., Szlachetka, M., Kępka, A. and Warchala, M. (2008) 'Co czują Eurosieroty?', www.gazeta.pl, 21 May (http://wyborcza.pl/1,76842,5233159,Co_czuja_EUrosieroty_.html).

Wojewódzki Urząd Pracy w Białymstoku (2005) *Sytuacja na rynku pracy w województwie Podlaskim w 2004 roku* (www.up podlasie.pl/default.aspx?docId=15954).

Zadrożna, A. (2006a) *Aktywność kobiet na rynku pracy – analiza danych zostanych*, Warsaw: Ośrodek Badania Opinii Publicznej.

Zadrożna, A. (2006b) *Aktywność kobiet na rynku pracy – badanie kobiet*, Warsaw: Ośrodek Badania Opinii Publicznej.

Zagórski, K. (2008) *Regionalne i społeczne zróżnicowania kondycji psychicznej i zadowolenia z życia: Komunikat z badań*, Warsaw: CBOS (Centrum Badań Opinii Społecznej) [Centre for Public Opinion Research].

Zontini, E. (2004) 'Immigrant women in Barcelona: coping with the consequences of transnational lives', *Journal of Ethnic and Migration Studies*, vol 30, no 6, pp 1113-44.

Zuzańska-Żyśko, E. (2006) *Małe miasta w okresie transformacji: Studium w regionie śląskim*, Katowice: Śląsk.

Index

A

acculturation process 9-10, 138-55
accumulation strategies 4, 65, 68
acquisitiveness 4, 35, 65, 98
age discrimination in Poland 47-8, 58
Ager, A. 10
Alexander, C. 151
assimilation 8, 9, 138
Australia 179

B

Bafekr, S. 163
'balance of family' and migration 179
Bath 141-5, 148-9, 157, 166n, 181, 237-8, 174,
    205, 227, 233
  data on 16, 183, 241
  Polish community 184, 187, 188, 189-90,
    228, 235
Bauer, T. 87
Belgium 31, 33-4, 69, 74, 145, 163
Berry, J.W. 9-10
Black, R. 9, 138
Blunkett, David 150
Bobek, A. 187
Bridger, S. 5
Bristol 80, 141-5, 147-9, 166n, 174, 205,
    237-8
  data on 16, 183, 241
  Polish community 184, 188, 189, 190
Burrell, K. 177, 183
bus drivers (UK) 142, 153, 157, 188, 227
businesses
  contraction in Poland 49-50, 75
  self-employment in Poland 50-2, 58, 63-4
Byron, M. 5

C

Cantle Report 8
caring
  and absent adult children 125-6
  quality of care and migration without
    children 92, 96, 97-8
  women's responsibilities 3, 29
  see also grandparents and childcare
Castles, S. 12
Catholicism 35, 163, 234
causes of migration 2-6, 120, 225-6
  and livelihood strategy approach 3-6, 229
    small-town livelihoods in Poland 39-60,
      63-4, 226
  'push' and 'pull' factors 2, 33, 40
CBOS (Centre for Public Opinion Research)
    54
Census data (UK) 241
Cerase, F.P. 197

chain migration 6, 13, 77, 86, 130, 142, 227,
    231
  see also migrant networks
child benefit 40, 56-7, 58, 83, 160
children
  absent adult children 125-6
  births at home and abroad 33, 216-17
  bullying in UK 148, 164
  and duration of stay 208-9, 227
  effect of parental absence 95, 109-11, 115,
    117-24, 127, 130-2
  'euro-orphans' 18-19, 98, 117-24, 131-2, 133
  influence on decision-making 12, 138, 236
    about decision to return 141, 201-2, 205,
      211-14, 222, 227
  and integration 14, 160-3, 165, 166, 228
    dual national identity 171-2
    language skills 160-1, 162-3, 234
    reluctance to return 211-12, 222
    views on ease of adaptation 84-6, 87
  loss of school friends 125
  see also education: migrant children; parental
    migration
choices
  and agency 5-6, 11, 235
  'herd effect' and destination 87
  and livelihood strategy approach 4, 229
    limited employment options in small
      towns 44, 63-4, 226
  and return to Poland 214-17
  wife's role in reunification 12, 106-8, 113,
    132
  see also children: influence on decision-
    making
Cieślińska, B. 58n, 76
cleaning jobs 13, 41, 46, 138, 151, 156-60, 164,
    231, 234, 237
  appreciation by employers 159, 164
communication factors 7, 74, 81, 169
  and family in Poland 177-8, 191, 233
  see also language
communist regime in Poland 56, 80-1
community involvement in UK 137, 144
  Polish community 183-90, 228, 234
commuting in Poland 53-4, 63
Confederation of Polish Employers 54
cooperation among Poles in UK 186-7, 187-8
cost of living
  family reunification and two households 109
  higher in Poland 160, 220-1, 226, 228-9, 234
  in Polish cities 54-5, 58, 207
  paying for higher education 69, 70, 71, 226
crime: migrants views on Poland and UK 86